Invented a Person

Invented a Person

THE PERSONAL RECORD OF A LIFE

LENORE MARSHALL

EDITED WITH AN INTRODUCTION
BY JANICE THADDEUS

FOREWORD BY MURIEL RUKEYSER

Horizon Press   New York

*Grateful acknowledgement is made for permission to quote from the
following material: from the* Saturday Review of Literature *for "The
Power of Words" and from* Arts Magazine *for "Patrocinio Barela."*

Contents

	Foreword by Muriel Rukeyser	7
	Introduction by Janice Thaddeus	10
1.	Circular Time	21
2.	Travel, 1914: The Actual Misery	27
3.	Travel, 1927: Unreal as a Postcard	40
4.	Travel, 1951-57: Fresh to Impressions Again	57
5.	Travel, 1969-66: The Personal Ash of Experience	78
6.	The Political Activist: Segregated Hearts	94
7.	The Political Activist: Talent for Extinction	113
8.	The Writer: Creative Writing Class for Children	126
9.	The Writer: Characters and Fragments	139
10.	The Writer: The Setting of It	162
11.	The Woman: Dreams and Scrambled Eggs	187
12.	Grandmother: The Trip	211
13.	A Good Death	249

Foreword

The balance of her life is of great fascination. Lenore Marshall's writing, published in novels and poems, is part of a landscape that is further mapped here in a collection of notebooks, journals, and the last amazing encounter. It is here, too.

The outward life—vivid, activist, full of people—is here, too. It would be easy to see it, as Lenore sometimes did, as an enormous system of waves pulling her away from the movement that writing meant to her. The outward life being a kind of travel, with real travel in it; a kind of making, of bringing people together so that the work for peace might be made, so that books might be made, and the pleasures that come from this kind of life might be there. This was happiness, with its huge load of stress, concern, unhappiness and panic.

Imagine a woman—small, attractive, incisive, loving, torn apart in herself, but holding the torn elements in the world and in her, really holding them, insisting that they belonged together—not only *belonged* together but are one. It was only in extreme tiredness that she saw one love as fighting against another love, the activist work at variance with the inner life and the poems. The keen intelligence, the penetration of her lifetime, came through in the work with scientists, the work with SANE (which was founded in her living-room), the work with editors (for she "found" Faulkner, in a burst of discovery when she first read his manuscript as part of her job). That intelligence went with delight, as every part of this skillfully-edited book shows. The delight came through to everyone who worked with her and knew her in her deep concerns. It went with the fears.

One deep value of this book, it seems to me, is that both the invention and the fear are given to us. This is the work-book of a woman poet, an American middle-class woman in the twentieth century. When she returns to America at the outbreak of World War I, it is peace and freedom that she thinks about, after the crush and horror and heat and dirt of an interrupted tour of France. This is not a woman who wants to change her bones, in the words of another woman poet. Lenore Marshall wanted to keep her bones, the bones of her life.

That meant to her that the inner life became "more intensely strong," the outer "under strictest rein." She accepts the split between the two, although she works at her strongest to bring them together. Deep in our century, we suffer from that split. She suffers, and asks why she was terrified of losing control, and therefore never fully entered the world. She speaks of the beast raging through the civilised good girl. She sees the beast as the fear of hurting, and here she joins the "two" worlds together at last. It is the fear of hurting herself and others, and there is no split here. There were many hurts done to her, as they are to all. I knew one that I remember as a clue, of an achievement much prized by her that she had been told she had and that it turned out was never given to her. Not the achievement, she had that; but the outward big splash of recognition that would have gone with it. And deeper personal hurts, in relationship.

But this was a woman with personal power—of character, money, place—all used as parts of generosity. The voices you can hear through these jottings are strong in actual creation; the fears are very strong, too, and you will see what happens through them. Her immediate family is here: James Marshall, her husband, whose life as a lawyer of great public responsibility provided her with love and strength and admiration and goad; her children, so clearly drawn here; and the children who are in that last voyage of great reality and fantasy. And finally Robert, the grandson who gave her her next voice, her next audience—if you will—the future.

These are the jottings of that life. Sometimes they give us the trivia of minutes, and then suddenly they will break, they will be without scale, they will deepen and open out into the marvelous life and death shared. Through open-handed poet's generosity, to be shared by all.

—Muriel Rukeyser

Introduction

In the Spring of 1971, knowing that she was dying of cancer, Lenore G. Marshall began to assemble some of her papers into a writer's notebook. She had been working on a novel—indeed, on two novels—but she had come to feel that the world required a more direct confrontation than fiction, and she was considering publishing her shorter pieces, fragments to shore up against the ruins. The cancer was too quick for her; she died in September, 1971. Instead of a neat manuscript she left behind clusters of separate reflections—accounts of her travels, outlines of stories, essays on the writer's plight in the modern world. She had been as she described herself "an inveterate notetaker," and the papers she left behind require seventeen boxes at the Columbia University Library manuscript division, including even the blank book she filled and illustrated at the age of eight. Her instinct that the time had come to publish selections from these notebooks was undoubtedly correct. Although I had known her for fourteen years and had read all of her novels, poems, and stories, I discovered in the notebooks a woman I had earlier only dimly perceived, the real woman at the end of a hall of mirrors. Reading through her papers was a new confrontation with a mind at struggle, more impressive in many ways than her previous literary accomplishments. In the selection presented here, I have tried to preserve this confrontation.

Lenore Marshall had achieved a full career as a writer, with three published novels, as many books of poetry, and a posthumous volume of short stories. She summed up the constant theme of her novels in a sentence whose complexity indicates her concern for exquisite craftsmanship, as well as her knowledge that human hopes are frail. This theme was "the secret drama of the forward-moving soul seeking its own truth, struggling to fulfill its own goal, learning to come to terms with its passion, its dream, to meet its destiny by burning to its brightest core what it wills to survive of itself, to climb through shadows and rocks to its own air, to reach, perhaps—and if so everything is worthwhile—its vista of light." Although she had clearly intended herself for a writing career, committing herself with that illustrated booklet at the age of eight, and pursuing her interest through Barnard College by writing the graduation poem, editing the literary magazine, and generally setting off on the expected route, she found that "domesticity absorbed me." The birth of her first child when she was 23 and of the second three years later pulled her away from her writing. When the children began at school, she had to move back toward her creative self through editing, first at the publishing house where she discovered the manuscript of William Faulkner's *The Sound and the Fury*, then as a poetry editor at a magazine, and at last by publishing her first novel in 1935 at the age of 40.

This novel, *Only the Fear*, is the story of Gabriele Kirk, whose ideal lover "Ivan," a figment of her childhood, interferes with her adult marriage until she finally exorcises him by a brief affair with her doctor. This subject matter was in that day unusual, and the reviewers were intrigued and respectful. Basil Davenport remarked on the novel's peculiarly enchanted atmosphere: "This is a novel of neurosis. It carries conviction as if by magic; but it has also the static quality of enchantment. The author establishes, at once and without effort, the dreamland atmosphere of a half-normal mind, where symbols melt into each other with a logic of their own; but it is also an atmosphere in which, as Alice found beyond the Looking-Glass, one may run as fast as one can and stay in the same place." Lewis Gannett mentioned the "finely mannered, sensitive prose," and many reviewers were reminded of Emily Dickinson. This was the novel she might have written. She too had known this sort of fear.

Two years later in her second novel *Hall of Mirrors* Lenore Marshall established a quite different atmosphere. The heroine Margaret Clay is a steady and strong woman, whose struggle takes place in the real world. She has been told that she has glaucoma, may go blind; her husband has quit his job as a matter of conscience; she is about to have to leave her own job; yet in the midst of all this she is a woman everyone can lean on. Her gestures are perfect. The book is a "hall of mirrors" because much of it has to do with these gestures. We see Maggie chiefly through the people she knows and touches: her husband, mother, servant, children, friends, employer, doctor, and dinner guests. Only at the end of the novel is she restored to herself. The method is pure Picasso. Maggie is pampered, superficial, fearful, but she is also admirable; she carries on, and the last words she thinks are, "It is wonderful how one endures."

Lenore Marshall's last novel, *The Hill is Level*, took her ten years to write and reached over three generations, centering on Abigail Arlington's repeated attempts to clamp herself and her family together. Published in 1959, this novel was greeted as "a woman's book on a sustained level of tense self examination." Besides responding to the subject matter, critics noted the book's more metaphysical substance, reminiscent of *Only the Fear*, but more various and new. Mary Ross wrote that "The course of the spirit rather than that of outward events . . . is the substance of this long, thoughtful story," with "a dimension unusual in prose fiction." Maxwell Geismar pointed out similar qualities, saying, "It is a novel of philosophical ideas and literary culture, of moral idealism and social criticism. The central theme is a woman's struggle to emancipate herself and to lead a good life." But he ended on a quite different note: "Mrs. Marshall is at her best in the tormented infighting of marital hatred, and here the novel gains validity and power."

Certainly Abigail's marriage is unfortunate. Her large and handsome husband Clifford drinks too much, cuffs her about, and at times is brutally insensitive. At one point when he is recovering from a bout of amnesia and she is deftly making his excuses, he asks her to shepherd her daughter and the servant through a protracted wildflower hunt while he visits with his mistress. She has never told him about her lover. She is always protective and polite. It is difficult to accept Abigail's decision to remain with Clifford, and some critics objected to this masochism, but the psychological motivations are carefully stacked. Abigail is attempting to undo the loss she felt when her mother whirled into the bedroom with a handsome French teacher and with a lame excuse closed the door on her "lesson." Abigail wants somehow to remain true to the ideal of a family, even in the midst of its ruin. *The Hill is Level* contains scenes of marital battle so vicious that Lenore asked me not to reprint one of them in an anthology. She could encase it in a novel, but the thought of seeing it separate and palpitating disturbed her. The novel, always seeking balance, the long view, returns to Abigail's feelings of continuity and place, her relationship with her mother and her aunt, her joy in her daughter. Indeed, the chief subject of this many-faceted book is mothers and daughters.

At her death, besides the notebooks, Lenore Marshall was working on two other novels. One was to take place at Columbia University, to include the 1968 riots, and she had made maps and notes. It was to be called "Chance and Choice," and a few pages are included here. Included, too, are some plans for a "Mystical Novel." This idea had been nagging at her for years, but one senses that she found its metaphysical qualities increasingly difficult to connect to reality as she felt it.

Meanwhile, she was also publishing poetry: *No Boundary*

(1943), *Other Knowledge* (1956), and *Latest Will* (1969). Her double sense of craft was clear, as Babette Deutsch noted in her review of *Other Knowledge:* "A novelist with the sensibilities of a poet, Mrs. Marshall is also a poet who has at heart the concerns of the novelist. The lyric with which this book opens, 'Invented a Person,' has for its theme the human need to establish identity. Other pieces deal with the conflicting claims that are made on one who is sharply conscious of private and public responsibilities, while driven by the demands of an exacting art." Stanley Kunitz wrote that her "modulated voice" possessed "distinction and authenticity," and that she had "an impressive command of the basic dialectical pattern, of the poem created, in Yeats' phrase, out of the quarrel with oneself." He suggested that readers tune themselves carefully to her cadences. John Hall Wheelock wrote that the book was "an addition to the poetry of our time which seems likely to survive"; he would keep it nearby "where I can reach for it and experience again the sense of liberation, of heightened awareness and realization, that true poetry gives us."

Lenore Marshall said that her poems were "varied in subject dealing with love, nature, grief, war, metaphysical concepts." Victor Howes with equal justice said of her last book of poems, *Latest Will*, that her "true subject" was "the paradoxical strangeness of the human condition"—a quality not quite sufficiently evoked by the term "metaphysical concepts." In her poem "Tree," for instance, after picturing an ordinary scene, where "They were felling the dead tree. It was necessary," she suddenly presents the eeriness of that simple act of destruction:

> There was an empty hole
> Roots stiff as corpses
> Sprang out, like arms and legs stiffened in the air,
> And unfamiliar.

Sometimes, her images are more shocking. In "Story" a wolf leaps free on a city street, where:

Four girls in a huddle who happened to have their legs
Bound, arms bound, mouths taped, are even worse
Off than everyone else, cannot even
Scream, cannot run.

What is most impressive here is the understatement—the girls
(patients? prisoners?) "happened" to be rendered helpless in
this way, an everyday event mentioned only in passing.

Lenore Marshall's sense of a world at the edge occasionally
found a lighter expression, as in her sestet "Safe":

I was happy, I could whistle
Till he got his anti-missile,
I felt better when I read
Anti-antis were ahead,
Now I'm safe again but can't he
Make an anti anti-anti?

She used to like to recite this one, in a tone of wry exasperation.
Similarly, from time to time in the notebooks, she would quote
herself, reapply an old poem to a new experience as, at the end,
with a terrible appropriateness, she quoted her line, "The full
of reach we measure to the grave."

I have reprinted two of the published poems here, in the first
and last chapters, because they so vividly illustrate the themes
of the pages following. Other poems in this book are early
drafts, sudden breaks from prose into verse. The end of the last
notebook opens into poetry, as if death had to be faced with
something wider than prose, without punctuation, all stops
released.

In 1972 *The Confrontation*, a collection of sixteen short stories,
was published posthumously. These stories range widely in
mood: an elderly man is pecked to death by the gulls he has
gently fed, a pair of aged lovers parts—not unkindly—after
their extended affair has somehow expired, a mother who has
timidly watched her son tear up his draft card bravely outstares

an escaped lion. These stories find their power chiefly in what E. M. Hall defined as the author's "insight into the deep significance of the small event, into the tiny points of time that are in reality watersheds of experience." Throughout the notebooks particular observations and phrases appear which eventually found their way into the novels and stories, small events which become watersheds. What is most interesting is not the similarity, but the metamorphosis. The characters in *The Confrontation*, for instance, are embarrassed by their interest in "causes." In "Dialogue on a Cliff," Felicia Jones meets an aesthete who invites her to hear his "made-to-order special etcetera stereo-hi-fi record player with its brace of speakers." He asks "What do you do when you're not on this holiday?" and the author summarizes her answer:

> She was something or other with some committee or other involved in saving the world one way or another. Her friends were trying to tip historical forces, no less; that's what they were trying anyway. Their preview of various dooms naturally became a bit of an obsession with them, a way of life, often quite enjoyable. They were minority-groupers, fighting-for-causers, on-the-brinkers, political back-seat drivers, in the thick-of-thingers, believers, that was it, believers whose ninety-nine percent of failure was presumably compensated by their passion of convincement.

Similarly, Cassie, a grandmother in "The Leaning Tower" taking care of her grandchild while her daughter escapes to a tryst in Bermuda, acts as everyone's Atlas and works for "the survival of the world, no less." The wry twist here denies Cassie's mission and her belief, and yet when by mistake she causes her grandchild to knock over his block tower, he decides to build it again. Still, this tentativeness is never the tone of the notebooks.

Although Lenore Marshall could condescend toward her

characters, her own will grew in strength. Her childhood had been sheltered, culturally nurturing. On her father's side there were, in her words, "several generations of liberal journalists and other professional people," and on her mother's "a streak of art took various shapes," so that the home of Henry A. and Leonie (Kleinert) Guinzburg was intellectually and culturally exciting. Her younger brother Harold Guinzburg became a publisher, founding the Literary Guild in 1927. The family traveled to Europe when she was fifteen, a trip which she encapsulated in a notebook full of exclamatory remarks. The next trip, in 1914, is in part included here, for this time the family stumbled upon the World War.

In 1919, upon graduating from Barnard College, Lenore Guinzburg married James Marshall, a lawyer and educator. By this marriage she gathered interesting in-laws. Her husband was the son of Louis Marshall, "a prominent constitutional lawyer, a leader in Jewish affairs, fighter for minority rights, humanitarian, and conservationist." Louis Marshall is thus described by his son George who is an economist and conservationist. The middle brother Robert was a forester and conservationist of note who mapped large tracts of Alaska before he died in 1939. By marrying James Marshall Lenore Guinzburg also acquired as uncle-in-law Judah Magnes, a forthright pacifist. His opposition to the United States entry into World War I forced him to give up his position of leadership in the Jewish Community. He emigrated to Palestine, where he became president of the Hebrew University in Jerusalem. Although he supported World War II, he always counseled the Jewish people to pursue their national goals through peaceful means. Judah Magnes was one of the four friends whom Lenore Marshall designated as "great."

James Marshall is also a conservationist, active in the Wilderness Society and related organizations. Besides his activities as a lawyer, he was a member of the New York City Board of Education from 1935-1952 and its president from 1938-42.

Among the several books he has published are *Swords and Symbols* and *Law and Psychology in Conflict*. The Marshalls had two children, Ellen and Jonathan, who in turn have produced six grandchildren.

Like many contemporary women, Lenore Marshall carried at least three roles—peace activism, career, and family—but she was exceptional in that instead of merely juggling these roles, she combined them. Quite early she "joined the Quakers, in whose attitude toward living I find spiritual meaning and purpose and faith where I feel at home." In 1957, with Norman Cousins and Clarence Pickett, she founded The National Committee for a SANE Nuclear Policy, which President Kennedy credited with being one of the major forces which brought about the Nuclear Test Ban Treaty. In 1959, during the negotiations out of which the Treaty finally evolved, she met in Geneva with the Russian Ambassador, Semyon Konstantinovitch Tsarapkin. When she introduced herself as a member of SANE, a mother, and a grandmother, Tsarapkin replied, "Then you have everything. The most noble cause, a career, a family." In reply to this diplomatic flattery, she pointed out that Tsarapkin too had "everything," and stood to lose all of it if the Bomb were to drop on his grandchildren. The peace-activist-grandmother enlarged Tsarapkin from diplomatist to diplomatist-grandfather, restoring the politician to his own humanity.

Nor was her career separate from her family life. Perhaps every writer chooses an audience—a lover, a friend, or Posterity—but for Lenore Marshall her special audience was her children and grandchildren, posterity particularized. Hence her only foray into children's literature was the book included here about the way a grandmother and her grandchildren can outwit the generation which lies between them. She recorded as well her daughter's reaction to reading *Only the Fear*, and the uncanny way her eight-year-old grandson Robert Marshall could understand her poetry and state his own role. "I'm your future," he said.

Of course, for her, as for other women, domesticity often meant diminishment, ideas scattered in a mess of scrambled eggs, but she never whined about her domestic problems. Although her position in society freed her from the chores which often baffle ambitious women, her heritage also oppressed her, requiring as it did habits of behavior, those "Victorian Kleinert niceties" she both needed and despised. She knew that her upbringing was a matter of clothes, polished tables, bouquets tastefully arranged—of veneer—and she worried lest the veneer crack away, leaving her defenseless. "Sartor Resartus, who is L?" Much of her life was a struggle against fear, nameless and named. Indeed, this book can be read as a gradual, unremitting conquering of fear. The most obvious example is her terror of airplanes. She could not bear to encase herself in a large coffin and leave the earth behind. Yet, after seventy years of automobiles and trains, a friend one day firmly escorted her by plane to Boston, fed her lunch, and accompanied her back home to New York. After that, one more ghost laid, she flew. Alfred Kazin wrote that she had what Henry James called "the imagination of disaster. . . . This was behind her unceasing personal struggle for peace." Because she shook with personal as well as social terrors, she fought for her causes, seeming in Kazin's phrase "wholly and yet unprovokingly the last idealist in the city of New York."

The clouds of nameless fears were harder to exorcise, but as she grew older she came to her confidence. She was able to face everything that came her way, even death. Like her Aunt Mince, she had wanted to die in strength, inviting her friends and relatives, drinking champagne. Lenore Marshall wrote the last pages of this book in full knowledge that she was dying: "The full of reach we measure to the grave." She reached it, and this book measures the way.

—Janice Thaddeus

A Note on the Text: Lenore Marshall's notebooks vary in size from 4x6 to 8½ x 11. Some are chronologically arranged, others alphabetically by theme. She reorganized her material often, moving chunks of experience from a travel notebook to an alphabetical notebook, from one context to another, blending fact and fiction. Confronted with such variety, I have not imposed upon it a simple chronological organization, nor would she have wanted me to do so. The papers she had begun to gather for publication were arranged thematically rather than chronologically. Her travel notebooks, however, always bore dates, and I have presented them in chronological order, moving from travel through public to personal self, from activist and artist to mother and grandmother. Within chapters, wherever feasible, I have maintained chronology. To aid the reader I have identified people mentioned, normalized punctuation, spelled out abbreviations where necessary, and corrected obvious errors, but I have maintained her occasional variations of style in numbering and spelling.

1 Circular Time

*There is no linear time. It is fake, inconsequential. True time is circular
—no beginning, no end—like layers on an onion, circles of a tree trunk
—concentric and excitant at one and the same time. Yesterday and last
year and childhood all exist in me now.*

Invented a Person

Invented a person named I:
Out of use and disuse
And the antique child who watched the new moon in the sky,
And a foot in the antique grave,
Out of faces cast off by mirrors eyeless under light,
Out of love and excuse

In need, on the screen of a dream:
The target of blow, the chosen of healing and love,
A marvel of fate!
Most trapped, like the wind in a trap
Sweeping forward and out, most curbed like the sea
Storming breakwater walls to the bay, like a bird that must
   break for the sky
Through all space winging straight

Longed to be:
Invented a person named I
With a place of its own
A certain thing to be done,
And in fear for that one.

A poem must be altogether right or it is altogether wrong. Each word must be exact for its purpose and seem unchangeable at last as if indeed the poem existed with a life of its own and the poet's part were to find it, to discover it from a clue wherever it exists floating around in particles in the air, and to reach for it, to grasp the illusive motes and put it together in its destined shape, like pieces of a jigsaw puzzle. This sense of inevitability of each component is not true of fiction; a page of a novel can be rewritten forever, sentence lengthened or shortened, total form altered. Even in the best passages of prose this may be true—there is never an end to possible revisions of a page, no gong strikes STOP at a precise moment. I am a novelist as well as a poet. Every paragraph of prose that I write invites endless rearrangement; such is the flexibility of the medium that if I were to say Once-upon-a-time it could quite as well become simply Once or In the year 1900 or In the good old days. "Big" will do for "large," "small" for "large," and no struggle involved. The poem too may be changed a thousand times in the writing, only, unlike the novel, at a given point it is finished, it is all there, the poet knows that it has arrived at its final destination.

If I open my notebooks to the miscellaneous scraps that I have jotted down—and I am in inveterate jotter-downer—I cannot define what makes certain phrases the spark of poems for me, what gives other substance to be embodied in prose. A bit of dialogue, characterizations, details for plot, these are easy enough to place. Another phrase says with equal definiteness that it may become a piece of a poem, the very germ. There is no confusion between the two notations, the two jottings, no interchange. I cannot mistake them. Yet, why? Why does a certain brief collection of words acquire a special intense impact, the passionate reverberation of poetry? Prose may have rhythms too, compression of meaning too. The heart of a poem—my own poems at any rate and their components as well—sinks inward and must extend outward to meet my needs. By this I mean that in most cases their crucial impulse is in personal experience or rather emotion; yet self revelation, in the deep sense of the essence of self, has large truth only when it is able to reach and to touch beyond itself, to seem part of the universe, almost abstract. A poem, when it is completed, must stand alone. It is still a vital part of the being of its maker and may seem to him to be his depth, yet also seems to him as to other readers to reach regions vaster than any limited by the individual, and this is its breadth. An upwelling is released beyond what was envisioned in that first line or image, and the tricks played by the unconscious during this process may contain dimensions and fullness which often surprise the poet himself.

In many of my poems the parts come at separated times until suddenly they spring together and become one. In between there is the sheer work, haunting, driving, necessitous, the experimenting, the rejecting, the seeking. It may take weeks or months to find a word, to catch a sound, to shape a thought. But after the urgency of the impulse and the labor of the making, there is the pure delight. The poem exists alone with its own life separated from the poet, and this is how it will stand in a strict selfhood forever.

"Invented a person named I." This line, scribbled on a page in one of my notebooks, stood alone for several years, no other lines or ideas accompanying it. Further along in the looseleaf notebook it appears again insistently: Invented a person named I. Each time I leafed through pages in one quest or another that line sprang out to me, struck a chord deep in me, and I knew it had become a poem; it waited, I hunted experimentally, beat about for its furtherance and shape. Occasional other fragments began to attach themselves to it: "A marvel of fate" and "out of use and disuse" and "longed to be." The line had become the embryo of a poem: it was ready to have a body given to it, ready for the all-absorbing labor that goes into the forming and enlargement and refinement that make it become a poem.

"Invented A Person" was first published in *Partisan Review* in 1955. It is the opening poem in my book *Other Knowledge*, and also the first I read in a Spoken Arts recording. It remains, from among my own work, one of my own favorites. Perhaps this is because beyond the truth about myself that it contains, my truth as deep as I can reach—a fact which alone is unimportant—it objectifies personal feeling. I could not change a word of it.

The analyzed meaning showed whole after it was finished. One might say it means the self who is the creature of our own minds, constructed from reality and dream, who lives in isolation and in longing. If that first line said "I invented" it would sound personal. Omitting the initial pronoun, as my instinct did, putting it last, "Invented a person named I" gives the double self and touches, I believe, undertones of that universality which poignantly links us all in our great solitary wish. I is myself known and lost and believed, compounded of memory and hope and death knowledge, all knowledge and mystery; it is the search for identity. "Out of use and disuse,/ And the antique child who watched the new moon in the sky/And a foot in the antique grave."

The middle section elaborates on the conflict and on the struggle: "in need" and "a marvel of fate" and "Most trapped, like the wind in a trap/Sweeping forward and out" and "like a bird that must break for the sky/Through all space winging straight." At the end the poem returns to the original line on a falling note of longing for the self's own basic place in life, its oneness, and of a sense of period to this frail "one": "Longed to be: Invented a person named I/With a place of its own/A certain thing to be done,/And in fear for that one."

(January 1969) Robert—8.* "I think 'Invented a Person' is one of the best poems in your book. It is about life—what life really is. It has a beginning and an end. All life is like a circle. Who knows, maybe there's reincarnation. Maybe people go on and are even happier after they die. Maybe my cat is my great grand-uncle . . . You are all your past experience. Old people can be as gay as children because they have all that past gaiety of being children in them." "Invented a Person?" "Uh-huh, I understand."

Robert—age 8. "The night is mysterious. It gives me such a strange feeling. Everything becomes soft and relaxed. . . . The line of that jet—you make me see it's mysterious too . . . So many things, colors for instance. What's the lightest color? Perhaps white or blue, but maybe invisibility. Chaos is mysterious. I love chaos! Out of chaos comes order after a while. I just love chaos. Action and reaction. Chaos and order. Have you read Ben Shahn? He's in the latest issue of *Ramparts*. He says something like that but I've thought of it previously too. Like that Chinese philosopher who talks about the future, do you know his work, he described ideas of action and reaction in science and said in a million years we'd still be looking for perfection. Like you say in your blind boy poem, you have to know your darkness . . . I'm writing a poem about what I give. There are different categories. The first is the things one should give and does normally. The second is more important things. The third is really the essence . . . I give to you in the way you say in 'Thoughts at Verona.' I'm your future. I can go on from you and so I give to you . . . One of the things I love about you is the way you say 'I see.' I feel you really understand. The thing is that you and I can say Uh huh to each other. I really love you. God bless you."

There is no linear Time. It is fake, inconsequential. True time is circular—no beginning, no end—like layers on an

*Robert (Robby) is Lenore Marshall's grandson, son of Jonathan Marshall.

onion, circles of a tree trunk—concentric and excitant at one and the same time. Yesterday and last year and childhood all exist in me now. Moreover, what I did *not* do yesterday and last year, but might have done and been, are as true as whatever happened. Robby would understand. He has the mystic's troubled vision of eternal truth.

2 Travel, 1914: The Actual Misery

I have never before seen a passion so intense as the international hatred here.

July 30   Streets

Paris is in a tumult. Not only the decision of a trial which has just ended dramatically, but also this continental war now so alarmingly threatening, stirs the whole city, and there is an air of excitement all over. The banks have stopped issuing gold and silver. People are leaving the country in throngs. Tonight we went to a café for dinner and afterwards rode through the streets. They were packed with people released from their day's work—ragged, weary people—showy, gaudy women—swearing, laughing men. And at every corner were drawn up lines of mounted police, giving a look of awful waiting to the city.

July 31   Tours

It is hard to write a few days later about what took place before. We left Paris for another auto tour—a long one—much to my disgust. I was so tired of traveling—so lonesome. The trip was to be in France first, then we were going to many other countries and finally end up in Munich. Well, we started in a

*Lenore Guinzburg wrote this 1914 diary at the age of sixteen when, for the second time, she and her brother accompanied her parents to Europe.

Delaunay-Belleville car with a nice French chauffeur, and everything seemed all right. We visited several lovely chateaux, passed through beautiful, peaceful country, and altogether enjoyed it, I believe, far more than we did England. We stayed overnight in Tours, which we found full of suppressed excitement. The city was packed with soldiers, our hotel piled with officers, and no one spoke of anything save the threatening unbelievable war.

August 1   Orleans

We left Tours early this morning to visit more chateaux. Finally in the afternoon we stopped at a majestic cathedral in a tiny town. Suddenly, as we were walking about beneath the great stone arches we came on a man ringing the huge church bell, his face flushed and frightened. Seeing us he screamed in French "War has been declared! War! War! We have just gotten the message! War! We are ringing the gong as if it were a fire, to let the people know!" And as we hastened out of the church, we saw the people flock into the street, the men all talking and running, the women sobbing and straining their babies to them. It was heartrending. I don't think I can ever hear a church bell again without seeing once more that terrible picture. When finally we sped into Orleans that evening we heard that every man had been ordered to join his regiment immediately. That meant that Henri, our chauffeur, had to get back to Paris at once. It would have been useless to have gone with him and perhaps be in the thick of the fight, so we decided to take a train to Aix-les-Bains in the morning. And then we were told that the last train left at midnight, and that in the morning every train and auto would be used as government property, for transporting ammunition and provisions. There was one thing to do—take the last train at midnight. We rested until twelve, caught the train, and left Orleans.

August 2   Vierzon

Fifteen minutes later we had to change cars at a crowded station. The carriages were jammed full, and Mother and I were pushed into a compartment heaped with men, mostly soldiers. It was terribly hot and uncomfortable and of course impossible to sleep. Then after about an hour we had another change to make, to catch a train that went to Lyons. At this station, Vierzon, we heard that the train was late, so naturally we had to wait there. Then followed a weary, weary time. The depot was mobbed with human beings—families that were going part of the way with their men, excited soldiers, weeping women, sleepy children. There was no place to sit down except on the luggage; some hay was thrown into one of the waiting rooms and people slept there. Such poor, smelly, miserable people! Oh, it was a dreadful hour! At last the train for Lyons arrived. We rushed to it, only to find it full to overflowing, with not an inch of room anywhere. Half-frenzied we asked what to do, but the few officials were as confused as we, and left us more ignorant than ever. In desperation we got into the emptiest train at the station—it was impossible to stay there. Somehow we heard that if we got out at a certain place, we could catch another train for Lyons, so about an hour afterwards, at three o'clock in the morning, we entered the fifth train that night. It, too, was sickeningly crowded and, separated from Dad and Harold, Mother and I were forced into an already packed carriage. No conductor had come near us on the whole awful trip—most of the people hadn't even bought tickets. The cars bumped and jolted over the tracks, it grew lighter and lighter, we shifted our positions in fruitless efforts to be comfortable, snatched a few minutes of troubled sleep, became hotter, dirtier, fainter. The train was due at nine o'clock, but the hour came and went, and we were still far from Lyons. There was no chance of getting breakfast, although our hunger seemed almost starvation to us—and still we sped on, on, on. It must have been one when we at last reached Lyons—when we stumbled out of the compartment into a stuffy station, were literally knocked up some stairs, and finally stood again in the fresh air! Ah how good it felt! There was no taxi in sight, but finally we procured a decrepit old cab and were driven to the Royal Hotel. We were in no condition to travel any more and get to Aix, so we took rooms for the night. It never felt so fine to wash before! All afternoon we slept—a line from the "Ancient Mariner" kept running in my head—"Oh sleep it is a blessed thing!" But when night came there was no rest for us. Mosquitoes were everywhere, but that wasn't the worst. At about eight o'clock bands of men began to walk through the streets singing the "Marseillaise" and yelling things like our basketball cheers at school, multiplied a thousandfold. The street cars ran just under our windows, a clock in the neighborhood struck every few minutes—the men ran screaming through the town—!

August 3

Morning came at last and we arose as worn out as ever. And then we heard that no trains were carrying passengers any more—it was impossible to leave the city that way. We searched everywhere for an auto—the government had taken all that could be had. At last we discovered a rickety old taxi, and a grumpy old chauffeur who had been overlooked, and for a ridiculous sum he agreed to take us to Aix-les-Bains. We seized the opportunity gratefully, in spite of many grave doubts as to how the tiny car would make the journey. However it managed to get there without any accidents, and after passing some beautiful country (Les Eachelles) we reached Aix-les-Bains at last.

Then new complications arose. Almost all the servants at the hotel had been called on to fight, and there was hardly a waiter in the house, so of course every person was an extra burden and the management didn't want to take us at first. After a little while, however, it was settled, and now we are installed here for an indefinite time. That doesn't end our discomforts though, by any means. Our trunks have not arrived, and as baggage isn't bothered about at present, we may never see them again. The supply of coal is running low, and they say there isn't too much food on hand either. The elevator isn't running and we must walk the long stairs. No newspapers come here, and we know nothing of the progress of the war. Only postals can be written, for all letters are opened. It is impossible to leave the place, as all means of transportation are gone. Of course these things are inconvenient but compared to some of the separated families, how fortunate we are! There are many people here whose men have gone away to fight—oh it is so tragic!

August 4   Aix-les-Bains

There are many Americans here, which is a relief. The Levies are among them, very much worried for the girls are in Switzerland and there is no way to get to them. The hotel is like a big home—all formality has been dropped, and, united by this common trouble, strangers talk to each other like old friends. In the dining room, guests help themselves, to assist the poor waiter or two, and no one thinks of the lack of elaborate meals. In some unknown way our trunks have turned up—they were the last baggage brought to the place, so we are quite comfortable. If only Aunt Hermie* were here instead of being alone in Germany, everything would be great. It is such a thrilling, real life surrounded by dangers and hardships—in spite of it all, I prefer it to the monotony of our previous lazy days this summer. Naturally, we do not know when we will get back home—so many of the steamers have stopped running, and the doubt, the desire, the uncertainty is worrying us all. We are absolutely prisoners of war—luckily, more-or-less safe ones, but prisioners all the same.

August 5   Aix-les-Bains

Well, here we are, and will be, for some time too, if the reports we hear are true. It all seems so natural, so easy to get

---

*Aunt Hermie or Mince or Mincie was Lenore Marshall's aunt, Herminie Kleinert, an artist who influenced her greatly (see p. 253 below).

accustomed to this new way of living that perhaps I am not sufficiently impressed with the horror of the war. It seems impossible that there can be bloodshed and misery near us, when I look out at this peaceful country, and the steep, cloud-veiled hills. And yet one cannot forget that it is all really happening—we talk of nothing else—only this evening our chambermaid said, between sobs, that her son had just been called on to serve,—they are taking boys of seventeen now!

August 6   Aix

What a ridiculous thing it is! That a mere political quarrel which most people have forgotten already, can bring such confusion to the whole world. The Americans here have meetings every few days to see how we'll get out, and many telegrams have been sent to Washington asking for help, but so far nothing has been done. Two thousand soldiers arrived today, to defend this town in case of need—how barbarous and uncivilized that those big, strong, brave men can be cut down like grass, in the twentieth century!

August 7   Aix

Things are just the same as usual. We haven't had hot water since we're here, and we use the same napkins several times, but the electricity is holding out well, and the meals, altho' everything is table d'hote, are awfully good. We are all accustomed to the different life—my, but people easily take things for granted! In the evening passports *(laissez-passer)* were distributed, with a place for your photo, name, sex, and a lot of other details.

August 8   Aix

In spite of all our information here being prejudiced and doubtful, there is an official report out that twenty thousand Germans who invaded Belgium have been killed. Imagine such brutality! Oh why doesn't Germany give in and prevent this slaughter, now that every nation but Austria seems to be her enemy? There are lots of soldiers sheltered in this hotel (mostly in the garage) and they are such a cheerful, quiet crowd. Some of the people have been making cigarettes today, to give away among them.

August 9   Aix

There has been another rumor out today stating that Germany has declared war on Italy now too. Either all her diplomacy and sanity have mysteriously disappeared or she must think that the whole universe will fall before her invincible army. Our few remaining chefs and waiters will have to go if Italy really intends to fight, but the report is still doubtful.

August 10   Aix

I have never before seen a passion so intense as the international hatred here. How fiercely they hate the Germans in this country! Our maid, Clodine, who wept hysterically because her son had been called to the front, remarked that it was a wonderful day, for many Germans had been killed, and the "concierge" muttered that it could have been a few thousand more, while they were at it. They can't seem to realize that the people who are their enemies are human beings also, that those masses of dead soldiers are leaving women who will weep as they do—are leaving lives of usefulness in their blind obedience to the state and in misguided patriotism to it. An enemy can have no feelings, is their firm belief.

August 11   Aix

There are some very queer people at the hotel, and it has been impossible to become lonesome surrounded by them. There is an antique French madame who tries to look young—she is almost too stiff to move and her voice is cracked and squeaky, but her lips are rouged and her hair a vivid gold nevertheless. There are pretty dressy Mrs. D.G. and Mrs. S.—a Parisian

countess who wears marvelous jewels and writes,—lazy Mrs.
L, and decided Mrs. B. One old man, Mr. J., is so amusing—he's
a regular gossip and his favorite expression is "Oh, you don't
know anything about it!" And we have "King Edward" who
shouts every word and marches over the whole place, and Miss
J. who talks of nothing but money from morning till night, Mr.
S. with a pale yellow mustache who paints, and Mr. M. of
Williams College who is a cousin of Roosevelt's. Then there are
several South American families, one of which has such a dear,
friendly kiddy, little Marie Thérèse, who calls herself Princess
Mary—and there are some people from Greece, Alsace, and
Italy too. It is queer how easily one gets acquainted in a time of
trouble.

August 12   Aix-les-Bains
The place is full of excitement and in spite of an intense heat,
every stranded Englishman or American goes tearing through
the town. News has come that Ambassador Herrick has
arranged for a train to carry the visitors at Aix to Boulogne
where a special boat will wait to get us across the Channel—and
then back to London! I little thought we should go there again,
but we are nearer the steamers that can take us home, so of
course everyone who can, will leave. It means, alas, another
long trip—twenty four hours for the usual ten hour journey,
but I am sure it won't be worse than the killing ride we had to
get here, so of course we can stand it. At least we will be spared
that famishing hunger which was ours last time, for we have
provided a large basket of fruit, crackers, and chocolate that can
keep us alive till we reach Paris or Boulogne.
    And to think that today, the twelfth of August, we were to
meet Aunt Hermie in Munich! I wonder where she is now.

August 13   Aix-les-Bains
We left very early in the hot morning with many other
Americans, for London. Almost everyone else at the hotel left,

and it looked quite deserted and lonely when we went away. We heard that seventy-five thousand soldiers are coming in a day or two, and that lots of wounded men will be brought to Aix too, so it is lucky we could go. The heat was terrific, and we were soon as sticky, dirty, and uncomfortable as could be. But we forgot our troubles when we passed long freight trains with soldiers huddled in like cattle, who were being carried to the front. There was hardly room for them to sit down, although in some cars they had thrown themselves on hay upon the floor and lay crowded together in their heavy blue coats. Soldiers guarded every bridge and tunnel that we passed, and at the stations we handed anything from wine and bread to bonbons and cigarettes out of the train windows to the herds of soldiers who were there. It was impossible to sleep at night, for the compartment was stuffy and small, and I sincerely envied Mr. M. who rolled his coat on the floor of the corridor, and slept there.

August 14　Aix-les-Bains

At nine o'clock in the morning we reached Paris. We had thought there would be time to go to a hotel and wash up a bit, but the train which was to take us to Boulogne was waiting so we were again piled into a roasting hot carriage. How terribly slowly the cars went, for every other train had the right of way. We gulped down water all day long in a vain attempt to keep cool. At last in the evening we reached Boulogne. As a porter took our bags he said that the boat would not leave till morning but we thought, because it was a special boat to meet our train, that he was wrong. But when we got on board we found out that it was true, for no ships leave after dark on account of the danger of mines. Then we tried to get a cabin but they had all been eagerly grabbed already. We couldn't even go to a hotel for the night because they said that we had left French soil and without passports could not go back. Finally Father and Mr. Fels whom we'd met bought up the captain's cabin together, and in these cramped quarters we tried to sleep, but Harold who lay down on a bench on deck succeeded better.

August 15   London

At about seven in the morning the boat left, and after an unpleasant crossing of the Channel we arrived at Folkestone where another train awaited us. We were terribly worn out, for the whole long trip from Aix had been terrific, so we were glad to breakfast even on such queer things as crackers, chocolate, and wine. And then finally we reached London at about noon. It felt quite like coming home again and oh, what a relief to get into a good hotel again, and wash and eat and sleep! I don't think I ever slept so well before.

August 16   London

There are several people from Aix here, in fact the hotel is full of Americans, all trying to get home as we are. It is good to get into calm, stolid England after our experiences with the excitable Frenchmen. In the hotel at Aix they trampled on the signs and advertisements of the Hamburg-American Line, and here, although the people are at war also, they are still sane. The English soldiers are so much finer looking too, so much cleaner, stronger, younger looking; they remind us more of our American cadets.

August 18   London

If we only had some definite news of the war, something we could surely believe! But there are so many wild rumors floating about—even that Ireland is having civil war and the British troops are all there, that the English fleet is annihilated, the President of France murdered, and that the Crown Prince has locked up the Kaiser to keep him from making further trouble. But there are no true reports from Germany. Father, with his usual luck and influence, has somehow gotten passage for next Saturday on the "Olympic" although thousands of people want it, and I knew we should seize the chance eagerly. But then we are leaving Aunt Hermie. It seems like deserting her, although we know she is safe and that we can't get to her, but we hate to go off without knowing her plans. Dad has sent letters by means of the Austrian Ambassador who has just gone home, has sent a cable of a hundred and forty words via Sweden, and tonight another one through Mr. Heilborn. Everyone seems to be worrying about some separated friend or relative and the whole city is plunged in a quiet, resigned despair.

August 19   London

Grandfather's birthday. How happy we are that he is spared the strain of this summer.

Even here, in quiet, thoughtful England, almost every man on the street is a soldier. We saw several thousands of them yesterday in Hyde Park—such boys, scarcely any over thirty, and most of them smiling and orderly. Oh it is dreadful to think of those fellows lying dead on a battlefield or being ruined forever, mere targets for the enemy's great, cruel guns. The tension at present is dreadful. Last night in the lobby a fool woman lit a match which made a tiny explosive sound as it caught fire and several people screamed and started and wanted to know what happened.

August 20

It has been positively decided—we are to sail on the "Olympic" next Saturday. I can't find words enough to say how happy I am! To get out of this miserable, unfortunate country, to be home again! Of course we are worried and uncertain about Aunt Hermie, but she hasn't sent one reply to our hundreds of cables, and we are as hopelessly far from her here as anywhere in the world, so we have gotten passage so soon. The city is overflowing with Americans who don't want to wait for the transports the government is sending, who are even willing to go steerage. Almost everyone has had some kind of adventure. One lady we met lost every speck of her baggage, every handkerchief even; another crossed the border in a hay wagon, and still others whose money was absolutely gone, were befriended by some strange English people who took them into their own home until they could get assistance.

August 21

Tomorrow we sail. Half reluctantly of course, for we have still had no word from Aunt Hermie, but very, very gratefully nevertheless. About fifty of our letters have gone astray, we haven't been able to buy most of the gifts we wanted, instead of touring Austria, Holland, Italy, Germany and Switzerland we stayed only in France and England, and in place of the fun we were to have there has only been boredom and worry. The summer has, without doubt, been a fizzle. And still, I'm glad to have lived through it. I will probably never again see events like these at present, or go through similar experiences, and although what we saw was tragic and what we went through nerve racking, still, now that it is over, it is most interesting and exciting to look back on. How fortunate we are to escape after this slight taste, without being touched by the actual misery all about us! And how many times fortunate in escaping to so free and peaceful a country as America!

October 4, 1918

Professor Baldwin* accosted me on the stairs today and to my surprise announced, "Miss Ginzburg, the glass of Rheims Cathedral is falling." I stared in silent amazement at the unexpected announcement. "The beautiful stained glass windows of the ruined church lie in fragments on the ground." Pause. I felt embarrassed. "They say the soldiers come and pick

*Charles Sears Baldwin, Professor of Rhetoric and English Composition at Columbia, author of manuals on writing and an *Introduction to Medieval Literature*.

up bits of the glass and have them set in rings. . . . There's a poem in that don't you think?" With which he marched off. "Yes! Thank you." I yelled after him, recovering my breath.

December 20, 1918

At lunch Bertha Wallerstein told me the most terrible thing I've ever heard, and I haven't been able to shake it off all day. No story, no matter how dreadful, has ever depressed me so. I feel positively weak from it. It happened to a conscientious objector at Camp Leavenworth. The way the conscientious objectors have been tortured I have often heard, but most people are ignorant of it, for the newspapers suppress that sort of thing. This is the most gruesome case I've ever heard of: they put this man in a tub of water in an ammonia room, till the water froze about him and he begged them to kill him. Ten minutes later he died. A tale like that makes me want to go out and kill. And they call that sort of man a coward! Talk of medieval barbarism, of German brutality. Just picture it! I've always thought I was an idealist and would have the courage of my convictions, but hearing this makes me feel that an idealist is the saddest person in the world—that it would be better to sell one's soul than live through such agony. Think of men doing such a thing.

3 Travel, 1927-40: Unreal as a Postcard

1938: In Switzerland the scenery is unreal as a postcard and familiar in the same way, dramatic and hackneyed. As for sightseeing, I get little out of the momentary glimpse except strain and exhaustion. I am of the kind who will look at one old codger with his beard and his polished white collar and his citizen-of-the-world air, and get more of the country from him than from a thousand rapidly seen sights.

Paris

1927: *Sacre Coeur* in Montmartre. Up the steep curved hill. Glimpses into courtyards, cobbled, puddled, green pots of flowers; kitchen with old man mixing a salad dressing on table, red checked cloth and ingredients in little dishes, a big book open before him, which he read with spectacles as he stirred. Modern clean apartments and bits of houses. The church with clusters of candles and black garbed people kneeling. Great spread angels on walls of dome. Intentness on faces as compared to our mundane indifference or inquisitiveness. Childish lack of self-consciousness.

April 8

Coming from Paris to Marseilles, leaving the damp chilly atmosphere, the gaiety, the Parisian insouciance, for a cosmopolitan city of burning blue sky, luxuriant foliage, as though each leaf were separately waxed, white stone, red tiled roofs. Spanish town in many ways—the flat low walls, little cobbled alleys, big squares. Much poverty yet on the surface little want; black shawled old women in the market place, selling flowers and vegetables. The square full of the outer leaves of cauliflower. A hot sun. Seething city. View on the heights. The vieux porte—boats to all countries. Senegalese—Japs— Chinamen. Black brave savages with shining teeth in European clothes, oriental costumes. The drive along the blue Mediterranean, white chalk or lime hills and goats nibbling at the sparse vegetation. Pink walls and colored shutters and white roads. All fishing villages, nets and boats, hills, steep streets.

Performing family on stilts. Two children on short ones, and the older girl up very high dancing lightly and easily up and down from the curb, her head held high and no expression on her haughty face. Even when the crowd threw pennies she did not unbend, but accepted it all like a princess, pirouetting loftily in her yellow skirt. The mother turned an organ which ground out gay tunes, and on a shelf beside her hurdy-gurdy, a tiny baby slept in a basket. Think of that infant starting life a few inches from the music, riding through the streets in that cool entourage. . . .

April 10
The *Rawelpindi*, sailing from England to Bombay, a P. & O. Line.* We boarded her at Marseilles. Slim small tight boat, very shipshape and modern. Steward who lays out clothes, stewardess and early morning tea. Passed Corsica, Sicily, Italy, through the Straits of Messina. Volcanic island of Stromboli, a dark gray steep hill of hard stone, menacing and bleak. The crater at the top was like a camel's hump. Below, it smoked

*Lenore Marshall's husband James Marshall accompanied her on this trip to Palestine in the spring of 1927. The trip lasted approximately two months and included, in addition to stopovers in London and Paris, Trans-Jordan, Syria, Lebanon, and Egypt.

constantly, a long cloud floating across the blue sky. A little white village lay at the foot curled along the coast. On either side of it skiing slides where burning lava of previous eruptions must have left a trail. No visible fertility—only a stubbly bare green evident from the sea. What a life—perhaps fisherfolk. Always beneath that unfriendly smoky summit.

Blue opaque water of the Mediterranean. Thick blue.

Hurricane at sea on the Atlantic. The boat dipping like a canoe. A steep roll and a whole room full of people, chairs, tables, sliding like an avalanche to the wall and in a moment being flung the other way. Passed a small craft, very near by, the size of a ferry boat, probably a fishing smack. It rode on the waves like a cork. A great water mountain would lunge toward it, lift it to its crest like a bull tossing straw on its horns. Then the whole little ship disappeared in a deep chasm, nothing in sight but the points of its masts. An awful sight, so lonely and helpless.

Mrs. L. on seeing the volcano, caressingly, "Oh, isn't it nice?"

Commenting on Jim's book: "I like it so much; what I like about it is the names you use, like Emmetsberg. That's so nice. How do you think of those nice things?"

April 13

Africa! seeing land from the boat was like living the Sunday picture papers—it really looks like that. Port Said is a poor flat picturesque seaport town, with the East and the West mixing on every corner. The place teems with beggars, palsied, blind, ragged. The men are barefooted, wear red fezzes, long cotton shirts. At the customs the porters wore white skirts and blue jerseys marked "cooks." Polite—all know a few words of English. Sitting at a café one is accosted by a continuous stream of peddlers: children who grab your feet to shine your shoes, men selling cigarettes, Turkish Delight, canes, trinkets. "Dis chain—only one pound, ten shilling." "Go on! You mean ten piastres!" "Ten piastres! No! I give you for ten shilling"—and so on to one shilling. Then they said, "You make toss for it! See! You a good sport?" The women—some in European short skirts, some veiled. A brass piece from head-dress to nose holds the veil in place. Story of the Prince's favorite wife throned on an elephant who became startled and jumped. The lady's garment ripped off by tusks as she slid down—exposed completely. The Englishman who galloped ahead so that he shouldn't embarrass the native lord sent back to enquire later for the lady, and received word that she was quite all right and the chief not at all concerned over the accident since the veil covering her face had not been torn! Indian fakir and nails in nose, out through mouth, read numbers on coins he never saw—card tricks. Little boy pupil with chicken and egg: said "one-two-three-golly-golly-golly."

Jerusalem

Sandy dusty stony roads, white square stone houses, excavations, old wall, Arab courtyards, red poppies and a quantity of other bright wild flowers. Outside of our garden the hill on which Christ was supposed to have been crucified. Every step has a familiar name and you feel with suddenness an almost physical connection to your past.

The Samaritan Passover

A group dying out now, who have kept separate from the Jews living in Samaria. Nablus, a two hour run from Jerusalem. A fair people, like Arabs but not so swarthy, bearded, wearing long shirts, turbans—entirely as one imagines Moses. They speak their own language, still sacrifice a real lamb, the paschal lamb. This is done usually at midnight but on account of the coming Sabbath we saw it at noon. A steep climb to the mountain on which they celebrate. Donkeys helped us up— slow, tough little fellows. Like a circus on top. Tents in which

the Samaritans live during the holiday; people from all over—
Arabs, English, Jews. We had a letter to the high priest and
were admitted to his cabin—a white bearded patriarch with a
tall dark bearded son. "Shalom," he said to us all and we sat on
rugs on the floor till the ceremony. Outside people crushed on
the walk in a circle, to see. English and Arab police kept some
sort of order. A deep hole in the ground held two kettles of
boiling water, and fresh boughs were constantly carried in for
the fire. Heat of sun and flame and people crowding. Queer
children and women veiled and gay in festive shawls and colors.
The six lambs are brought in and the Samaritan men, surrounding the pit, start chanting and gesticulating; finally,
before the slaughter, baaing like lambs, working to a pitch of
frenzy. The killing—then boys skin the lambs, pulling off the
wool, and at last they are thrown in the cauldrons where they
are cooked for supper.

Lunch on the ground outside the priest's tent. Beggars.
Children. Pilgrims. The son gave us matzohs—unbaked tough
doughy things. A wild man on the hillside going down, sitting
against a rock among the thistles, ragged and half dressed and
hairy, shouting to the passers-by. Trip home through steep
country, winding roads up and down mountains through Arab
villages, terraced hills and stone fences.

The Nebe Mousa*

The Arabs made saints out of all the old fellows, Moses
included. At Passover all of the different tribes flock into
Jerusalem. It was a triple celebration, the Christian Easter, the
Jewish holiday, the Arab festival. We saw the Hebronites
celebrating, with drums and fifes and shouts and chanting,
swords thrown up in the air, flags, speeches. The audience was
most interesting. The streets were lined with pushing dirty
people. Galicians in fur hats and purple robes or black satin

*Nebe Mousa is the Arab name for Moses, who is a saint in the Islamic
faith.

coats, black veiled women or others in gaily embroidered shawls, beggars with bare breasts and sack cloth. Women squatted on the crowded cobblestones suckling their babies, or slung the filthy crying little things in bags on their backs, among rags and covered with a cloth so that they must almost smother, an older child in their arms and one tapping at their skirts. The celebrating people then march for two days to the plains of Nebe Mousa near the Dead Sea where they symbolically gather up Moses' body and reburn it.

Dinner and Seder at Miss Annie Landau's. Fat florid English Jewess and her two sisters. Mixed crowd—big mixed room—very orthodox—was the fourth glass of wine filled, a great question, which made one Miss L. want the service repeated. "Eh?" The English mannerisms and the Jewish temperaments incongruous.

"Music at 9:30 at Government House." A formal function in a large palace, with pudgy Lord Plumer and her Ladyship, scrawny and jewelled, say "How-do-you-do? How-do-you-do?"* She is apt to burst out with such inept explosions as "Books! Don't you just love them!" People wore their decorations—men and women alike—gay costumes, amateur show and atmosphere. Flunkies dressed like the Arabian Nights.

April 23rd   Trip to Jerasch in Transjordania

From high Jerusalem (nearly 3,000 feet) down to the Dead Sea via Jericho, and across the Jordan, 900 feet *below* sea level. The air grew horribly oppressive and our ears hurt and heads ached. Steep curved roads, Old Jericho, a village of cobbled huts. Up and down on the other side for several hours, until at last we came to Jerasch, an Arab town settled mostly by Circassians. Old Roman ruins are being excavated there under the British government's direction, and lovely columns stand

*Lord Herbert Onslow Plumer was the British High Commissioner in Palestine, then ruled by Britain under a mandate from the League of Nations.

almost intact, two amphitheatres, a forum, etc., all on the wild hillside. Below is the little town, a stream making a green line through it. Arab hovels, primitive stone bakery—and our hostelry, run by a Druse in long white robe and stately of mien, bearded, and by a fat Circassian, neither of whom could speak any English. A courtyard, table in the center, three rooms at the sides, a pump and basin, in which we all washed and in which the dishes and forks were also more or less cleaned. Our room had a stone floor, three beds, a table; open unshaded windows, and it was reasonably clean. We had all of our own bedding and food. Ate our picnic supper under the stars in the court. Lots of fun. There were Mitchell and Codington from the American School, who'd gone down on their cycle; and our party, David, Hershkovitz, Jim and I. The Arabs watched us and were friendly. Little walk and to bed. Good sleep though the Arabs rose and started work around four and our proprietor probably came in and gazed on us asleep for our door was open in the morning. Breakfast again—at six—in the square yard, roses from the proprietor, kindly handshakes. It was a grand experience . . . Awfully hot going home. The "homseen" or sirocco blowing warm wind and sand on us. Passed many Bedouins camping or wandering in groups, camels with whole households on them and often a sheep or goat as well, strapped to the camel's back. Many of the Transjordanians go armed with old guns on their backs as they jog along on little donkeys—some have splendid Arab horses. Near the Jordan all is parched and dry. The clay is cracked, the sand piled in high pyramids. A narrow oasis of a stream flows near the road, oleanders and wild roses, wild hollyhocks, etc., making a lovely border. Groves of palms, fig trees, banana and orange and olive trees.

April 22nd

Beginning of automobile trip with Magneses.* *First day:* Jerusalem to Nablus and down into the valley of the Amak where the Jewish colonies are situated. Profoundly impressive, what these young men and women have done in five or six years. The settlements are poor and dilapidated, but most of them have gardens and all are based on agricultural development: wheat raising, cows, chickens, fruit orchards, etc. From swamp lands infested with mosquitoes they have made their settlements almost entirely free of malaria. Called "Halutzim." A fine straightforward upstanding lot—none of the Jewish inferiority noticeable in them, no smugness, no hypocrisy. Willing to work hard, unashamed, women good strong animals. Children provided for first and all looked clean and fat and happy.

In the evening to Haifa and up to Mt. Carmel for two nights and a day. A heavenly spot, like the Riviera they say, looking down on the Mediterranean. Pine trees and flowers here on the cool hill top; below, the town curving around the bay, and the indescribable blue of the sea stretching in a round line as far as one can see. A beach—boats in the harbor—good Kosher hotel with white balconies. Hills behind the town rising misty green and sloping down to the startling blue water.

Haifa to Safad, by way of hot Tiberias on the lovely blue Sea of Tiberias. Visited two Hasidic colonies in the morning. There you saw the other side of the picture. These were city folk, and older, mostly from Poland, entirely unfit for farm life. Sad thin faces and bleak cabins with gaps between the boards through which the winter rains must have poured. Had followed a "wonder rabbi" and lost their money in so doing. Young M.D. from Hamburg sent by Workers Committee and

*Beatrice Magnes was James Marshall's aunt. She and her husband Judah were living in Palestine. He was a rabbi, president of the Hebrew University in Jerusalem (see p. 199). David was their elder son and Hershkovitz their driver.

his discouragement in the face of all the misery, hunger, illness. One well of water far from houses so folk could hardly keep clean. Children all had lice . . .

Inn at Safad run by German girls. Old town—medieval feeling.

Across the Jordan and into Syria, bare country up to the great green oasis of Damascus. Dirty Victoria hotel, fleas. Proprietor, "They're harmless, they only bite a little." Weird shiny pictures on walls, steep stairs. The bazaars are the fascinating part of Damascus. Long covered streets and booth after booth, Arabs squatting and philosophically waiting for trade—no rivalry, friendly good nature. Every kind of shop: rows of cake, bread, fruit, candy booths (Delati's for candy), silk bazaars, brass bazaars, leather—everything. Water carriers, "Allah will quench thy thirst." Youths selling fruit waters from earthen pitchers, singsong chants, run shops with costly carpets displayed in the dark shadows; donkeys and laden camels patiently dragged through the crowds, smell of spices, pepper. Bedouins from the desert bargaining and spending, after a forty day trip through the sands to reach Damascus.

A Jewish home—walled in courtyard and apartments on all sides for every branch of a great family. Remote peaceful stone rooms, mosaics, platform at one end; fountains in rooms, and in court. Orange and citron trees.

April 26

To Baalbek, up out of Damascus and North through a cleft in the anti-Lebanon mountains. Green fields. Old Arab town—nice plain hotel and pleasant proprietor. Marvellous Roman ruins—Temple of Jupiter, and Temple of Bacchus. Pink weathered columns, Corinthian capitals, beautiful carving and mosaic ceiling—incredible work. Enormous stones, more than 70 feet long. Little flowers in crevices, daisies and red poppies—birds.

April 27
To Beirut. Climbed 8000 feet in the Lebanons till we were close beside snow patches—fine road and good view. Well-built summer houses on way down, through the clouds. Beirut on the Mediterranean, a more European city than Damascus, but with the flavor of the near East none-the-less. French speaking. Pleasant shops (Indian shop—things from Bombay, etc.) Fine harbor—American University on the waterfront with charming garden. Hotel Continental. O.K. Many beggars as in all Eastern cities. Poor. Camels galumphing through streets, as everywhere.

April 28
Left Beirut early for Haifa, driving along the Mediterranean coast. Through Sidon and Tyre, old Arab towns of small bazaars and crowded streets, friendly people. Along Phoeni cian coast, a sheep and goat-grazing land today where our alphabet started and the world's first shipping began. Blue sea all the way, hills and trees and streams. From Syria to Palestine. France to England. To Haifa through the ancient town of Acre—old crusaders' fortress and strong sea wall in curved turrets. Street cafés, old mosque and lovely paved courtyard. Looking through the arch of the gate, time loses its quality of progress. Arabs wander under the old stone, prisoners wave cheerfully in their stripes in the midst of the populations, women go to the public fountain to fill their jugs. Over the sands of the harbor to Haifa. Dr. Biram's school overlooking the bay—bright garden and children working it. Good school of the Berman order, with high scholastic standards. Tea on roof. No privacy for children: washstands of boarders in a row. Teachers entering childrens' rooms without knocking.

7:30 train from Haifa to Tel-Aviv (old Jaffa) changing at Lud, and escorted by Dr. Slozisti, because Jim and Judah motored to see further colonies, too strenuous a day for my taste. Dr.

Slozisti's enthusiasm for Palestine was very interesting. "It is *my* land—I suffer—I am willing to suffer—for my *own* land. In Germany it is different. I am happy here. In Tel-Aviv Shabboth is Shabboth—it is—it is Shabboth. This land is stronger than the people who come. It can change their souls. Can other countries do that? This land can make a new race. In America the pilgrims came first and suffered, the Jews long after. It is not their land. Here the Jews came first. They will suffer—get malaria, die, plant trees—it is their land. In other countries the Jew thinks, he talks. Here he must act. It is *his* land."—etc. "A fanatic of the soil."

Saturday in Tel-Aviv. Families walking the streets, stores closed except occasional drug stores, no vehicles. A real rest day.

The Good Hope

Play given by workers in Tel-Aviv for workers. The unseaworthy ship and the fishermen sent out by a capitalist—theme to appeal to these earnest young trade unionists, given in the great exhibition hall of an insurance company, a shed holding a thousand people. Audience all young—many hungry—many children because they couldn't be left home alone. Everyone attentive and well behaved, enthusiastic. Remarkable performance, unprofessional because these were all workers who rehearse only at night, but with a passion and rhythm and artistic instinct that was most impressive.

Jerusalem

Shopped at Ohan. University reception. Tea at Mrs. Gatling's. (Pacifist daughter of the Gatling gun—no smoking as she's an anti-tobacconist; pleasant gay English crowd). Receptions—Catholic Bazaar. Lady Plumer, looking like Queen Mary, opening it with a Masefield quotation; dinner at Magneses, Guinsbergs, Sacher, Bentwich, etc. Dinner with Bluestone's—nice man, competent in a difficult job, energetic;

call on Mrs. Ben Zvi who does nursery gardening: rugged hearty type, Russian, whose manners spring from within, not without.*

The Mosque of Omar, containing the dome of the rock, the ridged rock on which the ancient sacrifices were made. A beautiful mosque, with windows punctured to let in a pure light, fine stone and wood work. Most of all one loves the quiet of these mosques. You step out of the throbbing pushing bazaars of the old city, put on the flopping shoes they tie over your own, a step out of the glare of the courtyard, and there you are in a shadowy peace, remote as if by miles from the city. Great court-fountain—two mosques—wall from which one has a fine view of the city. The mountains of Moab, the valley of Jehosephat, across the Jordan, the flat roofs of the city, the Wailing Wall and a few pious Jews facing it, bobbing to and fro, muttering their unending prayers, hours on end, bearded, long black coats, flat black felt hats, some with longish hair coming into two twisted curls over their ears.

The bazaars outside are as fascinating as those of Damascus. The aroma of sesame, donkey laden pushing among the people, red leather slippers on sale, brasses, silks, peasant embroideries, meats, breads, sticky wonderful looking confections, many flies, heat. Persistent but good-natured vendors, laughing their few words of English. Nuts—pine nuts and pistachios and almonds. Saddle bags. Dirty-nosed children wandering alone through the melée. Gold chains and earrings.

The Holy Sepulchre still Moslem property. One ducks thru a low stone arch to the tomb, candles burning. Not very beautiful. Place full of holy spots, every inch with its legend.

Trip to Hebron with Mr. & Mrs. Max Schlesinger—8 a.m.

*Norman de Mattos Bentwich was attorney General of Palestine under the British mandate. Joseph Isaac Bluestone was a hospital administrator who was helping to organize the Hadassah Hospital in Jerusalem. Izhak Ben-Zvi, then leader of the Labor movement Histadrut, became President of Israel in 1952.

to 6 p.m. Through Bethlehem; women wear high head dresses there, as they did in the days of the Crusaders: styles and customs unchanged since then. Long white veil knotted at hem in back. Old narrow streets. The mosque at Hebron supposed to contain the tomb of Abraham, Isaac and Jacob, and their wives. Very hard to get permission to enter, but a note from Mr. Bentwich to the Chief Sheikh got us through. Interesting associations even to the skeptical; it hardly matters whether the tales they tell are true, for one place is as good as another as a setting to the picturesque old stories. The Arabs here were the worst we struck anywhere; a primitive savage lot who all wanted to guide us and would not leave us in peace. Shouted their few words of English—boys and men alike: "Listen, listen! Shut-up; Shut-up!" A disorderly crew, many half blind (the flies do that) some with cruel beastly faces.

Lunch at the Oak of Mamrhe, a shady spot, oak supposed to be 1800 years old, a very gnarled crumbing great old thing. Old woman of 80 there, selling post cards, who talked to us, full of spirits and vim.

The Synagogue of Abraham in Hebron is in the old ghetto. We went through the narrowest of alleys, in and out of steep curves and sharp angles. A fat squat friendly woman let us in, and other queer looking people followed. The tall old rabbi had something wrong with his bulging eyes; long garment, gray beard. Hard wooden benches. We went high up to the roof of one of these ghetto houses. Better than our tenements, for all their cramped littleness, because the walls and floors are of stone and can be kept clean, not mouldy and buggy. White-washed. Incredibly small rooms, steep high stone staircase, bedroom with covers and mattress heaped high, nothing else, but a low cupboard into which one could crawl on hands and knees to the basin to wash. View from the roof.

Glass flowers factory in Hebron—one of the few remaining hand worked glass maker's factories. A low hot cave. In the center the oven with four openings before each of which squatted a dark Arab, his long iron fork in the leaping flames. Some of the men chanting their rhythmic monotonous wordless songs. A twist of the hand, and the hot clay would become a bracelet; a blow of breath and a bowl or jar would form, a swing of the hot thing in the air and the shape would change miraculously as we watched. Very skilled, it seemed, and entirely primitive at the same time. Light, lovely, blue grass.

Beit Govrin on way home where very ancient caves remain. A hot walk up a rocky hill, steps down into the caves, mosaic work and painted figures on the walls, fairly well preserved remains of an old Roman villa; further on, painted and very ancient caves.

Cairo

Stopped over, at Shepherd's Hotel two nights and day, on way to Alexandria. Well worth it, heat and all. A large city, European in appearance in its business section, Arabic in its old streets. Hundreds of mosques, whose minarets and domes rise everywhere. Good shops, persistent street vendors of junk, flies, glare and heat at mid-day. Coptic church and museum—a branch of the Christian Church; early art, quite out-of-proportion and childlike. Lunch at old Groppe's, tea at new Groppe's, good restaurants with shady gardens and tables on verandahs and below trees. Lovely blue tree from India, high, flowering, fairy color at dusk. Great banyan trees with branches that take root in the soil and grow in thick clumps about the central trunk.

To three mosques—early, 800 A.D. Time of Saladin—circa 1200—and a later one 1500 (?). All quiet and remote seeming. Mosaic, stone, wood carving, simple arches, clear alabaster and marble.

Dinner at the Mena House opposite the Pyramids. I was astounded at myself—such a thrill seeing those ancient piles, and my reaction was wholly unexpected. One's indifference melts as they loom up in the evening, nearly 6000 years old, witnesses of so much greatness and littleness, themselves unchanged, never repaired, uncrumbling through time. Sandstone. We have not advanced in essentials since they were made, as symbols of mystery and power. Desert all about, camels walking with that peculiar rhythm of neck which precedes the motion of legs, a few dragomen and fortune tellers, etc.

The Sphinx is set in a slight hollow—one gigantic piece of stone (limestone) carved great and mysterious and impressive. Home in the moonlight—beautiful.

Arabic Museum—fine colored glass lamps, etc.

Egyptian museum—old wood carvings, stone work, etc. One understands this flat-appearing angular Egyptian art—in this climate everything tends to look that way. Tutankhamun wing—a marvellous display of splendor and preservation. Jewelry all unerased and exquisite, fine carving and engraving. Gold tombs and sarcophagi, inlaid with mosaics, enamelled, splendid. Minerally mummies, stately in their rags, their original garments. Chariots, gold wheels, beads, lovely fabrics, all still beautiful. Dry climate aids this.

Sailed from Alexandria on *S. S. Patria*, Fabre Line. An unpleasant boat, nothing ship-shape about it: dirty floors, damp railings, even the food—which we'd expected to find excellent on any French craft—turning out tasteless and smelly. Cabin-deluxe our salvation; we spent lots of time in it very comfortably. A cruise boat with a bunch of tourists on board, noisily gay and thick skinned. Loud French people predominated, men fat, bearded, moustached, women coarse, garrulous. The Americans were no better, a middle-class bourgeois set whose grammar was bad and who slapped one another on the back constantly or giggled. The group was finished by an English contingent, dull and tiresome with their "Oh Quites" and "rather nice" and "rather beastly" and "Stewards"-

Met a number of people. How do these dowdy folk get cash

enough for such trips? Mother and son—been to India, Egypt, Italy. Elderly couple from near Boston—she with horrid yellowy bobbed hair—travel each year to most remote places—friendly and loquacious. English couple and little boy, going home from the Sudan.

Stopped at Messina; the ship ran a trip up to Taormina so we joined the tourists for a day on shore. Sicily—what we saw of it—is what one would imagine: thick orange and lemon groves, leaves shiny and round bright fruit looking so rich and opulent, purple bougainvillea, almond trees, neat terraces and stone walls. Taormina is a charming village, near Aetna. Old streets, quaint courtyard, arched doorways, cobbles and steps, colored cement houses, pale green and pink and yellow lovely opulent gardens. Hotels for tourists big but seeming old and pictur-esque. Lunch at San Dominico convent—a real convent once, I should guess, from old arched ceilings, cloisters, big rooms, etc. Lovely there. Painted carts a delightful feature, two great wheels and little flat wagon gaily ornamented with pictures. Good steep curving roads. Ruins of a Greek theatre. Wonderful site on the hillside, looking over the Mediterranean and higher up, the hills and crags. Yet it wasn't as beautiful as other places.

I've seen Lynton, parts of Saranac, Mt. Carmel . . .

An old one-legged man sat at the roadside and played on a pipe, a primitive flute. Just right he was, fitting into the setting, with his jolly Italian face and his cocky expression and his merry tunes.

Passed Stromboli Island at 10:30 at night and saw her erupting. That was a real thrill, exciting as it was unexpected. So many of these unexpected adventures have taken place on this trip—more than any other we'd had . . . The night heightened the effect and they say Stromboli always smokes and throws off some flame, only against a brilliant daytime sky one doesn't see it. First we noticed a glow in the crater, then suddenly there came a great spurt of flame like mammoth fireworks rising in the sky. This subsided, but five minutes later another leap of red fire, a long tongue spreading and showering, and later another and another, till we had passed from sight. While we watched from our safe distance, yet with some alarm at the awful spectacle, waiting and watching, the little town of white houses that we'd noticed on the way out slept at the base of the mountain, not a light glimmering anywhere.

1938 Holland

It looks as tho the whole country is full of Mr. Reichenbach!* Daniel Websters—the men are sedate in black double-breasted suits (on the beach at Schevenigen!) into whose vests at any moment they may thrust their hands and address the Senate. Lots are bearded, with derbies or little caps on their heads. Sailors dressed up for a funeral. We get cheese for breakfast, thin golden slabs with fat bubbles standing out, and many kinds of bread in the basket—pumpernickel, rusks, raisin bread, zweibach, whole wheat, rye, white—and jams. How they stuff on the proletarian beach, bread and cheese, bread and cheese. Booths sell milk, kaffee, ices. Bath chairs. Blonde children dig. Ugly women, fat; harsh voices; no vanity. Families. Fruit. Guttural language spoken with open mouth. The peasant women are better looking and have great individuality; not only their heavy black shirts, shawls in triangles down the back and the ends tucked into the waist band in front, starched white cap poking out in back sometimes of sheer lace glazed and transparent, but their faces have a beauty—of independence—reliant, pink, calm, nerveless, and they hold themselves upright as though in virtue and strength. Children fly kites. Everyone rides bicycles, some built for two.

Of the dirty beach: they dug below the peanut-shell line to the cleaner damp sand.

*A rather fussy and stiff friend of the family.

4 Travel, 1951-57: Fresh to Impressions Again

1952: Our routines reduce us. Travel is like washing the hair, a layer of dullness washes off. We are clean and fresh to impressions again, less grime between us and them. How we limit ourselves at home to the same thoughts, the same round of emotions. We relax now and behold, there is something new, still, to be seen.

1952 Europe

Feel good because of sendoff.

Many people were thoughtful. I feel happy to have some good friends.

Ellen was warm and devoted and helpful and mature—also nervous for me! Quite keyed up at my leaving. Full of advice and charming. She's doing so well! I love her.

George, Nancy,* the Schermans on board. A cheerful gay dining table of 8. No motion to speak of. I couldn't have done this ten years ago. Make my arrangements with ease, no trouble with people. A bit amazed! Philosophical. Solitude, yes,—but decide to make most of it in affirmative way. No news of J & J. Wish they'd have cabled at least where they are.

A bang in the night. My life-belt, I think, collision. At the same time the fog horn blasts out. Put on light, jump up. My big suitcase has crashed from its stand to the floor.

*Lenore Marshall's brother-in-law, George Marshall, and his daughter.

The ship is rolling. I'm relieved—no accident—wasn't too scared though, only knocked awake. The horn continues. Moon gone. I sleep again.

At lunch. The usual questions are mutually asked—what one does, where from, etc., etc. Having found out I'm a writer there is much talk of books—"good" books, "bad" books. The lady from South Carolina, very pleasant, says "I just can't read Tolstoy, I know he's good but he's too depressing." Like the fog horn.

Fourth Day

I'm really enjoying it. So surprised! An adventure in independence. "Being timid she must always be proving her courage." Today is heaven. The mugginess has lifted. The air is sunny, bright. What a blue sparkling wide sea! I quote poetry as I walk the deck by myself. It is my own poetry, I find, and it stands up. "The girdling line, drawn far, drawn near/ Sometimes misted, sometimes clear,/Is somewhere always, troubled heart,/Keeping the sea and sky apart. Etc. "Bright patrician waters," "blue lawn" "silver flower heads," "plunge like bulls"—not bad—"a last abiding rim of peace."

I am enjoying it. The glorious air, sky, detached freedom. When I came to lunch today, the officer (purser) at our table. He is 52, looks 32, tan, sensitive, courteous, probably nice. He said: "Look at her eyes! I wish I could come down to lunch with such sparkling eyes." "I've been looking at the sea," I laughed. "It's not the sea, it's you." I tried to turn it. "Do you get out of doors much, Mr. Jolliffe?" "No, I don't too much like the sun. But I could be led." There is a burst of delighted laughter from the table. They're intrigued and I'm amused.

Dinner, drinks, movies with the Schermans. Nice evening. Harry says, "Your table is quite interested in you and curious.* They saw me wave to you and later asked me 'Who is this Mrs. Marshall?' I told them you're a writer." This accounts for it. I

*Harry Scherman was president of the Book-of-the-Month Club.

might be a Fiji Islander, a rare curiosity, whom one asks "What do you eat in your country?" They're pleasant enough people—two Carolina sisters, a couple, a Dublin government man, a Philadelphia shipper, the purser. It's easy to be with 'em—for a brief time. The flattery is superficial but the sense of security—being able at last to feel secure in the world in microcosm—that's new. It takes so long to grow up in these small unimportant ways. At the MacDowell* too I discovered it—being on my own and winning a ribbon. Why must one feel so afraid of the mass? Thomas Mann shows it in "Tonio Kröger." It's good to get over it and not to have sacrificed the self in the struggle.

Two nights of full moon. Black water, vapory clouds, silver path. Like Folinsbee paintings. All the same it doesn't thrill me as in youth. Yet I go out and watch by myself before turning in.

The rail no longer frightens me. Nor the big portholes. I walk on sundeck and forget the rail. Patterns fading. Thank God. Dining salon easy. Is it—? New understanding.

George is a fine person. This chance to be alone together is interesting. He was J's little brother too long. He is kind and attentive to me. But more—perceptive. We have long talks. He's a sensitive father and I can see that in spite of the prison thing that his children suffered he's given them a lot—very delicate with them, no domination, yet *there*. Nancy's interesting. Don't know her yet or how she'll develop. Burning eyes, firm, fastidious. Serious and gay. Not many young people. N. decides she must have a scalp; she and George plan a strategy. There is one youth she decides to meet and conquer. So G. takes her to the dance floor, gives her a whirl, shows her off. Sure enough, a man asks to dance, then the youth steps up. Now N. has an escort! G. and I watch in amusement.

---

*The MacDowell Colony in Peterboro, New Hampshire, is a haven for writers, artists, and composers, who apply for the privilege of working in bucolic seclusion. Lenore Marshall spent two summers there.

Friday

Beginning to be excited about the beauty and newness to be seen ahead. How different from the last time abroad. Then I felt I would never see Europe again. There was finality and dread then, coming home; all of this would have been impossible. Goodbye Europe, then. But now I want to cram all possible into these two weeks. All the cathedrals, streets, language, voices, art, get all I can, to feed on and to last. Resolutions to get up early, do all that strength allows. I must come again. Curious how a chance word can change one's attitude: Ellen said, "Get the most out of it." And I felt, yes, that's it. Have been studying, reading. More prepared now.

In Train—Monday, Cherbourg. I couldn't bear a single tunnel. I want to see and see! The stone houses, sloped roofs, people waving. Small square gardens, the red faces, berets; geraniums in windows, cobbled courtyards. Greenness like home. I love it. Porters manhandling luggage, a movie background in each one, sailor hats. Glimpse inside houses: children, quilts, an iron bed laden, black skirts, a street; the baby carriage even looks exciting, strange, but why? We climb. George and Nancy watch calmly. I am almost out of my skin with excitement. Red tiled roofs. I'd forgotten. Postcards don't give it. It's the sense of life behind the scene. This one must see.

Cyrus Sulzberger* met, last day on boat—hadn't known he was on. We ride to Paris together, dine, talk. My room in the Paris Hotel Raphael is elegance itself.

A suite—two baths each with two basins and feminine hygiene devices. No door between john and big dressing room. A two-foot-high little screen fronts the toilet. Blue satin walls, long windows on Avenue Kléber, high ceilings, crystal chandeliers. The salon has a case of books—Molière, De Musset, Voltaire, etc.—in fine bindings. Opening the door they turn out to be backs, hiding a mirrored closet. I'm too keyed up to sleep. Even luminal doesn't do it. The room tips. I think of so much. Want to write.

*Cyrus Sulzberger was a foreign correspondent for the New York *Times*.

Monday—Aug. 20

The romance wants to be shared. The independence feels good. Does it come too late? Not quite. The flat roofs opposite my balcony—small windows open out. Roofs of Paris! A city built for civilized people, relief of low buildings. Not so noisy as N.Y. Of course this is August. Cool. Pleasant. Must cram so much into this time. Into life—want to stay except for—lots! Come each year—but the farm. But work. The book gets perspective here. If I could stay 6 months I'd write better. Settle down and see in new terms. Two weeks too little, except for the thrill.

And security which means a lot, I find, to me,—getting on well alone. It isn't hard—meeting people or arrangements. "The attractive older woman," I read in a newspaper piece with a vulgar hostess today, "The attractive older woman" is in demand for an instant in time. At this point the "attractive" outweighs the "older." But in another few years the "older" will outweigh the attractive. Funny part is how little I care for this sort of triumph except in terms of development and shedding ghastly and inconvenient old fears. In terms of vanity or competition—no. Only in my own terms.

Later

I knelt at Notre Dame. To beauty.

Sainte Chapelle—all airy glass.

Chartres. The hand of God is at once upon one, entering. Not a light touch, definite. *"Dieu habite ici."* This is the peak of what man can do. The main rose window—it hangs in the air, above man. The color, the stone work, the buttresses, the shape. The symmetry and variety. The engineering, design, miracle of windows. One could become a religious madman here. One could stay forever and die in it and lose a sense of humanity and have only God. It transcends man. It smites me. I don't remember this experience before.

London: As in Paris my book friends live everywhere and it is this that runs beside me on the streets—was it here that Margaret and Helen of *Howard's End* lived?—were they near St. John's Wood or if not, who was it? The family in *The Death of the Heart?* But I think their house was opposite Regents Park. I want to know how and where my friends live as much as in life. Must check when I get home. Because now I know how the houses and streets are shaped and what they saw and how they lived. In Paris I saw the Boulevard Malesherbes where Chad Newsome of the *Ambassadors* had his flat and that was exciting—Ah *there!* Yes, very elegant, no wonder he didn't want to come home. And of course Proust everywhere. It was in this sort of wide fine court that the Hotel des Guermantes stood, with Mme. de Villeparisis at one side, the narrator's family at another, Jupien the tailor downstairs, etc. And Odette walks in the Bois, violets pinned to her muff. Where did the Verdurins live? All along the avenue Victor Hugo, d'Iéna, Foch, toward St. Cloud, all along the tree-lined boulevards, here is where Swann dropped cards on ladies who were at home on their "afternoons." And to come back to James, here is where Madame de Vionnet had her highceilinged gracious apartment—for the many well proportioned houses of the "best" Paris streets impress me; one seldom sees so many fine and variegated homes. In London too, the East End—bombed incredibly but there is no feeling of morbidity or paralysis in it. This East End we read of in Dickens and I think of Joyce Carey momentarily. Everywhere they are rebuilding and there is no litter anywhere. The streets are far cleaner than ours. The stones are piled up neatly. Even while the bombing went on they were tidying, building, making order, and now although all over are shells of houses, no roof, no floors, a gutted rectangle, next door is an inhabited dwelling; scaffoldings busily prepare new reinforcements, people bustle busily, queue up without complaint.

Southampton—dreary middle class shipping city. Drive to

Dorchester through the New Forest. Wild ponies graze tamely in the woods here, keep underbrush down, small horses belonging to nobody crapping at roadsides and right up to hotels. Never heard of this before . . . Dorchester again. But so different from 20 years ago. I am different. Judge Jeffreys Antiques—shop unexpectedly fine, everything first rate and shown with no clutter. Drive home by way of the sea in view of the Isle of Wight. Bournemouth—crowded, cheap, but people enjoying themselves, the beach and front full of canvas deck chairs. Beyond Milford-by-the-Sea and other small villages where the dunes and the few people remind me of Cape Cod. More sun and bracing air and quiet and a shore running into the water far and wide—these look like our kind of people.

Ship. Proper elderly lady with her polite smiling poise and orchids at cocktails. Waved gray hair and conventional orchids, no expression. But on deck sleeping in her chair the face is drawn into a network or desert of worry and despair.

Baldwin boy, 12: "Mommy, what is rigor mortis?"

As the ship pitched the passengers at the Captain's dinner clutched their silver paper dunce caps.

1954 Mexico

Looking from train window things are cut out of cardboard. But maybe it's *we* who are the stuffed toys. Gnarled trees, Arthur Rackham arthritic shapes. Such poverty! Small station-beggars *really* in rags. Five-year-olds carrying three-month-olds in shawls wound cripplingly about them both. Cripples, aged, professional-station-beggars, tiny dwarf people who were the three-month-olds in shawls fifty years ago. Argentine Ambassador and family on train, five polite independent children, no pouts, no problems, lively and no one pays much heed to them but they are scrubbed and friendly. I can't help thinking some of their sophistication is better than our own products of concentration-on-problems.

The Ambassador from Argentina has yellow suede shoes and

after two days of travel knife-edged trousers. In the long run this must be the requisite of Ambassadors—the pressed pants under all conditions. Four little boys, a girl and a wife compose his entourage, unostentatiously in his background. The "diplomat's pouch" is a pouch!

Taxco: Hacienda Del Chorrillo is here since 1539, built by Spanish smelters, with all the elegance that made the conquistadors bring architects, engineers, etc., with them. We sit high on a hill, among pine trees, several miles out of town. My room might have been made for Empress Carlotta, vast, beamed, galleries outside, fine heavy cedar furniture. Esther Sullivan* a genius at decoration in key with the ancient walls, arches. Outside stone stairs lead to my room. Fountains drip in stone troughs—ancient tiles of gods. Birds sing ostentatiously. Tall old walls enclosing the court are laced with vines. A cerise bougainvillea is gigantic in the center in a clay pot. Music usually comes from somewhere. This is a wise life because it is beautiful.

What have we done with ourselves? We are squeezed into grotesques by pressures. If I could have a good hospital and a good school that is all I'd want to live here and bring my clan and stay forever.

I feel my clichés from home dropping off like veils in a strip tease. Values straighten out, the big separates from the little.

I pick up words, make myself understood with laughter, gestures, mistakes. The little maid sings as she does my room, a graceful Indian girl, she steps out on the terrace and carols at the mountain. I ask her to teach me her *canción* and we both rock with mirth. Such straight simplicity in this people! Such a strong old land. Being here is a dream but reality is closer here too than among the twists at home.

The steep cobbled town, narrow streets, steps everywhere. A shop with a little grain, a little tawdry pastry. Basket shops, silver. *"Con ochos de fria plata."* *Plata*—I beam at the silver shop.

*Esther Sullivan and her husband operated a hacienda in Taxco, Mexico.

The girl who went through Mexico on one Lorca poem. I study functionally not as a student. But I am ashamed of not speaking Spanish better. What soft balmy air. What flowers. How could anyone born and raised here survive in our northern cities, in our dirt?

The guests at the Hacienda: gay male decorator from Toronto with wife, child, and boy friend. Has clever rapid speech. Boston couple—proper, aging, an osteopath and wife, he watercoloring on holiday. The Sullivans are perfect hosts—such taste, efficiency, a charming air of casual houseparty to the place. No newspapers—I rarely wonder about the news but I wonder if the bulbs are up at the farm.

Every morning I walk, throw open the shutters, step out on the balcony and say "How lovely!" There is the mellow air, there is the bluest sky, there below is a cobbled courtyard with an angel mosaic wafting over the tiles.

Invisible to all but a few buzzards from the mountain, I sun mornings on the rear stone terrace, clad in bra, brief pants, a sombrero. The Sullivans are real people. Solid, talented, kindly, and something very true behind it all. Ideal hosts—things run to perfection and never a sense of bustle or trouble. We dine à la dinner party at a long table, have drinks for an hour first in the charming bar with Sully as barkeeper and everything on the house, no keeping track. Architecture, decoration, food, conversation, spirit of the place, all in excellent taste. The little maids serve us as though they enjoy it, busily. Other guests as per usual, except for that chatty Toronto decorator, Irvin, with his fantastic memory, gossip, information—please mind about art, theatre, diplomats, places, clients, society etc., all rattled off with gay insouciance.

Bunny's* house—A terra cotta bath tub on whose ledge rests a great pottery jar holding a huge plant. Such taste in everything. The kitchen, charcoal burners set in a deep shelf, clay pots hung on wall, plants, the smiling Indian cook. Dog house

*Bunny Kassler was a sculptor who lived in Taxco.

with air chamber under the tiled roof! Cat house! Gardens, views, tiny spaces planted with lettuce and strawberries. Table set out on the terrace under the mountains. All on $1500! New walls and fountains and stone grottoes and orchids, all built on old slap heap and looking centuries old.

Saturday is beggar's day in the Zócalo. They are out with tin cups, the crippled, the blind. If you put a centavo in the cup they recite a poem about the Virgin of Guadalupe . . . The nuns are not allowed to wear their robes in public but some get around it. How does anyone *not* break a hip on the steep streets? Buses, cars, tourists, all on narrow perpendicular cobbles.

How does one catch a sight in words? "The sharp original guard from treason, never to escape."* The sunset light crowning the dry mountain, a shadow—round—under each tree in that cone of light on top and underneath the dark half, the other half of the self. A platter of shadow below each green tree. How show the stone and plaster wall across my patio, its fifty or a hundred foot height, or even one inch of it, the colors of time, gray, fawn, rose, olive, pocked into shaped sockets, oval orange, lavendar round, but I must look to refresh my mind even now; the eye is needed and then the metaphor. No literal translation can be enough. Facts are barren vessels that must be filled with interpretation. Even in photography this has become so. Without the symbol there is loss, poor deprived facts, the tongue cut out of them or born without tongues.

People on holiday have the same sort of voices everywhere. Resort voices. Casual, floating, waving lightly as leaves.

The tourists are all manufactured in one place. A button has made some brassy and some mousy, one lever for Helen Hokinson's, another for Marcel's, but it doesn't matter. We Americans stand out and not too well always.

Ride over the mountain with Bunny and Vail to the house of Valentin—architect, painter, Renaissance character, weekend

---

*A quotation from Lenore Marshall's poem "Memory in Winter," with the wording slightly shifted.

lodge where he retires after the week's work in Cuernavaca or Mex. Utter isolation in the hills, only a few Indian mud huts spotting the opposite mountain side, and here his luxurious hacienda, built by himself over ruins, immense halls of rooms, glorious Chinese and Spanish furniture—a stone outside chamber with open top slatted by bamboo where he raises orchids—they bloomed in clusters and varieties everywhere—and great ferns, fronds, etc., too. He lives, evidently, with pretty Mexican boy. The young Indian sits silent on other side of house; he a charming worldling. Tale of the old Salinas clan—200 years ago the son of the powerful Catholic house sent away to Spain for education and to become a priest. He returns, steps from his coach, the great priest now, and beholds lovely blonde girl. "Who is that?" to his father. "Your sister." "No!" "You have not seen her in 17 years." Next day servant to master, "The Senorita should be whipped if she goes to priest." Nine months later a baby; the mother dies. The priest never talks again, builds shrine in his room where he says mass. 200 years later the revolution; house destroyed, they find mummified body of girl behind gold altar. The Salinas family become anti-clerical. It is from this family that President Obregón comes. . . . Oh, oh, the road to Valentin's. (He a Salinas too—and Catholic anti-clerical. His tale of village priest, baptism where he is to be godfather, church where he refuses to go, wants it in home. Priest refuses, then when he says he will pay priest holds him up. "Ah you want it elegant? I give you 36 candles," etc. "How much?" "200." "How much for the least?" "2½ pesos." "I'll have that." He gives rest to choir boys, priest is his enemy.) Oh yes—that road! Unsurfaced, pebbly, precipices, and so steep I hold my breath in terror and my head presses inside. The others take it casually—what a coward I must be—so I say no word, try to be a fatalist and stop my imagination, admire the stupendous view. But am glad—and worn out when it's over. Valentin built the last part of road himself. There'd have been no means of communication otherwise. Avocado trees. Lime—tiny intense blossoms. Bananas—huge ribbed leaves, clusters of fruit, flowers. Avocadoes on ground, heavy in branches. Flowers—flowers! The dark underhalf of mountain at sunset, the bright upper self, clear light. Each pine with its separate platter of shadow, worn creviced rock. Remember how I knelt at Notre Dame to beauty. . . . I am secure in the world of strangers. . . . Read *Bhagavad-Gita*—in spite of renunciation it comes down to Freud, the self, stern self-knowledge in order to attain peace. The differences superficial—or at any rate under them I find timeless goals and disciplines. Laden burros. Sweet children lead them. This corner of Mexico is enough for me to take in on one trip. There is so much! Wonderful reassuring letters from home today. The children are so beautiful, so big hearted! Good letter from Jim.

No straight lines in Mexico except the perpendicular lined rock mountains. All else spirals—roads, trails winding up hill, a flight of stone steps leading down from the road into a valley, curving steeply.

Eleven o'clock at night. I am working. Bunny knocks, brings in a night-blooming cactus. Long white petals curl backward to an outer fringe of rosy tawny. The center is spun glass, a million fine stiff threads, crystal pale, each tipped with gold, a calyx, a deep cut that hold the passionate pollinated stamen. A heavy scent unlike any other, lemony, intense, with an under-perfume like an intoxicating poison. I can scarcely bear to breathe it. The stalk like intimate flesh, dark flesh color, thick, crenellated, evenly grooved, and tufts of needle-fine hair grow on it, increasing downward to a base spiked with iridescent spines.

Talked to Jim tonight. He leaves tomorrow!

Well. One gets perspective. And at what cost.

A week-long pre-Easter fiesta. New types of people have appeared in town, little people from the villages, thousands of them, crowding the tiny town, they will sleep on the cobbles beside their poor wares. Faces of old men hewn out of rock, lined, brown, patient. Women carrying babies wrapped in shawls. Beautiful boys, soft cheeked girls. Gay colors, burros. Clay pots, copper pots, chamber pots set out in the narrow streets and they squat beside them. Paper flowers, big musical instruments like cellos with ribbed angled backs. Fireworks— the "castillo"—a wick burns slowly up a pole on which all sorts of straw, etc., figures are set, ending perhaps with the virgin. What a mob like this might do in an emergency— but they are friendly. So clean. The scrubbed white garments.

The universe is close here. In New York we are hemmed in by petty details but here we are part of the universe. I never saw so many stars. Bare night outlines of mountains.

A man bearing aloft a chunky cactus stem on which, like the chancel of a church, is built a multiple tin pinwheel whirling like birds in the sun. A real mobile. In front of Berta's bar on the Zócalo a group of women sit on the sidewalk with two mangy pigs tied by ropes. They talk, there with their black ribosas wound over heads and shoulders while within the open-fronted bar a couple of musicians strum and sing and tourists drink and chat unconcernedly. At last the native group rise and cross the square, one old lady leading a baby pig by its cord, behind her a younger woman tugs at a more recalcitrant larger animal. Another woman walks behind, occasionally kicking the resistant animal in its rear, to speed it on, and shouting. Perhaps there was danger leaving the pigs unguarded and alone at home while the clan was off at the fiesta; or they would be sold for a party. . . . Travelling musicians in every tiny cantina. All bars and shops are three-walled, open-fronted.

Margarita of Casas Figaro—lovely Mexican girl, vivacious, exquisite clothes and jewels, sad (Indiana husband deserted her), guts (rescues American man who falls on a child and the crowd yells, threatens, might kill him). Elizabeth Anderson, one of Sherwood's wives, lives up a perpendicular hill, too narrow for cars, we struggle to keep upright on the slippery cobbles. What a darling Bunny is! What style, gallantry, taste. Her charming house, studio, dinner in garden. She makes waffles in the kitchen, her food always good, tequila under a tree. Valentin Vidranritta there again. In a.m. Bunny sends me a glass dish lined with her strawberries, fresh picked from the little row, and a colossal bunch of white lilies, longer-throated than our Easter or Madonnas, opulent, not so chaste, the hidden prize deep down. Like taffeta. Perfume. Bunny's strength in her sculpture. Abram, her man, sculpts too, real old Indian feel. Valentin chain smokes, sophisticated, urbane, sad-eyed, tells tale after tale. The parrots: "What do you think I've been praying for all these years?" Inez Amor's family in Mexico City. Seems that three generations ago the name was Segoritas (?). A brother and sister had an affair. When the baby was born they didn't know how to legitimize it so they went to the Pope. Pope said, "Love conquers all but you must change your name. Then you may marry." So they became the Amors. There is a second daughter, a poet, who is impossible, was a brat. [This seems dull in retrospect! It was Val's telling.] At 15 was late for lunch. "Why late?" asked mother. "I have been in bed with a torrero." The mother fainted. A few days later the same happened. "Mother I told you I am having an affair." A few days later daughter was late. Mother began "Listen—" stopped—never asked again.

> Never in memory this same light
> Only now and gone
> A fleeting glimpse tomorrow
> Next week a struggle a wrench a lack
> And a sense of strangeness.

The patio with its high worn wall and weeds and flowers flying a hundred feet up from a crevice.
The mosaic angel wafting over stone floor

And twin bougainvilleas, red and cerise, tall twining from clay
sunken circle—
The blue sky—above all the sky, and the mountains, and the
line of light cutting and crowning the mountain. Light above,
dark below, two selves—

> Never in memory this strumming music
> The passion flower's mauve star
> erect and intricate
> Never trust memory—Go to the source
> Go to the light

The muscular sage. Stone figure resembling Chinese art, all
power, Mayan art at the Belles Artes, so intricate, perfect,
timeless. Where else but in the artist's mind does civilization
show its eternal oneness, the timeless vision?

Never in memory this same light
Only now and gone
A fleeting glimpse tomorrow
Next week a struggle a lack
And a sense of strangeness.
The patio with its high worn wall
And weeds and flowers flying a hundred feet up from a
    crevice
The mosaic angel wafting over stone floor
And twin bougainvilleas, red and cerise,
Tall twining from clay sunken circle—
The blue sky—above all the sky,
And the mountains, and the line of light
Cutting and crowning the mountain—
Light above, dark below, two selves—
Never in memory this strumming music
The passion flower's mauve star erect and intricate

Never trust memory—Go to the source
Go to the light

June 10, 1955   Andria Doria to Naples
Strange. Utterly alone this time. Not a familiar face or name
on board. I have been hiding in activity. Now I must come out
into the stark universal solitude. The sea where the individual is
lost and found. The towers of New York were like El Greco's
Toledo.

Neither unduly nervous or depressed, as I'd feared I might
be, but bored in a good way. Means maybe grown up. Having
met nobody especially interesting I am content to avoid the
crowd and read. Dancing, nightclub, games, etc.—
balloons—paper caps—how absurd for me. This would take
just the right companions, otherwise forced and false. Read
Burckhardt last night. Am poorly placed at table but this too
does not matter, as I look about I see nobody who attracts me so
I shall remain.

How horrid that money gives confidence! My clothes must
have been building me up in my position and attitude before the
world, for years. I can be comfortably alone in my clothes.
With an orchid on my dress I stroll, a proud and amiable
stranger, a woman of the world who protects Lenore. Sartor
Resartus—who is L?

Read late, slept with the help of a pill till twelve, pulled the
curtain, and there was an immense island, a rock with a village
at its base rising from the sea. People say one can get from
pictures and books a sense of place—yes, but not this thrill. I
could not believe it, here in the middle of the sea! Rushed into
clothes and on deck—the Azores! A word suddenly imbued
with excitement because of what my eyes saw so unexpectedly.

At night sometimes I have qualms and wish the trip were
over; by day I enjoy myself now. Met various people
casually—feel freedom, nobody but me to consider. So I am
beginning to unwind yet scarcely have time for the books, the

letters, the walks, the movies that compose the pieces of this
life. At my table: the French ladies and elderly Jewish dame
claim me. We drift at home with our own pack; here I find
interest in the differences we all represent and I need no
younger group or gaiety. Man on sun deck—noticed first his
powerful stocky middle aged body and face—this type appeals
to me; I no longer see attraction in the handsome youths. Then
watched him read a mss., decided he was most interesting
person I'd noticed. Yesterday he picked me up—Geo. Radin of
Washington, lawyer, co-ops.

Long talk—met his family; he invites me to cocktails. I am
gaining confidence again, at least in relation to the big world.
But what of my work? Have I the learning, the originality, the
impudence?

I am already—feel different than on other trips. The suggestion, like the true seed, in each new thing. We are passing
Spain. Isn't that miraculous? I see a hilly coast line, now it
stretches long and far, this is Spain! Imagine how Columbus
felt when he left all shores behind, even the Azores, and then
there were all the days and nights of water! Imagine how he felt
when he saw his first shoreline from out of space, the new world
appearing, land again. Such poles of experience apart, water
and land, such poles apart of emotion. The safety of land, the
mystery of water. Gibralter! The beetling rock, brow like an
emperor's over a second height, a steep face second only to the
bulging sheer upper head. And Spain spreading below. Lights
go on. Diamonds rope the hills, map the shore. Little boats, the
tender alongside. Africa somewhere opposite.

Rome: Fountain Steps—in St. Peter's. I have not the religious experience of Chartres or Notre Dame. Beauty and love
there, but in St. Peter's Grandeur. Power. Beauty is truth,
truth beauty . . . but grandeur is power here, power grandeur.
Except for the Pietà, the wounded boy in his last breath, caught
so, in his mother's arms. Priests, priests, all kinds of garments.

International yacketty yack. Bright rinsed hair, diamonds,

idleness written large. And the vast servant class, brushing fallen leaves with brooms, spreading awnings, bearing trays of perfect food. Very poor—"You are all so friendly." "We are brought up with the tourists. Of course we are friendly. We depend on the tourists." There are no young men in town with money enough for girls like the masseuse to marry.

Headwaiter my friend, tries to teach me Italian. "Ah madam, America is wonderful. There you have great wealth. But"—proudly—"here we have art." This has been only a preparatory experience. I have not gotten any one master deeply enough. There was too much.

How sad it is when strangers leave, she thought, one feels more alone. In the last day three different tables have been vacated and new, even stranger strangers supplanted those on whom her eyes had lingered for a week. The Yugoslav couple who sat near the door, "not married" whispered the headwaiter with a shrug "c'est un ménage." They had a grey poodle, one could tell without seeing a pedigree what a fine poodle it must be, it sat on a chair outside of the dining room waiting and never stirring while its beautiful mistress and distinguished master dined, leapt to playful attention when they strolled out. The woman whose body was strikingly lithe bent down with a sweeping motion, making a loop of her arm through which the poodle jumped. There was the Hollywood group, three men of whom one—but she never knew which—was the president of a big company. They were elderly men all and looked harassed and hurried even here, with them were two wives and again she did not know which man was without a woman though if they had stayed longer that along with other things might have become apparent—two women were elegant, jewelled, and one was much younger than the rest of the group—the young wife of an old rich man. She might have been an actress, fine straight carriage, high heel, poised. Then there was the French family, perhaps the father, the son, the daughter-in-law with a certain smoky pallor to her skin. All these people were gone and although she had never spoken to them and knew nothing of their lives she had invented lives for them and had become accustomed to them in certain chairs. How sad it is, she thought, I shall probably never see these strangers again. They have vanished. I did not even know they planned to leave. Yet tonight a family with a pale girl child (and the fat boy) sat where the Yugoslav lovers had been. An emaciated elderly man, alone, with an intelligent death's head face, sat at Hollywood table and banged with his fist for the waiter's attention.

Overnight to the Riviera. Comfortable *wagons-lits*. The lulling constant pound of the ocean. Mountains somewhat like my million Mexican mountains—ridged rocky and with trees, perpendicular. Blue blue sea, sails, red tile roofs. . . . That minute of waking—I have experienced it in Mexico—open the window, lift the blind. Then sun! Blue! Here I see a harbor, the Mediterranean, mountains dropping abruptly to the sea, a shoreline of villas, white in the brilliant light, small ships bobbing. I am not worried during these days. Life is full. I must write, I must write, I must write! So much to put down! But I must live! My enthusiasm is greater than in youth and all my capacities. There are miracles. The lull and thunder and hush of the sea. No hush so great as the moment between thunders.

June 2, 1956

And now the *Flandre*, on this strangely personal trip—pro and con. After the inner torments. But decision today and quiet and curiosity. Smallest ship I've been on, like a private yacht. My seventeenth, I think, crossing. For two and a half weeks— flat—then back in New York. Taxi to dock through slums and billboards of smiling girls advertising laxatives—a sign: Happy Boys Club. Closed. The motors start, whistle blasts, orchestra plays, Manhattan is a fantasy, fading. Go to the bar for sherry. Again the smiling stewards, linoleum corridors, flowers in the way—one eyes one's neighbors—is there anyone who will be interesting? Will it be safe—calm? But J. seems pleased so I am glad I came.

7th
Tossing, pitching, too small. Really frightened last night. The frame shivers. Our table fell over twice during the night, crash. Nothing stays—impossible to walk. Don't like this ship. Excellent food, service, informal get-together gatherings and dances, but too little deck and exercise space. Rolls too much.

Rebecca West—see a lot of her and cultivated charming husband Henry Andrews. Big intelligences—he full of references, reading, easy courteous erudition. She friendly and chatty but I suspect too much ego, sense of power, hysteria through need to keep her powers semi-bottled. Suffering face when she sleeps on deck. We are invited for a night with them in England, should be fascinating, a new side of England not of the hotel or sights, a new kind of woman, the success, the mistress of her own life, free. He with the mannerliness of the true gentleman, the great scholar.

Anne Fremantle, a dazzling creature, radiant swift mind and body, must have been fantastically beautiful, is still exciting to watch. These disciplined people make me feel the gaps in my education, my training, my ability to think hard and clear. But to the Woods of U.S. we are small lions; they are well read and pleasant but she—in Bell system public relations—avid for meeting the names in Art and takes notes on even me, to send to the Provincetown paper!

1957: Woodstock
Finishing revisions on Book I the night before—the deaths: Grandfather—Adam of the book. Mother, Mince tomorrow—"memorialized" in a house, a room, the paintings, the names in bronze.* Only the living count—but who now is the one. Abby knew the essence, and I too. Love, she said.

*In memory of her mother and her aunt Herminie, Lenore Marshall gave a room at Woodstock, New York, for exhibitions of paintings and performances of small concerts. "Abby" is the principal character of her last novel, *The Hill is Level.*

I have created a world. There are people. There is wisdom in the book—did it come from me? Yes, wrung from me. It moves me tonight. The chapter ends—the author is the loneliest one among his characters. The characters begin and end. The author must live on. The characters refuse to have anything to do with him ever again.

5 Travel, 1959-66: The Personal Ash of Experience

1960: Last lap—what does one look forward to, at my age, in the world's despair, in the personal ash of experience! Nothing as much as before—not pain, not joy. Yet ready for "home"—glad the long trek ends.

1959: Taos

Insecure in this outpost but indifferent to insecurity, so perhaps really not. Out of everything we learn—or should. I have a comfortable room, a patio. The tiny patio has mud walls uneven as a child's clay ashtray, adobe, low, flat, charming, on the outskirts of nowhere, mesa surrounding, mountains ringing, later it will become beautiful.

Floods make the sand rut road impassable. So everybody is marooned. The sand lane, questionable at best, is now a lake, loses its shape. Thus quickly, constantly, one is cut off. Inside is the charming house, many good books, good food, good manners, alone in space. My room is furthest from the others, no bell, no phone, silence, one could write here if one were at peace. Nothing impinges but the self.

Night of panic quickly relieved. Sensible M.D. They suggested her, not I, sensible pills, evidently everyone was worried, brought me flowers, dropped in, solicitude and real kindness. And the awaking after a few days—venturing out on the sandy land and behold the mountains. Behold what you have been blindly not seeing—beauty. Not beauty again but beauty eternal. I walk, cleaned out, wanting to stay. Here is the universe once more. New York is a fantasy, but not those one loves. Therefore there is something wrong about being away. Dear God, to live again and do what one now knows. The children, mother, Mince. Mince's self-effacing sensitivity. I understand her whole now. Too late. Purgatorio appeals most, the human book, the sinner who did not mean to sin and strives forever. The parody songs—Wagner, Sullivan—how Mother and Mince would have laughed, how vainly I love and see them now. Sagebrush mesa, storms on one mountain, sun on a peak, the cleft slanting between two green crags through which the sun rises, beaming first. Always one long line—the mountain. Indian, Spanish-American, Anglo-American civilization. (Mother—Mince—I have *given* too little love. I *felt* it. I could not *show* it. That was the sin.)

No describing the mountains. They ring the sand and sagebrush mesa, near or melting into horizon, into dream, but holding the mesa, burning it, ending it, walling the world. If I were a painter I could not do it representationally—here is where picture postcards triumph. It would have to be abstract, a jagged circle of lights and shadows, near and far.

The trader, Gil Mitchell, drops in for the night, straight from Hopi and Zuni reservations, car loaded with vegetable dye rugs and wonderful jewelry. He was once a playboy in Chicago. Drank for weeks—divorced. A lower class woman saved him, he gave up drink, moved out here to a remote village, devoted to the sick wife who has had operations for cancer but is always cheerful. He is a strong trader now, his life among Indians, mountains, spaces.

Brett—deaf, kind, yellow pants, blue smock, red Indian blanket coat, paints Lawrence with halo, another painting in Mexican art tin shrine, Stokowski paintings as mystic, messy house, books, jars, bones for dog under table, crucifix, Buddha,

Indian dolls, battered sofa, bed under curtainless windows because Lawrence told her she would be peaceful if she looked at stars.

Frieda Lawrence* and Angelo the younger new husband. Charming house, Angie's bright paintings and Lawrence's sex paintings, sad animal men and women in various scenes of naked passion. Frieda old, still delightful, warm, powerful, welcoming. Vines growing within house. Angie builds rooms, everything, ceramist, flirts, male. Tea and plain Mrs. Wurlitzer comes in, rich, elephantiasis, great legs, and a straw farmer hat decorated with flowers that Frieda made her, fantastic. The wonderful mountain views the creative people! This evening so beautiful, worth being born for this. Then sweet chimes over the sage brush and alfalfa mesa, from remote adobe chapel; I rush out—the big close mountain is purple, mountain purple, and then the ridges are mountain gold where sunset falls, and far off at the edge of the flat world it is shimmer color, champagne, bells tinkle, baled hay lies at rest. It breaks the heart with joy. The far mountains roll green. One is transcended. The person you love hardly matters on such an evening. It is love itself that counts. I talked to Jon, how sweet he sounded and glad to hear my voice as I to hear his beloved presence, bless him. For this night I am glad to have come.

When they enshrined Lawrence's ashes Freida didn't see why it should be lugubrious, she decided to have a do, with wine and foods and a party. Brett was so angry she threatened to steal the ashes. . . . Before Frieda and Angie married someone in town who had it in for them reported to the F.B.I. that they lived in moral turpitude. The F.B.I. came so Angie sent F. out and they found him living alone, he denied F. lived with him. But the next day the FBI man returned and there was Frieda. "Do you live with him?" asked the man. "Yah!" cried F. with warm gusto. "Of course we live together. Come in and have coffee with us."

*Frieda Lawrence was the widow of D. H. Lawrence.

Millicent Rogers who was here with maid, chauffeur, tutor, two boys and bag full of diamond jewelry worth $1,500,000. Too broke to pay bills, ran them up, paid Dick $500 at a time. Once when she needed money sold a Degas for $25,000—to her son!

Patrocinio Barela

A thin little man wandered in and crossed the patio. He wore jeans, his face was hewn full of character and old legends as a mountain rock. An object bulged under his tattered jacket, protected by his hand. On an impulse, "Are you Patrocinio Barela?" I asked.

I had seen Barela's wood carvings in galleries and homes around Taos. Examples of his work are spread from New York's Museum of Modern Art to the San Francisco Museum but he himself is as innocent and indifferent to this as indeed he may be of the very existence of these cities. The carvings, varying in size from a few inches to a few feet, are religious, austere, elemental, fatalistic, some compassionate as a Rouault, some grotesque in pagan humor, some looking as though they might have come straight from the studio of Henry Moore: madonnas, angels, animals, family groups, death-men aiming spears or arrows. His output is prolific. He has little contact with the Anglo-American group of artists in the neighborhood. He is the real primitive, if you wish to think in those terms; he is also the sophisticate if native insight contributes to sophistication. He uses cedar branches, occasionally pine, precious chunks that he carries all the way from the forest or finds among logs in the woodpile. The deep red core of the cedar is sometimes used for a body, the white outside lining of the wood may appear in the enveloping wings of an angel, rhythm of grain is skillfully and naturally manipulated.

He had taken the bulging object from his jacket, a shepherd tenderly holding a lamb. "I never went to school," he said, dignified and friendly. "My daddy sent me to watch goats in the hills. I no read or know my ABC's. One day my daddy was going to trade a piece of land he had. I say, 'Why you do it.' He say, 'Twenty-one, get out.' So I go here, there, nine years, dig potatoes, coal mines, railroad. Then I married with this woman, she's my wife." Long pause. "I work in WPA then, haul dirt, ate breakfast, went out. One day the priest showed me old figure of Saint Angelo, broken, he say, Pat, you think could be fix? I say, Padre, we can try. We work all night and fix. That santo was done in joints, pieces put in with pipe. I came home and lay on bed and think How can you make it so it's in one piece? All one. I can't sleep all night. Next day after work I eat supper quick, go out where I got pieces of cedar wood, I choose some with no knots and I begin with my pen knife. My wife call, 'You no going to sleep?' I no answer her."

This is how art begins, I thought. This is the raw material. He spoke lengthily and lovingly of his work. "It is beautiful work," I said. We had strolled out of the patio and were watching the sun set over the mountains. "You a painter?" he inquired as though noticing me personally for the first time. "No. A writer. But here I should like to be able to paint." He looked at me hard. He said: "Maybe you can catch it if you try."

The next day I visited his studio in the Spanish-American village of Cañon down the road. The studio was a shack, perhaps a woodshed once, here he worked and slept beside the small adobe house where his family lived. The dark interior of the tumbled slatted shed had for floor the sandy earth of the mesa mixed with shavings and chips; a stump of tree rooted in the center, board walls gaped, cardboard cartons were stuck over some holes in an attempt to keep out rain, there was an iron bed without sheets, a mess of quilt, a disintegrating mattress; from under the mattress protruded a bottle of Tokay wine. A shelf held a paper bag of corn, rags, peaches, pits, cans, lanterns, a smashed stove, an auto tire. An extra pair of jeans hung from a nail. At the door was his workbench and here in orderly rows, contrasting with the disorder of the shed, were laid his tools: rasps, chisels, bits, knives, a hammer. Tool handles to hold the rasps had been made from sawed-off pieces of deer antler, polished from usage. Three newly completed figures stood on the ground. Above the bench was nailed a carving unlike his others: a double portrait plaque of Senator Chavez and FDR decorated with stars and each man wearing a respectable, respectful tie.

Pat lay on the bed more in stupor than in sleep. He staggered to his feet, coming back slowly, talking out of some other world, out of some deep, far unconscious, a Dostoievskian world, talking altogether to himself, moving a figure on the ground, a death image with arrow flying. "You see, that's what I dreaming. It came from a dream." He tried it in different positions. "Maybe this way, maybe that. Like in your own life; you stand, maybe too straight, maybe crooked. Make it simple. I don't know — I kill you —." But he was studying the death figure, living it. He picked up a chunk of cedar, bark still on it, it took on form as he placed its chopped off branches on the earth, caressed it affectionately. "See, Sister?" "Yes. An animal." He nodded, stripped the bark, "cleaned" it. He turned to an angel with outspread wings, traced its shape with his finger. There was about him a transformation into a world of visions that appeared to him: of "an angel behind a person, perhaps an angel behind every person"; he muttered that he wanted to carve into a great trunk of cedar that he had, but must wait to see if first it might develop a crack.

He describes his carvings in a kind of poetry: A King's Subject Being Killed, Heavy Thinker, Man Praying Deep for His Own, Man Who Stands by His Own, Death Looking for the Good Ones; he elaborates in this same poetry. The allegory in his poems unites them with the spirit of the Bible or the work of Mayan and Aztec artists of centuries ago or the traditions of the early Spanish-Americans who were his ancestors and whose effigies were the art of the Morada.

Pat had come back to the outer world, now he was entirely at ease, alternating between joking and seriousness. "I like to have a vice," he said simply. "Can do more better."

The last time I saw him he stood alone in his doorway, thin, pathetic, immovable, next to a pile of lumber, and I remembered what he had said at our first meeting and I thought that he had given voice to the hope, the passion, the longing of all artists: Maybe you can catch it if you try.

Poem ?

Experiment in sound waves. Man in closed room makes speech, recording made 2 hours later. Do the waves dissipate or are they always around us? The Sermon on the Mount still vibrates in the air? Los Alamos—G.E. portable box for heating the sitter in the chair—skillets hang in air frying eggs 6 inches above stove. A giant hand threads needle. The cliffs like tents—sphinxes—one of the billions of nature's experiments or perhaps like the aqueducts of ancient Rome—man-made ages ago—the formations of nature of prehistoric man—indefinite, merge, question. Our little daily newspapers give a spot perspective. The old narrow-gauge railroad abandoned along edge of cliff. My peach tree smelled sweet ripe in the tiny paved patio. Farewell my mountains. If Mince could only have seen this land. Known this life. Work—but never hurry. The universe—not the city. But whose life is hardest, hers, Pat's or—'I'—the fortunate for an hour, wearing the heavy mask.

1959: Mexico

These people bore me, except Bunny who is very fine. But it is worthwhile for that moment in the morning when I throw open the long wooden panelled doors and step out into benign sun to face the mountains. The incredible mountains. My own grilled balcony, vine-wound, a sort of blue morning glory. Bougainvillea petals drift over the swimming pool and must be skimmed off.

Being free of the novel makes me remarkably free to read, to think, what can I do of most value to others, to myself? Will it be in writing?

When I read the papers I feel we are balanced on a knife edge yet this is ambivalent, the mountains are eternal though probably as frail as the Empire State Building. The people too, knife edge and house party, unaware, and the little sweet natives.*

Flower-laden buffet and busy bar. "Only in Mexico," says the lady to me as we squeeze past the truck that blocks the street. Bunny's man, Abraham, walks slowly along the aqueduct, stops, white shirt flapping, faces the mountains high up with the great drop beneath him, but unaware. Abraham with his new machete, crouching behind Bunny at the terraced cocktail party, to escort her home. The tourists talk a tongue I have never mastered but I have mastered indifference to it. Lava rock with streaks of black. Twin perpendicular steeps, little neat green trees on upper fields. Goats, burros on road, streets, hill. Patient men and patient animals. A rocket or firecracker in the night. The morning moment: through my open door sun on a high stone wall, a balcony, a tile roof, bougainvillea, roses. Green trees above, rock, blue sky. Glare of sun, sharp shadow forms. Birds and silence.

Hotel Telva—terrace for lunch and what a view! What a hill to get there—cobbled of course and perpendicular and narrow and twists.

Tonio Kröger—but I really don't feel bothered by my isolated stance, as once. Feel very independent, wandering around alone. Astounded as I view myself in the cobbled streets, content as I view the mountains and the natives. Evening at Bunny's. I think of my Mince, what this life would have meant to her. How she was deprived, living on thin fare. Not much worry about home thoughts. Bunny's lovely house, all open—kitchen open to the garden, hung with pottery, vines indoors and out, big leaved, dogs in the dog house built like a

*This is the germ of the short story, "Dialogue on a Cliff."

little home, cats in the cat house. Boxers and Siamese—she mixes the cats' meal, milk, honey, things in the pottery bowl, tastes it, serves them—12 kittens, all prize. She puts on my record, turns lights low. It sounds wonderful: the incredible market. Week before Easter. They walk from the hills— sometimes three days, or bump on burros, hundreds of pieces of pottery tied in bales of straw, they unpack on the steep cobbles, mothers nursing babes tied in shawls, cooking or selling simultaneously, a bit of charcoal, on the streets where they will sleep, hundreds of them. No children cry. No drunks. Dignity, some friendliness, some stoicism.

Fiesta of San José at the Cathedral on the Zócalo. Little boys, *ninos*, with chicken feathers covering their white overalls—a mass of chicken feathers! Little girls as though they were to be confirmed, white dresses, flower wreaths, staffs. They dance on the porch of the Cathedral, singing the same song over and over, and an Indian musician, handsome, young, kindly, plays his fiddle, another man wearing a mask dances with the children. Another band approaches across the Zócalo, a brass band playing, in front a man carries a silver plate with flowers on it, into the church. Inside a mass is being said, the people are kneeling, wee urchins come in, cross themselves, kneel. Two-year-olds leading one-year-olds! Child beggars, sad eyes. The dancers sing outside on the porch. It is pagan and wonderful. What a drab civilization we have! Their church is their friend. A blind man begs on the step, filthy, a shabby rug over his shoulder, he kisses the corn, crosses himself.

That winding mountain drive from Taxco—burros strapped with faggots, women's heads laden, sometimes sitting in rest on the road, a quiet baby or two. The patient beasts of burden, one with nature—*Cuernavaca*, Casa de Piedra. Fairyland again. Mansion—my big room, crystal chandelier, French needle-point chairs, big gilt clock on marble bureau, best of all a wide balcony with table and view outside the long doors. A German ex-countess, Rosa Hayden, married to an American.

Superb gardens. European tone—small tables in garden. But
the Fromms! Their house perfect. We talk till midnight. The
brilliant man—he undermines me even while he builds my
beliefs up again. I do not often feel envy but I envy this—his
life, her life. Everything is right. Immense gentleness, peace.
Productivity. Wide ranging interests. Scholarship vast—his
political-historical talk flows with passion, so full I can scarcely
follow. I live behind 20 ft. stone walls in a baronial estate. The
snow-capped volcanoes, Popo and another, the bride, among
green mountains. Hyacinth blue, dream-blue jacarandas, blue
pool, stone terrace. We have not lived well—we do not know
how. Too late. This is the promised land, glimpsed but not
achieved. Repose, courtesy, beauty. I feel alone. But not
lonely. When I am frightened I am not *too* much frightened.
This independence is an achievement. But never the whole.
"You, longing to share the moment"*   the heavenly morning
hour. Open long doors, red stone wide balcony with table,
vines of blue flowers, blue jacaranda, pool covered with blue
petals drifting over from night—my sun, my mountains. My
breakfast! in my elegant Louis XVI room, papaya, pastries,
coffee, etc. This is my favorite country. Old world
grandeur—gardens of bread fruit trees with blue flowers,
orchids, copodoro—great yellow lily cups. The crowded narrow streets, bazaar like the orient. The Fromms' perfect
hospitality. He lives fully every minute. His life is arranged for
this. With all the comforts and beauties, and the end is
productivity and usefulness. He knows how to love. His wife,
people, life. It is in his shining eyes, his brilliant flow of words.
He undermines my previously held beliefs. All in the green-
and-flowing region. An armed watchman at the gate—Love? In
my terms, my term of time? But beauty. Allen Haden, "The
American chicken may be responsible for our increased
homosexuality." "Hormones." "Camacho had 28 mistresses.
All had children except one who was a pianist." Said, "Darling,

*From Lenore Marshall's poem, "How Will You Show It."

don't give me emeralds for Xmas, give me a grand piano." So in 1942, midst of war priorities, he ordered 28 grand pianos. Imagine 28—with whooping cough, measles and diarrhea in each house. Erich—I feel I have known a great human being, like Einstein. Beauty and wisdom of personality. Closely connected with life—not his ego.

1961: Sarasota

Florida—empty hotel. These people seem merely rich. Talk of travels in terms of hotels, of golf, at night they play bridge. No real relationship with each other. No relationships at all, resort curiosities. Elderly, smiling, relaxed, no one carries a book, they talk quietly in the lobby, gray and not even a single bright dyed head, respectable, accepting as their due the exceptional food and service of the three-fourths empty hotel, looking alike in their fine clothes, no one walks along the ocean, dull, dull, content.

The approach to the Taj Majal is as long as "two golf shots." Who are they, these people? Where is the real self, in this controlled environment? All smiling servitors. No one admits it if it rains. I am reminded of Steve aged two making the rounds of an elderly group of mother's guests, saying to each "Are you happy? Are you happy?" Of course—he saw behind the friendly smiles.

I—how rid myself of the Victorian Kleinert niceties—the maid in beach dress—cannot, of course.

I love the sandpipers. They skitter on their shadows over the bright sand, quick as a wink, in groups. Like eight-month-old babies, creeping, quick as that and funny, into the edge of water. Millions of shells each gleaming. A few of us beach-combers. I can't resist looking down at the shells, walk reluctantly as on violets in May. Then I am oblivious of the ocean. But then I look up and there it is—the long view.

Resorts . . .

Why doesn't a sociologist do a study from the resort angle? X HOTEL IN THE CATSKILL MOUNTAINS—Alas, my snobbery! I am spending a day and a night here, liking people but I feel like a sociologist—in other words, an outsider. I always wanted the experience of one of these Catskill hotels. The X must be seen to be believed. A caravansary—nearly 3000 guests: at night an anthill of sequins. The anonymous masses, here they have everything that a multi-millionaire could command, all run with vast efficiency. Noise, cheap humor, good natured; a dozen tennis courts outside and another dozen inside; a big pool out, another in; orchestras in four rooms at once, a floor-show here, dancing there and there. "Swingles" weekend: Rosie, a dyed blonde mama, calls out "Only singles" for the dance floor. "They go in single, come out double. Next year they come back triple." At 2:30 a beauty contest, at 3 a swimming race, at 3:30 a mass dancing lesson. Food! As many portions as you wish, they ply you with it. Lavish, but no esthetics, no attractive rooms, no bowls of flowers. The ladies at night are weighed down by their wigs and fake lashes. A pink leather evening dress with pink dyed fox collar. Ostrich feather skirt on a wobbly behind. Silver gloves, silver stockings. 3 chins—gazes in mirror as she passes. Stands at bar but nobody talks to her. Young girls out of *Esquire*— sequins on wobbly bosoms. Hairdressers, chiropodists, appliance men, delicatessen owners, teachers, real estate. A Daumier parade into dining room, the line stretches half a mile, it seems. A good time for most—easy—friendly—10 or 12 at tables jammed together, first names basis. "We are Sol and Bee Schwarz." The mama waitress takes empty seat to take orders at breakfast—plies 'em with heavy food. The appliance man orders 2 hamburgers, a fish course, veal and noodles—says he likes to try everything, eats half, then pushes away for something else. "You'd get hungry by night. At home, you *nosh* all day, here nothing between meals." My snobbism is confirmed. I feel like an outsider. Men in turtleneck sweaters, fashion-model men with hard jaws, weak faces. One gets an awful feeling about the human race. Fierce and lonely empty faces . . . who comes to a "Swingles" weekend? The pretty girl and middle-aged man on a lobby couch. He: "I can get you three partners on the dance floor in a minute. If not, I'll dance with you myself. Honey, you're choice merchandise. You really are, choice merchandise." She seems troubled—at last gets up, hurries into Swingles dance hall alone. To meet . . . whom? Mr. Schwarz wears Friday night skull cap, Saturday night a black jacket and dinner bow tie outlined in red. Girls saving up for a dress in order to be picked up here . . . no butter or ice cream (with meat).

Resort Town

America Anonymous—wide open spaces and narrow closed minds. Everybody is from somewhere else—nobody from here. The old woman whose husband is in the hospital: she says, "No, I haven't gone to visit him. It would only upset me." She may be seen wandering aimlessly at any time. "Weather bad"—it is cool but I referred to storms in East. "I'll go listen to the news. The news must be on," and off she walks a dozen times a day, briskly, aimlessly, for something to do. Mrs. Simes, in the elegant, mostly empty, dining room, her low-voiced but audible monologue to old husband: "I did *not* wake you at 8 o'clock. I came in to see how you were. You were a sick man, that's why I came in. I did *not* wake you, you always blame me, I did *not* wake you at 8. You blame me for everything," etc.

The train going there represents a strange freedom—cut off from routines, I write and feel young.

Resort in the Desert

Many rich old people at resort hotels could not get along without weather. At resorts where the days are a succession of blue and gold warmth they ask anxiously of the waiter who bears their iced and steaming breakfast trays: "How is it out? How will it be?" and to each other when they meet later on the putting green they remark severely "There's a breeze today"—

and if this continues they may even discuss some other winter-free place further to the South. Their performance on the putting green, a rectangular carpet of sward edged by petunias, is of almost as much moment. "Bother!" "No one's had an ace yet," "You looked up"—and thus, no longer haunted by the fairways of yesterday, with dinners, dressing, naps, a card game, another golden day goes by. There are events, of course; the bony smiling chambermaid, whose daughter died recently of tuberculosis, loses her temper at one of the oldest guests, talks back, one is sorry for her but she is discharged. A boyish clerk is seen to blush suspiciously when the fat gentleman leans across the desk to talk, as the gracious gentleman often does; the clerk too departs and his replacement mixes up mail and names for several days. These events do not emphasize the many-leveled order of the resort to its inhabitants. Everybody knows that these days nobody is responsible for the way things are, and that one makes the most of life. After all it is not nice to become old and to be reduced to weather and putting greens instead of fairways.

The Racecourse

Saratoga at night. Trotting. Middle age middle class. The people are unsmiling crowds in slacks, shorts, shirt sleeves. Stupid faces indifferent come alive when the race starts, dropping paper cups, stopping in the midst of a bite of hot dog. As the horses pass our section of grandstand and Bullwinkle pulls up from behind, although Noble Belle has a clear gain and passes her for a second, the crowd is galvanized—becomes one. Roar. A flag goes up on a pole. A trumpet blares. Playing music stops. A bum near the rope separating us from the reserved section of boxes and club sidles up to a man on the other side of the rope, spy glasses at eyes. "Won't make enough for a cup of coffee tonight, will we?" They all move to betting windows between races—"Place"—"Show"—"$5"—"$2"—Lights stream. A million cars parked waiting.

1966:   Yellowstone Lake Hotel—Wilderness Society Meeting

Came in conflict—wish to write. No prospect with these good people and scenery of grandeur. Yet wish to accompany J. this time. There *is* grandeur, of course, but not mine. Not the thrill of leaving the ship at Cherbourg and there are the little villages, gardens, people, seen from the train—and the French conductor! This is John Q. America—big ugly hotel, jolly folks who wring your hand, thousands of tourists—young people, children, old, to stare at nature's wonders. Fine that they come—but I approve, I do not participate. Old ladies—with cotton hair protected by prim nets. They line up in queues at the dining room. Rambling yellow firetrap of a caravansary: vanilla ice cream with white whipped cream columns. The young staff have nice faces, all college students, brisk, elevator boy is reading Armageddon on Berlin Crisis. Hopkins' "inscape" is what I have but here there is too much landscape for instress. Because one wants to share inscape one is isolated (but not last summer with Linda in Italy)*—I feel alone. I need to be yet want more of a fellow spirit than I have.

Trouble with travel is you waste so much time locating your room—key in your bag. Things like that. Rummaging for the stamps. Three Chinese philosophers, of vinegar: "It is sour."—"It is bitter." "It is fresh." I have learned—yet how much more I must learn!—to see it, know it—as fresh. . . . But this place is not for my inscape. My citizen-self says, "Great! All the tourists, seeing nature's wonders." But my artist-self finds little warmth in tourists or bears or moose, or the genial extroverts in plaid shirts.

It is better to be an extrovert than an intro. How they smile, these Wilderness Society People, how much energy they have, full of vigor and good will. Not I, alas. My introspection doubles among them. Old ideas, for no new ideas come in this milieu.

George again—quiet honor.

*See below, p. 202.

It got better. Much. My gradual adjustment and improved health—at first the altitude had me short of breath, some pains, etc. Later at Jackson Hole I began to write again and at once I liked the place too—even took it in. Mt. Moran with its skewer of glacier—mound of shadow half way down, and the Tetons, ranging up down—up down—"range peak cleft rock tree"— what a good poem that is—"Stare at one grain, stand before thicket"—*

*Quotations from Lenore Marshall's poem, "How Will You Show It."

6 The Political Activist: Segregated Hearts

1935: I am an artist and a moralist. I want better conditions for mankind. I will work for that and try to understand the efforts of others, and their causes, their ideas. I will affiliate myself with honest men if I believe with them, yet keep my own soul clear for myself and my work. Because I have no gift for politics. Therefore why must I take part in their way?

Sunday, February 17, 1918: I smoked a cigarette purposely to shock a few of the Respectables and succeeded beautifully. Why is the world for some people bounded by such straight, distinct lines?

Thursday, March 7, 1918: I don't think I shall ever catch up with my work. Just now I'm trying to find time to rewrite themes—Brewster* makes me do over all my best things, while the worst ones he labels "brisk and lively." My good opinion of him is falling . . . I walked part of the way home with Mrs. Grant today, and she told me more bits of her life. I'm so sorry for her and should love to ask her here for lunch or something, but I always feel guilty about inviting poor people into a big, comfortable house—I feel it isn't fair, and as though it were

---

*William Tenney Brewster, Professor of English at Columbia University and Provost of Barnard College, author of *English Composition and Style* (1912) and *Writing English Prose* (1915).

exhibiting forbidden fruits to them. However, that's probably cowardliness on my part, so I guess I'll invite her over some day.

1935:   Southern Labor Trip

I, who came in fear and despair and excitement, to get away from my life, its insoluble problem and moral dilemma, I find myself bright-eyed and eager too, with them, drawn into ideas foreign to my life but absorbed by these lives, this movement bigger than I am. I'm taken to their hearts—they are friendly and poised and hospitable. They answer my questions. And I, on my part, am proud and triumphant for I can be one of them, no inhibitions or differences keep me from them, I am easy too and friendly and simple and they could not suspect my different origin. How much they give to me.

In Greensboro I have the chance of a lifetime to study both sides. The drama of contrast. Conspiratorial atmosphere—for I am with the union crowd, at a Labor Board hearing, with the biggest boss in town, and must play my cards skillfully.

I dine with Strickland, the organizer, gaunt, middle-aged, from Durham, go with him to find the meeting. Cold, dismal room, swing door, folding chairs. They are talking of their weekly entertainments, setting up a committee for a dance, to make a little money, and for fun. A few negroes sit in back. They have a meagre entertainment—the girls blindfold the boys, then dress up their hands like babies, pull off blindfolds, loud laughter. Candy is passed. A boy does a trick. "We do have good times!" says Mrs. Holyfield. But they are worried. Membership is falling off. Plants are shutting, laying off. You can't strike now. Just wait—try to hold on.

At breakfast with Mrs. Holyfield when Caesar comes,* curious about me, to show me his town, his plant, his ideas. We go to Labor Board hearing, sit down, and Dowery the organizer

---

*Mrs. Holyfield was a labor organizer in the Cone Mills; Caesar Cone was their principal owner.

comes in and taps me on the shoulder gaily. He is the Big Shot in town. Keeps whispering to me "Listen to that! See how they favor the Labor lawyer every time." I see my last night's friends in the room. Caesar says, "The rabble have more violent emotions than you and I." Mustn't educate too much. Would shut down rather than unionize. Won't let the government run *his* business. These agitators tell the workers Roosevelt wants 'em to organize and they're ignorant and fall for that. But how can an intelligent New York girl believe all that? All manufacturers are humane, he argues—they couldn't get good work done otherwise.

Shows me the town. In the slums he says of every hovel— "But that one isn't occupied, it seems." Or, "If they prefer to spend money on cars and electric refrigerators instead of paint for their houses, why should you pity them? See—there's a car before that house." Then shows me his own palace set in a park, red brick and marble and lawns. His father's mausoleum is on the mill property—marble and evergreens fenced off. Touching, the old man wanted to be buried near his plant. This was his life, his creation . . .

We see the Y.M.C.A. and the smiling healthy-eyed director guides us. I am to be impressed by bowling alleys and pool and signs saying "Spirit," "Cleanliness is next to Godliness," "It Can Be Done." On top floor he has Friendship Room: bits of the Holy Land collected in cases for the instruction of the workers. Here is old lace from Hebron, oil lamps, a parchment scroll, an embroidered shawl. "Even," says the confident, brisk Mr. Arnold, pointing to a sprinkle of gravel in a dish, "even sand from the desert."

The Mill is a monster; we enter its maw; the Fidelity Plant. Caesar knows every machine, every process: he can knot the thread that breaks as quickly as a worker and he explains painstakingly what happens as the fine combs fly back and forth, the threads tighten against one another into cloth, the long packages of carded ropy cotton dip into vats; it is all familiar to him. Some rooms are ice cold—the next, where a different process goes on, may be hot as a furnace for the air must be kept humid to prevent the cotton from becoming brittle. They work eight hours, no time off to eat: a man goes through the plant selling sandwiches and they eat at their machines, tending the needles and levers and pistons, in the roar and hum of iron monsters, bits of fluff from the cotton circulating like snow through the room, blown by the tubes. Caesar acts as though he were performing a public civic function by owning this plant; working these men is his noble contribution to humanity. Many of them know him and call him by name. He is the kindly slave owner.

All day long he is on the defensive with me. At night he is still fearful and suspicious although always hospitable and pleasant—"Well, Mother, Mrs. Marshall is going to write a novel about us and you'll be the duchess and I'm to be the villain."

His house is huge but simple in its feeling for all that—a kindly mother, a smalltown evening with neighbors dropping in for bridge, a nice dinner with visiting grandchildren. We talk of servants—the colored butler has been there 37 years. So nice!—and so established, everything, and so secure in the belief that this is the way things should be. So convinced that the workers are children for whom they will care as they see fit, except for those few wicked ones who are out to corrupt and ruin the others.

Mrs. Holyfield: she is so good for me. I who am deep in my own grief and struggle feel my heart go out in gratitude and warmth to her. At the union meeting she is "Mother Holyfield" to all those boys and girls. One young man brings her a tray covered with a napkin. She pulls it off, her blue eyes bright. "Um! Oysters!" she cries. She bears it proudly down the rickety steps. "We'll all go home and have one!" At eight next morning she is there for breakfast, dignified in a simple black dress and coat probably belonging to a daughter. Night before in gingham dress & old tweed coat. Such handsome healthy polite children. I envy her, seven of them, all vital and strong and pink-cheeked, how did she manage it? "Come to see me this afternoon," she cries, "And we'll play the piano and sing and have a fine time."

She talks seriously of union affairs. The youngsters in the union reproved her for talking to the company-union girls who went into the plant when they'd been on strike but she had answered, "I'll talk to whomever I please, whenever I please, wherever I please." Proud and great integrity, humanity, and humor. I'd like to be like her. Strong and fine . . . I break away from Caesar and call on her for an hour in the afternoon. Her four-room flat above a grocery store. Ten of them live there. She and Mr. Holyfield, who is ill, in kitchen at stove, on straight chairs. She kisses me goodbye. "I hate to think of you girls staying at the hotel. We sleep three in a bed or I'd make you stay with us. 'Course we got hooks in the closet—I could hang you up on one of them."

1938:   Womens' House of Detention

Bulletproof glass and iron bars in a neat modern design compose the vestibule. A door is unlocked; we enter; it is locked behind us. We too are locked in.

White-dressed matrons with gold badges. Humane—they talk of the "girls." It is almost like a boarding school at times—any institution. We are shown the shops—they weave—they cook—they work in the laundry—they have a chapel—a roof for exercise, a gymnasium. But there are the cells. Little cubicles, neat, clean, a bed, a toilet with curtain before it, white virginal walls, a table, a small cupboard. But we can see inside: thru bars. Heavy bars divide us from these rooms and we may look right in. We walk down the row. All alike, yet with tiny human touches of difference: a piece of colored cloth on one table, a ribbon tied against one curtain, a laundered handkerchief hanging neatly across one chair, a red pillow slip on a bed—infinitesimal human feminine differences. "Just like most tiny hotel rooms," says a woman of our party brightly. White rooms, one size, one shape, open to the corridor behind bars.

I see individuals. Their dust-colored uniforms all alike cannot hide them as individuals. There is a girl with blonde hair and a speculative hard un-afraid face. She looks at me and I look at her. She sits at a table with others who are weaving, the others negresses and whites, dull looking, impervious, they look at us curiously or indifferently. But she is hard and pent up. Her hair is fluffy and light, maybe she is twenty-five, rather pretty. She stares. But does she resent me, coming from the outside, to look about and go outside again? Does she hate me for coming in my stylish suit and gazing thoughtfully about the room? I dare not smile, I dare not be friendly to her as I might smile at the negress beside her. She would scorn me for friendliness here in this place. Would it be false and pretentious to her? But it is not to me. Does she sense my sympathy, that I too am different, not cold, not impervious, not sentimental— does she wish that we could talk? We regard each other deeply and with no expression. Then I go out.

In another room, where the rest are sewing, one girl sits all alone; she is painting bowls and vases. "Something of an artist, that one," says the matron. "An addict. She's a bad egg. Beyond redemption." She has straight black short hair, a gaunt face. She was caught with three men in a hold-up in which a man was killed. She was their outside aide—a narcotic victim. Her face is cold. She does not glance at us as we praise her painted china. "It's something," says the matron of her painting. "It gives her something. But she's bad, that one."

The Head's charming apartment within the jail. A hatchet-faced woman, but warm, sincere, idealistic, competent, modest. Dark rings under her eyes. Delicious charming lunch, the uniformed maid is an inmate too—a trained nurse caught in the abortion racket.

Key West—Florida

The Keys. Driving through the dark in a great bus at 60 miles an hour, through flat dark country, the water on both sides of a narrow strip of land or occasionally wide level marshes, a shack, a roadhouse, one single light. The most isolated land, secret, mysterious, with an Ancient Mariner atmosphere of something strange lurking. Who are these people, what can they be, driving in from nowhere for a drink, a few single cut-off individuals at a bar in the night, miles from any place? Here is a collapsed building, boards strewn near the road. "They blew that up last night," says the bus driver. "The proprietor tried to put a guy out but the guy wouldn't go so he shot him. Later the fellows' friends came with dynamite and blew up the joint." A six-mile bridge, narrow, rattling under our wheels. We make it in a few seconds. Colored people in the back of the bus. A few Cubans. Some old garrulous ladies. An old man going to see the sights. At the terminal at the end he asks for a cheap hotel. "Two dollars a room? No, I can't afford that."

The hungry girl who can't afford to get out. Rosie buys her a sandwich. She comes around next day at ten and has a highball on an empty stomach. Sits and talks and doesn't think of going.

Key West People—Outcasts

A Saturday night like those in Montmartre, in the '20s; among the expatriates. The frustrated and clever at the bars.

There is Canby, handsome and crippled, symbol of them all, helpless from the waist down, dependent on his wheelchair, blue at moments but at other times content and talking suavely, drinking from ten in the morning on. Esther used to act; now she spends her time in sea resorts with him, in "barracks"— except for a few months each year in New York. Pauline Hemingway with a youthful pretty boyfriend. Drink, drink, bowling, poker, beach, drink, drink. A young man, Eddie Bacon, is trying to finish a novel but the life makes it hard. The lifeguard, Jerry, in blue jersey and blue slacks, makes $30 a month; he only drinks beer; gets into a fight with Tommy. The

Naxtons—she from Australia with pale yellow hair and a big hard Valkyrie face, he with a beard and a Semitic look—he says he is Swiss; their baby died and she went gaga, but now they run a children's camp in Connecticut. Worse is the little slovenly blonde we meet in Sloppy Joe's. A dipsomaniac, now a poor wreck of a character of Key West. She married a few years ago—she is a Dane—the man had TB. Their child, three years old, died of meningitis. She took to drink, fought with her husband, they would throw bottles at one another, he cleared out. Now she is left, laughing and ordering at the bars, joining parties, unwanted, sending back her drinks to have them made stronger. And George Abel, newspaperman—Don Juan they call him and he likes it—very handsome, dark, a small mustache, his family founded the *Baltimore Sun*. His six-year old child, whom he had stolen from his divorced wife, he brought to the island of Sark in the English Channel, but one day she landed in a privately chartered boat and with detectives and kidnapped the child from his nurse. Now the child is with her. As he drinks with me at the bar we talk of Washington radicals and his emotions break loose. "They're such bores!" he cries impotently and furiously. He holds my hand and refuses to let the bearded bloke, Naxton, with whom I had made a hit, come near me. His fury at his ex-wife and her crowd—he is on the opposite side, oh a fascist all right: "I bet this made them mad all right," he says and takes from his wallet a clipping and it is an account of a party given in Washington by George Abel, writer, to forty guests, to celebrate the fall of Barcelona. Suddenly he is repulsive to me, a cad, and I get away. Slap him.

Key West—holiday island—amongst balmy palms—under a blue sky.

Title: Under a blue sky.

Ca. 1940: Factionalism. She is the victim of two opposing camps, each accusing her of favoring the other. Evelyn* and the

*Evelyn Scott (Mrs. John Metcalfe) was a prolific author in many genres—poetry, novels, juveniles, essays, autobiography. She was, in her own words, "afflicted . . . with an ardor for social reform."

Communists. Her obsession makes her misinterpret me. Because I try to be fair I am a Communist to her. Because I have friends and acquaintances whom she suspects of a career of persecution she thinks me duped by the Communists. She writes me involved letters full of implications: I don't understand the evil surrounding me and which is trying to use me.

The Communists (Betty) on the other hand think I am surrounded and influenced by Trotskyites. Or I must be a reactionary—since I don't agree with them!

Neither can believe—or is willing to believe—that I see them both, lost in a tangle of conflict, trying to draw me in where *I know I don't belong.* I am an artist and a moralist. I want better conditions for mankind. I will work for that and try to understand the efforts of others, and their causes, their ideas. I will affiliate myself with honest men if I can believe with them, yet keep my own soul clear for myself and my work. Because I have no gift for politics. Therefore why must I take part in their way?

July 3, 1961 or 1962:   Communism

Recently I have been struck by the indiscriminate use of the word "Communist." It is the easy conviction with which the word is made to include irrelevancies to which I refer, the application of a stereotype to wholly inappropriate occasions, which seems to me of consequence within the negative thinking of our time, yet another part of the psychological climate that is an outgrowth of fear and hate and produces more fear and more hate, and thus even more international tensions. The label "Communist" is employed as a facile epithet somewhat as Boche or Bolshevik were in the past, in connection not with a system or any specific meaning but in a broad blind weighted sense; it means Them, not Us. I am of course at present not referring to informed language although there too a tinge at once colors the word because of the world situation, just as presumably the word "Capitalist" even when correctly employed has a certain emotional overtone in the Soviet Union. What must be reckoned with, as well as informed usage, is the general, the common, the careless tossing off of the word and its impact upon prejudice within our society, its contribution toward the difficulties of finding a *modus vivendi* between two systems in a period of crisis.

"Communist!" an ill-tempered farmer yelled at us: we had driven by mistake into his private road, having lost our way. "Communist!" a storekeeper said of country neighbors who wrote letters to the local paper protesting against this or that. "Communist!" said the lady at the hairdresser's, picking up a pamphlet on disarmament that had been left among movie magazines. "Communist!" said the teacher to a foreign-born obstreperous student (I heard all of these); and "He's not a Communist, he's just a bookworm!" said a school boy in defense of an ostracized lone-wolf chum, to his pals on the baseball team.

Well, it's trivia. It would be ridiculous if it weren't also deadly.

There's a sort of boomerang effect: next time these speakers meet the word in any context it will have become invested with the surplus meanings of the first time. Even when properly employed it will have attached to it certain nuances,—it will be self-infecting. The snowball effect may thus set the framework for political events: after all, politicians aren't deaf to public opinion. How does one break into such a self-fulfilling cycle?

In Erich Fromm's book, *Marx's Concept of Man*, he points out Marx's humanist philosophy versus the positivistic-mechanistic thinking of much of social science. "The alternatives for the underdeveloped countries," Fromm says, "are not capitalism and socialism, but totalitarian socialism and Marxist humanist socialism." And again: "I am convinced that only if we understand the real meaning of Marxist thought and hence can differentiate it from Russian and Chinese pseudo-Marxism, will we be able to understand the realities of the present-day world." Which way socialism? Which way *next?*

The way will be determined by attitudes as much as by anything else. Men motivated by fear and hatred will of course tend to extreme and paranoid actions. A word won't change the world. We writers wish it would—maybe that's the writer's nth degree dream. All the same it should be possible to restore a word to its truth. If it is freed of extraneous barnacles, if its realities, its formal meanings, are emphasized, we may be able to give the idea behind it a fairer appraisal.

What I suggest is that a concerted attempt be made to diminish some of the blind prejudice and surplus meanings that swell the word Communist, and which may even create further schisms due to irrelevancies. Such a project should not be only on a purely intellectual level although its formulation would start there: it must reach people at all levels. What are the stereotypes that are not true? And what are the truths?

Needless to say such central problems as Germany, Cuba, China—heaven knows how many—are beyond semantics; or are they? That prejudice in which semantics plays a part should not be overlooked.

A clearer image than the current one of the word Communist should be presented to the public. I'd feel better if the farmer yelled Bum instead of Communist at me next time I took a mistaken turn into his driveway.

The Segregated Hearts   *1964*

I begin to understand the Negro's hatred of the white liberal. The rank reactionary or segregationist is too easy an enemy, too obvious a target for hatred to linger on. Yes, he must be defeated, exterminated, by law, for the law at last recognizes him as criminal, and his like must be prevented from ever again having power . . . propagating . . . but fear of him and hatred of him (even the white hate him) make him unsatisfactory as a target: there is no dispute about the reactionary, no question involved. But the liberal, the white liberal, is worthier as foe for the new Black . . . a subtler quarry. Trust him at first, be surprised at his sympathies, take comfort in his committed acts. He (she, I) marched in Washington! He supports CORE. He knows Jim Farmer.* He went to Atlanta. The Negro's skepticism at the validity of a white ally, his wary consent and admission; then sometimes his too-great transference, becoming like a child to the white, over-expecting and feeling entitled to every concession, once he is willing to trust the white. He takes advantage then, under the cloak of trust, irrational and irresponsible to his own commitment. The semi-intelligent, half-educated Negro is self-deceived. And how natural this is! After generations of injustice the lid is off at last. He may assert his rights now; it comes all at once; the white is responsible for the past which built up unbearably. Yes, the lid is off. A levelling process starts. It cannot come all at once, the intelligent Negro knows it, yet let an individual instance take place in which the white does not baby him with extra consideration and he will twist it into injustice. Wilhelmina, my maid, a compulsive talker, ambitious, desirous of culture, helpful, at first is delighted and astonished at my liberalism and friendliness. She is thrilled at the job. She begins to talk too much—I do not like to stop her. Then Wilhelmina misses the suburban train on which we were to meet. Comes to Trenton late, but after waiting an hour for her in the station, I have left for home, tired and not knowing whether she would come at all. An hour later she phones, not apologetic for tardiness but furious that I would not wait indefinitely. My "Get yourself here by taxi—I'll pay" is interpreted as "You expect me to walk from Trenton!" Hysteric tirade follows—the pleasant woman is now the wildly unreasonable accuser—in her own eyes the oppressed victim. I have become her white oppressor, all the worse for having misled her by my liberalism into believing in me . . . the Good White! (When her boy friend did not get a job for which he

*Jim Farmer is James Farmer, formerly head of CORE (Congress of Racial Equality).

applied she said it made him "bitter"—implying he was turned down *only* because of color, although he was unqualified.) The paranoid wave. She does not *want* to believe in me and she almost did—she caught herself back in time, so that she too can hate again and return to a racial paranoia. It is easier to work for someone she can hate and indict. The past is too strong to allow admittance of any white to her *segregated heart*. The white liberal is not really one of them and so he is a traitor (And I find in my heart a new segregation of my own: despair for her and our relationship).*

Many "liberals" have sympathies but do not take action. This is the age of impatience. We must have more than right feeling.

1964: Scenes from last August's Washington march flashed through my mind. One recurrent flash was of the night before the march: Washington's breathlessly silent streets, the atmosphere of pending, of suspense. Another was a moment during the march of forty people abreast, filling the street, and of an eight year old boy walking beside me; he held his father's hand and with all the others he sang "America The Beautiful," a rapt expression on his lifted shining black face; "America, America," he sang, "God shed His grace on thee,/And crown thy good with brotherhood," his face, heir of generations, exalted and forever unforgettable, his voice pouring out love of his country, his country. There was a two-month-old infant borne in a sling around his mother's back and there were snatches of talk—"Anybody who's *any*body" . . . "Naturally nobody would stay home" . . . It was orderly and dignified. It was full of hope. We were part of millions. We were not only one. Archimedes said of the lever: "Give me a place to stand and I can move the world." If you were white you felt less guilty that day, you held your head higher; if you were Negro—how did you feel? We whites who had done nothing but sympathize,

*Lenore Marshall embodied this theme in an entirely different situation in her short story, "The Segregated Hearts."

nothing but contribute our dollar, we faced our passivity at last. *I* felt more integrated that day, more a part of the human race, forgiven by a boy who sang "America, America." In the afternoon another young couple, this time with a baby of about eight months, passed in the crowd. I had the illusion that the morning's two-month-old infant grew up quickly; now he smiled, gurgled, even had a tooth. His nice young parents had discarded the canvas sling and toddled his feet on the grass, let his back straighten, all within this day's hours. His head too was held high.

For an article . . . The Theys: *1966*
What can a novelist do about Them in the face of life today? The raw stories are around us in any newspaper column. Usually we find as we read that a certain kind of They are well behaved except, it seems, when outside agitators get busy among them. Then the Theys who have been living unobtrusively among us revert to some violent identity within themselves, show their dark underbellies, corruption quickly finds fertile ground. They show a bizarre dissatisfaction with us, their protectors, so that in fact our state is scarcely protector any more, we are overrun by hordes. In my newspaper (*New York Times*, July 17, 1966) I read that the mayor of an upstate New York village is bewildered: migrant Puerto Rican farm laborers on the outskirts have rioted. The mayor, standing on the lawn before his ranch home, says: "They walk by here on the road and I wave to them and they laugh and smile. One time I was going to throw away an old rusted broken-down bed—it had been my mother's long ago, I guess—and I offered it to them. You should have seen them, carrying it down the road on their heads. Real happy, you know!" But the police chief who is to be tried for assault in an incident connected with Them says: "I get along fine with the boys. Hell, I have to, that's my job. I would say there's some outside agitation going on here to produce the trouble we're having here." And his wife adds:

"This place is a paradise compared to what they're used to living in. Of course you and I wouldn't want to live like that, but I believe they like it fine." What is it they like fine? One of the condemned migrant camps contains in 11 shacks and houses more than 40 persons. The furnishings are beds crowded side by side and cooking gas rings; no running water, only 2 outside toilets.

And how do people adjust to new systems? In Czechoslovakia there was not long ago a most democratic government, an independent people. After war and change these people had to adjust to a new system and in order to do so, knowing their old ways and tradition, they had *doubly* to believe in the new necessity . . . My Airedale dog always ran free in the fields, at night sleeping in the barn. I wanted to make a watchdog out of him, get him to become a house dog, so I bought him a fine pillowed basket to sleep in, put it in the kitchen. I took a steak bone and, opening the door, tried to lure him into the house. Inch by inch I moved the bone through the open door, from almost his mouth toward my house, into the house, stood there bone in hand saying, "Good dog!" I thought he would have a breakdown. He wanted the bone, he could not bear coming into the house which had formerly been forbidden territory. At last he dashed up, seized the bone, turned, leapt at the closed door, pushed it open and—whoops!—out he raced. The door slammed behind him.

This is supposed to be a new age. Recently I was told that the previous age was the age of fragmentation but just now we are in the electronic age which means the age of unification. We are bound together by new communication systems, thus farewell to fragmentation. Even before that this was the age of anxiety, etc. Once ages lasted ages, take for instance the Paleolithic Age, the Pleistocene Age, even the Middle Ages. But now 10 years is an Age.

Whatever our Age is, there is a deep dissonance between my lane, my love, and my world of news-events.

1966: The Writer

One could wish to be a Negro. The Negro novelist may be both artistic and concerned with social justice: he carries his problem and his race with him every minute of his life and these must be amalgamated with his art. But we are not White novelists. We must find disguises for our "savage indignation" lest sociology obtrude in our work and make of it a tract.

It is often said that protest demonstrations do no good. Despite parades, groups, meetings, Madison Square Garden rallies, Washington conferences, despite draft-card burnings and statements by prominent persons and prayers, the political situation—the Vietnam War—remains unchanged. No, there is a change: youth speaks out now and is a factor. This generation is the best: the *good* ones are the best. And we older ones, we the innovators of SANE or whatever it may be, we are not futile entirely: we created a climate in which these young people at last have come up.

Article: 1966

We fight the cliché, the stereotype. When I was first concerned to the point where I became active people said, "What can the individual do?" Later they said, "Nobody likes such things," implicitly accusing us of taking over dislike of war, abrogating it to ourselves, whereas they were as much in it as we. They weren't. They were passive, outsiders. Content with words and not even strong words. Always a big But in their voices. Always the word Freedom is used, to clinch matters. What is Freedom? Ours? Or the other fellow's? They are infidels. We are noble. They are aggressors, deserving of any fate. We feel *righteous* wrath. They feel only wrath.

Not only our morality is corrupted—but our words! Headline: 420 Dead in Greatest Victory. "Victory"? How can this be? The words further corrupt our morality. Greatest Victory consists of numbers dead. Literature deals almost altogether with life and is therefore humanist. Even *1984* shows the state of humanism in reverse.

The mathematical infinity rung by the arrangements of the letters of the alphabet. Out of 26 letters have been conjured the unlimited mutation of language and literature. Infinity (for novel),* the unending repetitions that can be rung up on an initial theme. Shakespeare and a laundry list, the Bill of Rights and a grocery bill—all combinations of those 26 letters. Infinity—something that has no fixed sum? Could a computing machine work out language?

The stereotypes about the Chinese are heard more often: more people are saying things like The Chinese won't sign an agreement—It's the Chinese I fear: with some reason of course; Chinese statements of position commit them to aggressive opposition to capitalism. But if the Russian-U.S. tension eases and we can no longer vent our clichés on Russia, if suddenly the image changes to the Jovial Krushchev—overnight we acquire a new friend, a whole nation is changed for us, we shake hands and shout for joy. (Maybe! May it be!) But must not our *hate-image*, so long directed at Russia find egress elsewhere—to China of course, the new yellow foe? Where would the hatred go? Can it evaporate? Our John Birchites, our Goldwaters, do they not need hate, thrive on it? They dictate uniformity, they are ferocious in their demand that all be like themselves. They fear the stranger and so exterminate him. How they will turn on the Chinese. But really what do they know of the Chinese? Do they think of the temperament, tradition, do they remember the past or have any curiosity based on reality? Any wish to come to terms? Were there always such hatreds? During other wars, governments quarreled over borders or incidents or trade: then men fought. But was there hate of whole populations, hate-mongers consisting of small mean fanatical power-mad men?

What is kindness? Is it the intention to be kind and the belief in one's own kindness? This is well meant but sentimental. It

*She is probably referring to the novel outline on pp. 182-183.

can actually turn out to be cruel. There is no imagination in it, there is, rather, an inflated ego, self-protective, demanding recognition of its virtue. There is a difference between being unkind and being ungentle. To be ungentle implies being unkind but one may be unkind in quite gentle ways. The ungentle person has no identification with others; he snaps his answers, "Well what now?" When he makes a mistake he barks "We won't discuss it"—he is never sorry—he is angry. He may thrash, lacerate, pummel, murder, but convinced of his own good will and rights, he never recognizes that he has injured.

Writer

What did he want now? To wake people up—illuminate—to make them feel their world, this world, see it, want it. He had no wish to preach to them: if that, he would write a tract. No use. There would be more use if you could sing to them—reach them. He had to get off the ground. Their hearts, for their minds didn't seem to count. Mental health wasn't mental—it was emotional. There were writers who pondered technique. The novel was dying. How resuscitate it? There were anti-novelists. They threw out stale outword forms; by shock they made new again. Or—once there had been the stream of consciousness novel—the psychological novel—the inner. Now the outer worked inward: it *didn't matter.* Yes, style mattered but if it was good it could be a book by Tolstoy or Proust or Balzac or Dostoevsky—style was a tool and whether it were the carvings of Chartres or planes of the Lever Building it had meaning, it had reason, its own stamp, it was connected to its purpose. What purpose now?

The political world? That was only part. Because the danger was more complex. There was a deadline approaching. The danger of an explosion increased, sped daily forward. He had only himself—his strong right arm—his pen. What megalomania! Would he deflect the deadline? That was really what he wanted to do—just that. With no megalomania but only soberest wish to make his life count, to channel his art into his life, into life—to preserve life. Good or bad didn't matter in these terms. Of course it should be good, it is intolerable that it is so bad "the best lack all conviction while the worst / Are full of passionate intensity." But it is Life. It is force. It must go on.

These days—revolution—youth. How parents must question themselves now! Bright affluent cultivated young people make bombs. They plant bombs. We the parents brought them up to this revolutionary stance, with our liberalism, our Peace Corps, our social justice committees. Our words have become their distorted action.

Dostoievsky's Ivan has seen the evils of the world; and though the earth may someday reach the millenium, he cannot justify the evil that has accompanied, and will continue to accompany, progress toward the New Jerusalem. He envisions the inevitable superstate, the loss of personal freedom, the loss of spirituality. But his comment typifies the very spirit of isolation in contemporary man: "Good Lord, it's no business of mine."

Disenchanted with old ideologies, too old to live within the new, yet agreeing with them.

There was something noble in the old idea that a poet was to be known less by his craftsmanship than by his vision. The large vision of humanity is essential to the poet and the poem.

Political feeling is very different from partisanship. It is closer to a feeling for humanity. Poems against the Bomb or proletarian poems may be invested with passion and magnitude that the trick verbalisms lack.

What we read first in the daily newspaper tells something of our character. Today, before the headlined news of the Israel-Arab war, of unemployment, of the Nixon speech, I read that the lost head of Aphrodite by Praxiteles had been found.

7 The Political Activist: Talent for Extinction

1963: Who knows how to live? Now what emerges is barbed wire, depravity, the rationalization, talent for extinction on a grand scale.

The Establishment of Poets

There's an establishment of poets and their self-placed haloes. The critics who make certain laws for criticism, and set a style—their style, their literary scene, and woe to him who does not fit the formula. The establishment has grown up subtly in a few years. It acknowledges that it has not always a relation to merit. "That poem of A's in X Magazine was poor," one says of his friend. But he will still not hold it against the friend because they are cohering elements of a group and will support each other. Nor will an editor turn either down; he will read the name and this is enough. This does not mean that the charmed circle cannot be pierced: a newcomer may be published or send some poems to one of the group with a well-phrased letter of admiration. If thus he becomes a protégé he is on the road to being an insider, a junior insider at first, for whom a senior will write a blurb or a preface. The opposite, a failure to realize the importance of practical steps, may be disastrous to a career. One young poet of my acquaintance was highly praised at the appearance of her first book, by a foremost anthologist who announced that he would put several of her poems in his next edition. The statement was made in the hearing of her editor, her publisher, her husband, etc., so that the fact of his promise, to which there were witnesses, is not in question. Yet this poet, an individual somewhat innocent or perhaps high-minded about strategy, was not only never included but also snubbed by that maker of reputations.

The morality of politicking in poetry has its shocking, if human, side. In what way does a poet place that halo on his own head? And how have poets risen from a much-neglected group in the writing fraternity to one which is honored sometimes quite out of proportion to its due? It has academies and societies for the good and the mediocre. It has patrons, prizes, forums, unlike novelists or essayists who have not all of these and surely none with such special heavenly auras. Is there an extra need "to compensate" among poets, an extra lack of security that makes them surround themselves with high glass walls behind which they exercise their pinions, voices, and wings, exhibiting themselves as birds do in bird-banding stations? Yes—in many cases the answer is yes—some of our best poets have gone through terrible breakdowns and their sensitivity may often be on a more precarious level than most, though plumbers too inhabit asylums.

O why do we write? For fame? for power? prestige? Sometimes, whether in love, in hate, in compulsion, there should still be a further reason. What are we trying to do in this world? The writer (the serious writer of course is the only one who concerns us) wants to impose his order on chaos. He has a direction, a goal, to give shape, to form an entity which is *his*, which represents himself. But today what order is possible? Is it realistic to believe we can shape this chaos, is it honest to set out as though what we have to say will bring clarity or hope or change, do we dare to believe or pretend that our word will be significant, faced as we are by unmanageable disorder everywhere while the great question, overshadowing all others, is the survival of the human race?

1971

Sometimes there is an agonizing conflict for the writer who takes part in a movement in which he believes. The writer hasn't all the time he needs, not ever, or the tranquility for his work. He may have to make great sacrifices in his career, write fewer books than he otherwise might have. He wakes up at 3 A.M. in a panic about the book he is writing. He wants to stop all this do-gooding, as it may be glibly called, having talked maybe all day with scientists or politicians or educators about, for instance, the shafts that have been dug 6,000 feet deep in Alaska, for nuclear weapons tests. These will be the largest tests ever held, and they are planned for this year of 1971 in earthquake territory. What dangers do such tests invite? Are we tampering with nature? What of earthquakes? What of pollution? What of tidal waves? The writer wants instead to go back to the heroine of the book that he is writing . . . to that heroine and how she solved *her* problems. He is terrified that perhaps he will never even finish his book.

The Hill is Level took me ten years to write. During that time I was co-founder of the National Committee for a Sane Nuclear Policy, now known as SANE, and I helped launch it.* One wonders sometimes who one is when one feels torn limb from limb between the inner and outer lives, for one can't help it, if one believes passionately in a thing, one has to commit oneself to it. We hear about searching for our identities these days— identity crises. Perhaps we now have to have more than one identity or perhaps the different sides really do compose into one. Who are we really, we ask. We would like to pursue a direction that is simple and clear and to arrive at our life's work. But our idea of our self-hood and the facts of it are complex.

What about the writer, the poet and novelist? SANE was born in my living room in 1957. That is what I think of when I talk about practical matters, of the poet as peace worker or of

*SANE was established by Lenore Marshall with Clarence Pickett, who headed the American Friends Service Committee, and Norman Cousins, the distinguished editor.

the writer's divided life or the divided writer's life or the writer as activist. SANE started really through a conversation with a friend who was as concerned as I at that time about the madness of the arms race and the growing possibility of the destruction of our civilization.

At that time the United States was testing nuclear bombs in the Pacific, and we laymen were beginning to hear about fallout and the terms Strontium 90, Iodine 131, radioactive poisons that could mean death. I said, accidentally enough, shouldn't we stop, shouldn't we do something about stopping this? The result of that meeting was a meeting several weeks later of a few more friends, about thirty of us, and the formation of SANE, small at first, but soon growing large, taking the lead in trying to halt nuclear bombing tests. Other organizations joined us and our efforts contributed several years later to the nuclear test ban treaty.

The difference between the period in which we founded SANE and now, between yesterday and today, is that there was very little support for a peace movement then. We were considered kooks, cranks, nuts. Just one step above Commies because, they said, if you believed in peace, that could help the enemy, so obviously you couldn't believe in peace.

At any rate, when I asked some of my writer friends to join SANE, or in some way speak out against the arms race or nuclear weapons, they would say to me, your job is to write your books. You shouldn't be engaged in these activities. Start your new novel. Of course, it was just what I was doing and wanted to do all the time. Now there are people everywhere who agree with the peace movement. Formerly there was very little to read on the subject. Now there is a large literature. Now people inform themselves about the issues. In the past, the youth generation was silent. Now there is a youth generation that *leads*, and the best of them—not all by any means—but the best of them are the best young people that we've ever had.

Writers

There are those people whose success is won at the cost of self-betrayal. In writers, above all, the tragedy of success may be most poignant. In Her,* her failure was caused by the opposite: she had to make her life the first truth, even though the art suffered. She had to be a woman first, her *own* person, her own *kind* of person. Not only her reputation but her art was the price. For every day of living was difficult, a struggle, and not enough was left of her for her work.

Today the writer cannot write as before. A giant nostalgia in his heart pulls him back to the poems and novels of his past, but he lives in a world on the brink of self-extermination and the loves of yesterday dwindle in comparison. Everything must be related to this over-riding fact and the over-riding goal of preventing war. The intellectual technocrats have brought us to this: all human values are distorted. We can split the atom— why?—to destroy ourselves. We soar into space—into a bed-bug cockroach planet where man had died of radiation *knowing what he was doing!* No realism in that, the realist is not the mechanic, no matter on how high an electronic level. He is the man who keeps his vision of man and relates it to what he does. Then how write books as before? Only books with a theme close to our crisis are true. Art has always been the Great Truth, transmuting. . . . Now it can no longer aim at Eternity—but at Today.

1955, Montecantoni Ferme: Arthur Comptons came for lunch, driving from Firenze to our elegant huge wandering hotel. He big, imposing, friendly, lecturing abroad on Brotherhood, Christians and Jews and—of course—we-must-be-strong; she large, garrulous, bossy, interrupting, not to be outdone by a Nobel prize husband, always says "We worked," eats too much, greedily. After lunch we adjourn to the gravel-walked garden among oleanders—palms and pines—

*This seems to be a sudden reference to a heroine in an unwritten novel.

here he launches into his story, Roentgen rays, the making of the bomb, the *using* of the bomb. They polled the men who'd worked on it about its use for, you see, there was a split in Japan, the Emperor wanted to surrender but not the war party, the war might have dragged on, they tried to find the Emperor's speech offering terms but just then the Tokyo electric system failed in the night, they couldn't find it. "They" was the war party—the surrender might have taken another year or, at least, guerilla warfare—whatever we hear. The conscientious righteous man. Compton, the masked man successfully fleeing from his guilt, goes on with his success story, while his boss, his big horse of a wife, interpolates without a doubt. At last the four men were asked by our government Compton, Oppenheimer, Fermi, Lawrence. They said use it. At this point Mrs. C. opens her bag, takes out a mirror, examines her large aging ugly face, powders, looks again. She dives further into her bag, produces a tweezers, there in the garden, on a bench beside a stone cupid, we talking, people strolling, begins carefully to pluck at her eyebrows, and then she proceeds to her nose, pulling out hairs while the impressive mustachioed man goes on about the bombing of Hiroshima; about how all through history new weapons have been used; after bows and arrows, gunpowder. We suggest we might have announced our possession; no, he says, nobody would have believed. Suddenly I want to get up and walk away. I want to say: sorry, I cannot sit with you. You are responsible, you virtuous man escaping behind your Brotherhood. It comes over me, I doubt that I can control it. But I stay. Perhaps for Jim. Perhaps my own courtesy to guests. Perhaps thinking I have made some point that might be lost, made obliquely what would be destroyed by his fury if I acted thus. His astonishment would then justify him by branding me a crazy woman. Perhaps he saw that I questioned his judgment for he says "We did our best." "Only God could know," I say. The lady puts away her tweezers and rejoins the talk importantly. She guides his words, his career, in fact it was probably *she* who made his decision. Yes. What would he have been like with another wife, this man whose conscience sits *almost, almost* easy, helped by the tweezer wife. A "good" man is harder than a Hitler here; he has no aggressions, he is sure of his nobility; in fact a Nobel Prizer. "True there's the danger they'd get one off first but we'd protect ourselves and knock them out with a stinger." I wish I'd said, "You might have saved morality, you moral man. Maybe civilization. If I'd been God I'd have decided differently"—and walked away.

March 10, 1959, Mexico: My million Mexican mountain again! Through it all, it is here!

Poems well up. Words—lovely words—well up. But not the bitter words that I had been writing—not those sad disillusioned themes—the true untrue—this is eternity again, these mountains are all one mountain, one is all. It is the same, from the upper terrace of the Hacienda—red rambler roses all over the rail, earthenware pots full of plants, sun, sun,—beyond it all my mountains shape, sheer, perpendicular, green, trees upright from rooftop to sky, bold, assertive. The earth and the universe and the little humble people. Rightness. No ersatz city civilization, bumper to bumper, exuding fumes, dressed up to hurry and wilt—here all is bloom, strength, fundamentals. I miss Jim—sorry for his cares at home. I want to share miracles and refreshment with him. The old civilization—stoical faces, mud huts, thatched, open to the elements, like villages in India, plaintive-eyed child beggars at stations. From the train the country unfolds, mountains begin, ringing the earth. Could the Bomb pulverize here? This isn't man's country. It is the universe. Stars real and abstract—

Peter Sachs of Chicago—above the Chorrillo. They built their new house, complete with a private funicular up the cliff—a basket on a cable. It rises slowly and terrifies me. I take the steep mosaic steps. There are great formal beautiful rooms—Picassos, Chagalls, Braque. A stereo phonograph playing music as if the orchestra were in the room. Around us the peasant huts of mud—invisible on the mountain side, while music pours through the portals, the hostess turns out all but one light, puts her feet on the coffee table, the host runs his fingers over his record collection, whisks away dust with a handkerchief, takes off a record when there is a whirr. The music is too loud and exciting.

There is evil in this inflexible *âme* secluded from the world, my atom world, talking of art to me: the past, the present, the future—writers do not write enough of the future. The rich German esthete—man of ideas and taste—where is the evil? for I feel it powerfully. The contrast is too dramatic for my blood: hidden in the mountains the humble huts, straw, mud, the million little toiling people blotted out by night, while our music, superb, rolls through the heights and caverns of darkness, and we sit, we six, dropping a few intelligent words to each other, sure in our Picassos, unsure me! The violence of this land around us in the darkness, precariously perched on our ledge, the stars above, the mountain fortress around, the eternal night not covering our strange presences, my enormous fear.*

1959, Geneva: I go alone again in the morning—wonderful feel of independence again, a strange city and I am able to speak, to understand, to make my way, to walk alone, LGM, I, in the Palais des Nations corridors, searching for Salle V. There are big conference rooms, empty at lunch. One man sits alone among papers at one place, working. Charlie Chaplin should do Kafka—in the U.N. (Thurber should illustrate the sewers of Paris, man chasing woman thru the world's underground.) I see Ambassador Wadsworth for SANE.** Cordial—we have a nice jolly talk. I have gained so much confidence with people. Ease. They seem to like me. I'm trying

*Compare the short story, "Dialogue on a Cliff."

**James J. Wadsworth was sent as the United States Ambassador to negotiate a nuclear test ban treaty in Geneva. Semyon Konstantinovitch Tsarapkin was the Soviet Ambassador to negotiate a nuclear test ban treaty in Geneva. Lewis L. Strauss, a personal friend, was chairman of the Atomic Energy Commission in 1958.

to see Tsarapkin—appointment made with Mr. Verontov—
cordial—in the Soviet Villa, tomorrow. Wadsworth seemed
cautiously optimistic. "Talk and talk but sometimes they give a
little bit, we give a little bit . . ." Ts. is referred to as
"scratchy." W. calls him a devoted family man, adores his
grandchildren. He's of course under orders from Moscow but
probably "wants an agreement as much as anyone." Underground tests are the real block, hard to check. Strauss is a "good
enemy to have"—no use for him. McCone is better. W. gives
me name to approach at Soviet Embassy.

June 26
Russian Villa—Tsarapkin—5 Avenue de la Paix—opposite
Palais des Nations—near Red Cross—set in a garden. I am
cordially met by young Mr. Vorontsov who speaks perfect
English, ushered into small reception room, round small table,
comfortable chairs. Ambassador Tsarapkin, pleasant looking
and friendly. We talk for more than a half hour, and in fact
when Mr. Vorontsov reenters to say there are people waiting he
detains me five minutes more. I say I am on SANE, a writer,
mother, grandmother. Ts: "Then you have everything. The
most noble cause, a career, a family." L.: "SANE and my
children are linked." Ts.: "I too have grandchildren. Two. We
must protect them," etc. Shows me letter he received from crew
of a phosphate ship near Australia, movingly urging a ban and
calling on God to put in men's hearts the wisdom necessary. He
is deeply sincere and stirred and upset. I tell him more and more
people are concerned at home and are calling for a ban. He is
much interested, says however there are strong U.S. forces
who *want* the bomb, the Army, A.E.C. I say I assume it is the
same in Russia and in all countries. The "you have to be so
strong that nobody will dare attack you" fallacy of the military.
He says: "No. *Everybody* in Russia wants a test halt." L. "We are
concerned about fallout; when I give the children milk I wonder
what I am doing." Ts.: "Is there an increase in strontium 90 in
milk?" He looks thoughtful and worried. Tells me how the

meetings have gone on and on—over 100. It is time to write a treaty. There has been procrastination. L. "Our people want it but they want confidence. Your people must also say, "Can we trust the Americans," as we say the opposite. I myself think we must trust, but many people want more assurance. However, each time there is more flexibility and a step is taken, people are more confident in the possibility of a ban, and they in turn influence their senators. A treaty must not only be signed but ratified." T. asks "Will it be ratified?" I say I believe so, but Congress naturally wants controls and the Soviet U. also must want this. Every step helps. He says he has not seen any SANE reports or publicity lately. I assure him it goes on; I will send it. I bring up the Berkner report: "My understanding is that new methods and machinery are indicated, not necessarily more men stationed on territory." At this point he becomes somewhat excited; we are standing because now Vorontsov has returned, the time is up. T. talks animatedly—the methods are more complicated than would at first appear, they involve further depths in the earth, much more time, much more money. A ban must take place *at once*. Berkner means more delay which cannot be allowed. I say we want the most effective ban and soon also; our people long for it. T. "Tell that to your Ambassador Wadsworth." I say *we* believe in W's sincerity and that he is devoted to peace. T. "I too believe that. Ambassador W. is sincerely striving for a treaty." I thank him. He wishes we could go on but it isn't possible. He sends regards to my group at home. L. sends best wishes to his children and the Russian people. He sends best wishes to my children and the American people! For another five minutes I talk to Mr. Vorontsov. T. has talked English carefully and well. V. is fluent. He wants to go home, says they have been here away from their families too long. The treaty ought to be signed in a few weeks. I repeat what I said about a *total* ban and about safeguards. He too talks of our military-minded influences. I say, "But Strauss is out." We agree on Strauss; he mistrusts the Army, however; once more I say there are crazy men everywhere, the more reason for control. He was in the U.S. for four years, we agree that U.S. and Russians have so much in common. He says we are much alike, there is every reason to agree. I wish I could go to Russia. He says why not now—*this* summer? I invite him to visit when he gets to U.S. again, I call Ambassador Wadsworth and report, ask, "Was I okay?" W. "Yes ma'am! Congratulations!" Later I wonder if I put enough stress on *total* ban. They are obviously eager to get a treaty signed *soon*. Will they be patient enough to work out controls? Will *we* be flexible enough? Their earnestness impresses me.

July 1963   Notes   The Writer in Novel?*
How does one live in the world today? One is a woman, aware, living fully, alone and with others. Much of good, too much of bad, lying behind and still all around. (That's all personal—it counts in one way, not another.) But how does one plan one's life? From now on, in this world of 1963? For it is unlike every world on any level before. We have no precedents. Over my head a bomb is flying, and under my sea and in the roots of my grass and it will explode one of these days, wiping out—me? The garden where I sit, a nest of green, seven tall maples, a clean white picket fence, red lane, bounding dog? This favored world of mine. All the contrasts, personally alone as I sit here, surrounded by a network of evil. *The Garden of Eden is ringed with serpents. It is a snake house. That serpent had a million descendants.* Behind my trees, under my lawn, in back of the rose bush, the Negroes are rising. Good. They are gathering somewhere, marching, sitting-in at a lunch counter, braving the police, some are being beaten. All are holding up their heads at last, squaring shoulders, feeling like men at last. The days of gradualism are past. I cannot be a gradualist any more—human dignity—where have I been since the Civil War while black

*As on p. 117, these may be notes for a novel about a writer "who had to make her life the first truth."

children have been shamed by white-skins? While they swarmed in fetid tenements I have cultivated my garden. While atomic submarines were launched I have sat at meetings, the flattered girl-friend of busy brilliant men, scholars and activists to a point, as well meaning and almost as futile as I. What shall I do? Be honest from now on. Write every day, like this, even with nothing to say—automatic writing—maybe something will come. Try not to forget. Not to despair. The sickness proliferates. Talents devoted to killing by the million. But *isn't there a law against genocide?* Gamesmanship that forgets the stakes. Then that Profumo scandal in England—a whore and a politician—but behold the panorama of high-life degeneracy, governments dependent on sordid procurers and bitches. Sick world, where have you lost yourself? What can we give our young?

No news of beloved Bob C.* Personal death (I pray not) death of the good and true. In the sea of life-and-death there is life, and death, personal, individual.

We are governed by the laws of nature and of society. Animal nature, instincts, drives, which we stuff into a box marked Law and Order. Twisted into a mould that becomes second nature to us, but sick, for it is superimposed; no wonder we are a neurotic civilization. From infancy all training is superimposed on the poor kicking protesting animal. Soon he learns. But he must break out. Where are the people who have done it best, when, at what time—who know how to live? Now what emerges is barbed satire, depravity, the rationalization, talent for extinction on a great scale.

But ah, the individual death. Dear true gentle civilized Bob. His gray eyes, rather prominent, smiling, intelligent, tender. What agony the human animal must endure. Torture and failure of the body and mind and spirit overtake us.

No—this is not idea-writing. I am growing old and disor-

*Arthur R. Cohen, a psychologist, was a friend who was dying of Hodgkin's Disease.

ganized. There's always a leak in a faucet or files to straighten, to keep me from writing. Diary stuff, phew!

From the Porch (for an article)

My autumn lane winds down hill bordered by yellow maples, some tipped by scarlet, some flanked by summer-green oaks. Across the narrow red earth road there is a network of interlacing shadows and that is best of all, under the mellow sky and clear sunlight, and touched off here and there by wild asters at the roadside. How can I connect this, or my joy in it as I sit on my porch or on the soft grass, head turned this way, that way, to take in every inch of it, with the newspaper lying beside me, and its account of a baby bitten twenty-three times by rats in a Harlem tenement, its mother taking it to a hospital where she must wait four hours for attention . . . with boys beating a derelict to death on the streets . . . with napalm bombs burning villagers and villages six thousand miles away? Yet this is what I read as I sit on my porch, eyes up on the lane, down on the newspaper, this is what I read when my eyes drop to the page . . . And this connection is what we are called upon to make within our present world, our ever-present modern world, wherever we may be, we fortunate ones, whatever we may do. Both of these worlds are mine. I live in both.

8 The Writer: Creative Writing Class for Children

We all have strange dreams . . .

Creative writing class for children: *1942*
Estelle says: "Miss Marshall, we had to write a letter of sympathy to a girl in the class whose father died. I wrote just two sentences—'Dear Sadie, I was sorry to hear about your father. It's hard, but be brave and have courage.' Was that all right?" I praise it but the other children are stormy in protest. It's too grown-up! It would be all right if her mother had written it—but one child to another—no! I say, "But one human being to another! Why think of yourself as a child? Say what's in your heart." Beth is especially stormy. She says a letter of condolence would only make things worse. She wouldn't want to receive one. She'd want to forget! Not that letter—especially. I say, "But what did *you* write?" "Nothing. I couldn't." "What would you say?" "Oh, it would be easy. 'Dear Sadie'—I don't know." " 'Dear Sadie'—let's see." 'I'm sorry'—no—!" She is tormented—cannot express herself. "Oh," she cries in despair, "haven't you any imagination?" "Yes," I say, "and this is the problem of writers. Our words won't fit our feelings. But we must try. That's what writing is. We can't count on the imaginations of our readers." Beth is stormy and sadistic and confused. Says she has the most awful dream. Whenever she has a fever the same dream returns. I

draw her out. But no, she can't tell! Too awful. I tell her to think of it as material for a story. I tell her of Poe. I say we all have strange dreams. Then she tells me of dreaming of going thru a long dark hall and coming out in an open space and many men stand around—big dark men and short men and they come closer and closer and she is in a bed and they frighten her and then she wakes up. But telling me helps her—she is one step removed from it now. Can there be a technique of group therapy? Telling dreams and fantasies, getting further from them, robbing them of their most inward sting? Children are closer than adults to the past.

. . . . "The trouble with teachers is that they are evil-minded. Suspicious and evil-minded! They say 'Don't cheat' when you haven't thought of cheating. It just puts the idea into your mind. I think a teacher who is suspicious is worse than a girl who may cheat."

Belle's mother beats her, she tells me. The mother tells B. she has had more trouble raising her than her four other children. "But I try to think of all the times she was nice to me," says B. "My mother's so smart," she tells me the next week, as though to make up for what she told me the week before. "You ought to meet her, Miss Marshall. She's not like me—she's smart. But I could be smart too. Only I don't know whether to be a great actress or a writer." She's the most disorganized of all. Signs herself "Miss Belle Slatoff."

Beth—destructive, dramatic, temperamental. Belle describes her fights with her sister. I suggest she try to make her sister her friend. "Aw," says Beth—"why don't you just knock her out?"

Denise, 9 years old, younger sister of Estelle. Wide-eyed at writing possibilities. Says "Can you write about something that has happened?" "Yes." "Can you write stories about things you think?" "Yes." "Can you write about anything? Oh!" thrilled.

Crush on me. "Parting is such sweet sorrow."

Theme of true stories, when I ask for episode out of their lives: getting lost.

Imaginary theme: love stories. 18 yr. old boys. "So then they were alone," etc.

Villon story: I read few paragraphs, have them use this start as a stimulus for their imaginations. Stevenson gives snowy night Paris Villon: they have Villon find infant in snow. Then: "18 years pass. The lost child was now a beautiful young girl." From there on it becomes practically the fantasy love of any of them: the girl and her boyfriend go for a picnic alone one Sunday, practically to a suburb of N.Y.—1942!!

First thing Belle told me was "I am the type who starts things but never finishes them." She cannot even finish a sentence, I find, without rambling off excitedly to something else. Her stories are fragments—suggestions—random phrases. I get her to make an outline of one with me. I show them how, first, using familiar Cinderella story and outlining it. Then force from Belle a sequence, which I outline, using her initial ramblings about "A Southern Belle was she, Kathleen, who killed a wandering Yankee," etc. I insist on logical progression. She becomes wide-eyed at what she is doing— thrilled—almost fearful because her belief that she cannot complete anything is being violated. Step by step! Force decisions: "Then what? if she becomes a spy what does she do?" "Does she love this soldier?" etc. She must choose, decide. She is deeply excited. When other girls interrupt with their ideas she flies at them like a wildcat: "This is *my* idea! this is *my* story. *I* was just going to say that!" At end I tell her she must decide whether it is to have a sad or happy ending. She is troubled, says, "A sad ending is just as bad as a good one." For her any ending is impossible. But for once she achieves it.

Their dreams. Much in common. Being chased by a man with a big head. Falling or drowning; being pushed into the water and sinking. Denise ("long ago when I was about six I had this dream many times")—a man put her up on a long pole.

Then he pushed at her with a long stick until she fell down. Then she always woke. Leonora too used to have an identical dream many times. Belle, who is most confused, says it is always dark in her dreams so that she cannot see. She is lost in dark. "Even if by chance I get into light it never lasts. I always go into the dark again." She dreamt she was back in Brooklyn where there was a boy she adored. The other boys liked her but this certain boy paid no attention to her. But in the dream this certain boy was so nice! "And this certain boy looked just like my father." Little nine-year-old Denise: "I dreamt we were on a picnic, this boy and I, and we went swimming and played ring-around-a-rosie, and he ducked and put his hand down and found gold." She is sweet and bright—likes nature. Writes, "In spring the trees and flowers are nature. I like nature. Don't forget the birds are nature too." Says to me pensively, "Are bees nature too?" She has a great crush on me, says, "You are the kindest person." Says, "Is your book finished yet?" "You have such pretty clothes. And I love your shoes." Belle, poor child, says, "I think I'm a very lucky girl. I seem to have everything I wish." She says this after showing me her report card, very poor; she has failed in several subjects. "I don't know, the teacher is so *stupid!* I don't know why she marks this way." Then she tells me why she is lucky. "I could do so many things. I could be a great dancer. Or a singer. Only I never know whether to sing high or low. When I sing high it doesn't sound so good—otherwise I'd be a great opera singer. And when I walk on the street people stop me and tell me I look like Jeannette MacDonald, the movie star. Don't think I'm conceited, Miss Marshall! And I write so well." Here I stop her and tell her she must learn to write better; she never brings her stories, always forgets them.

They have an awful teacher who swears at them. They don't like to repeat the words: "I can hardly tell you. Remember, this comes out of her mouth not mine. She says, "Go to hell" and "God damn you." And there's a Greek girl she hates. She always calls her "You foreigner." She tells her to go back where she came from. And every day she tells us, there's going to be an air raid tonight, and she hopes there will be."

They play word games. I show them how to vary sentences: "The girl ran down the hill"—raced, flew, etc. Then we use new words in sentences. Belle: "Miss Marshall, is emotionally a word?" "Yes." "Then I have a fine sentence! The fire engine stopped—emotionally—at the hydrant."

They write verses, bring them. I: "In what mood are you when you write poetry?" Denise: "I like to sit up on top of the Frigidaire! Then I pull up my little kitten in a paper bag. Then I pretend the Nazis are after us, and I write poetry."

I ask them how many American writers they recognize. List Emerson, Hawthorne, Alcott, O'Henry. Denise: "I know that! It's a candy!"

We make up and act out a one-act play in club. They invent a play about ten girls (themselves!) on a picnic. (Like Jon once. "Let's play. Let's pretend we're a mother and her son.")

Maria—energetic Philippino—smart as a whip: "When you're poor you feel you have everything. When you're rich you're not free—you're discontented."

Estelle always talks in big sentiments: of Fairness, Love, Truth. She is outraged when I explain socialism, when we discuss a better world. "I don't believe in that! Because when I'm big I want to be rich so that I can give money to the poor."

I: "How many of you know about Kipling?" Denise—"Yes! Yom Kipling—a Jewish holiday."

Belle: she is miserable at home. Her mother beats her, prefers the little ugly sister Dolores who is really nasty and bad. But Belle is pretty and like her father; is that why the mother hates her? Won't give her a penny for candy, says, "You're fat enough." Belle must sleep with Dolores—"Ugh, she's awful! If she were only bigger! You'd know she was there. But she's slimy—like a cat." The family plays the radio all night in their tenement and Belle can't sleep. The mother writes and tells the father, absent, working in Delaware, how bad Belle is. He used to love B. Now he scolds too. They won't let her go back to Brooklyn—her glamour—past—where she longs to visit her old friends. They had to move from there—owed money. The agent comes there to collect. "Oh once we were rich! My father drove a taxi. And he played the horses, and I guess he was a bookie, or something. Then once he got into trouble. . . . My mother says such awful things! She shouldn't do that to us. I don't know—people can be so smart and so stupid. She says she'd like to leave us all. She doesn't know why she lives. She'd run off, she says, if it weren't for us kids. She shouldn't say that." When the mother was young she was very poor; used to be sent out begging by her father.

Leonora in love with her pretty chum, Estelle, and dominated by her. Leonora is always touching Estelle's hair, her arms, her blouse. Belle: "Oh and the boys in Brooklyn are so much nicer than in New York. They're tame and gentlemanlike." We stand on the corner an hour after club. She writes theme for "Why I am Glad I am an American" contest—disorganized—brings it to me to correct, saying "Isn't it wonderful, etc.," so I know she is insecure and fearful; she always starts that way. It begins: "So you're asking me why I'm glad I am an American? Don't you know? Don't we all know . . ." etc. And "Am I fighting with Doug McArthur?"! etc. I correct it, give her ideas. I say, "You mean . . . free or suppressed." She, " 'suppressed'—oh, that's a lovely word. Will you write it down for me?" I do—that and more—in margins. Next week Belle doesn't show up for first time; she's out doing the town, delirious with joy. She has carefully copied all my corrections and won the contest! She—and I—have won a trip to City Hall to shake Mayor LaGuardia's hand!

Marie helps in her father's restaurant. The truck drivers come in for coffee. Belle: "Oh, I think that's the sweetest job!" Belle says, "You know, my mother hates me." I cannot give her false assurance. I tell her, though, what she *does* have, looks, health, etc., and that many people don't have these; that someday she may profit by her experience and be a more understanding woman because of it. Leaven her mother's lack of love for her. "Yes," she says suddenly, "and I can write about it." I see that she *has* learned; the club has given her some insight and hope. She has faced a problem.

Creative Writing Club—II
Colored children—age 12

It is harder to hold these childrens' attention than the former group—perhaps because they are younger, but also because they are more disorganized. A curious combination of ignorance with a wise old street-knowledge. They are restless, often leave the room, interrupt each other, but goodnatured.

Jason: an eager, psychopathic, rakish, raffish boy, has been at Bellevue for observation but this he does not tell me. Instead he says of one of the girls, "LaVerne was born in—what's that place? Bellevue. In the psychopathic ward." I ask them first to write stories about themselves, histories, so that we may become acquainted. Jason: "Teacher, I have no history about myself." One child boasts "I have a complete Shakespeare home." J: "I have an *in*complete Shakespeare." I ask them if they know who is acting in *Othello* at present, imagining that Paul Robeson is a great figure. But several reply "Bill Robinson." I ask them to tell stories, and suggest stories of dreams. Jason: "Do you want a Frankenstein dream or a jealous dream?" Then he tells us an elaborate story of a dream of two boys. "I was the handsome guy, he was the ugly guy. I was calling on a girl" (he whistles and cocks his head). "So Tom jumps on Jim and makes him ugly. So then another feller comes to see her. Tom and Jim they both fight him. Pretty soon he ugly too. She say, 'I don' love you no more.' They went in a cab to kill her on the outskirts of town. So there was her boy friend's house. She say, 'Fight for me.' They fight. Later Tom goes to the doctor he fixes his face. She say, 'I like you again. Will you marry me?'

Later she wanted to do things. She stood on a windowsill, make all the people think she goin' to jump. But she had strapped herself. They cut the strap holdin' her. She cried O! O! O! So she hold on to the flag pole an' save herself." Later he says, "I wanted to go make me a monster. So I got my snake poison. An' I went to the graveyard and' dug up a skelical." He says to me, jauntily: "Teacher, I'm a moron." Jason's stories are all about murder. I say to him: "You know, you write well, Jason, and you tell fine stories but I'm getting a little bored with murder stories. Why don't you write about the nicest thing you ever did. Did you ever do anything especially nice?" His face lights up. "Oh yes, Teacher! I was on a farm!" "Then tell me about it," I suggested, but he cannot sustain his inspiration, he starts his story on a farm but in a few minutes the hero has a knife in his heart and the farmer is going to the electric chair.

All the children remember—or at least tell about—being dropped when small. "My mother once dropped me down the stairs. Once she dropped me in the coal cellar." Many act up. One girl leaving the room says, "Good-bye, you charming people!" I tell them something about Poe; had they ever heard of him? "Poe? Sure. Like Mark Twain and Shakespeare." "They buried Shakespeare in Westmoreland Abbity."

I walk down Eighth Avenue, a stranger in a strange land. No other whites around. This is the black world, drab, dingy, cold, mean, but theirs, not mine. I am the alien in these blocks. And I get a glimmering of how *they* feel all the rest of the time in *my* world. The rest of the city in which they are always the strangers, the dark aliens, conscious of the color of their skins, black in our white world. On a cellar door it says, "Peace. Ice." On a dirty window, "Peace Express Co." A sign says, "Herbs. Spices. Candles. Oil. Religious goods." There are stones in the window, and glass jars of spices and powders, there are paper dream books, images of a bride and of Christ. "Peace. Fried Fish." "Best Furniture"—and it is out on the sidewalk, dumped, a rug, a kiddie car, a broken bed.

Jason shows me a set of drawings he has made of childbirth. They are impersonal, no heads on the figures, simply female reproductive organs containing the foetus, showing process of birth, infant being slapped, etc. I ask him where he copied them. He says the museum, that he goes to the museum each Sunday. He keeps his stories and pictures, giving me only a few; the others like to give them to me.

Edith and Dolores write of Hollywood heroes. They do almost identical stories of 'dreams'—of Alan Ladd asking them to marry him, they say "Yes," they have twins, one named after the girl, the boy named Mr. Alan Ladd. Romance is a movie star and twins. A love story is a triangle story, of violence. No normal adolescent romance. Instead a woman, her boyfriend, and her husband who usually pulls a knife and they fight. Edith sucks her thumb steadily. Says: "Mah mother likes to dance the boogie woogie blues. Nobody can do nothin' with that woman." Charles Reid tells love story about a feller and his girl say Will you marry me but he don' want to cause she's not so pretty as another girl so he say he goin' to marry the prettier girl, but that night all the pretty girls he knew got married so he marry his girl. Helen has a cousin who is the black sheep of the family. He has been in jail five times and he is only sixteen. His mother comes to the door, tears streaming down her face and says, that boy is gone again, and then she goes to the City Jail and bails him out.

Helen is supposed to mind her aunt's three babies while the aunt works but she goes home, feeds them, then leaves them alone while she comes to Club. George says if his mother died he'd kill himself the next day. Yes he would. A girl in school has no mother and when anyone talks of mothers she cries and tries to choke them. George, a sweet orderly good boy, who writes fairy stories: "How the Devil's Daughter Becomes the Beautiful Princess of Love and Friendship," etc. "What's the best thing to have?" Helen: "Courage"; Jason: "Calmness"; Dolores: "Cabbage and rice"! "Clark Gable he don' love colored people."

"Rochester's mah color anyway." "Ah do love mah men." "There weren't no peace and quiet around Hitler." Edith sucks her thumb when she listens. Talks with great speed, description of a fire in a tenement, one of their friends had her clothes burnt. Her brother ran around crying, "Save mah $5.95 hat." Sign in Harlem, "You'll feel brighter if you look whiter. Use bleach cream." In their love stories the woman always is the one who proposes marriage. Edna says she is going to the Catholic school. The others scoff but she defends it. "They teach you everything there. History and everything. All about how when Columbus was discovering America all he thought bout was God." Lenny would like to write a love story—a big attractive sleepy adolescent girl. I say "Why don't you write it then?" She: "I dunno nothin' about love." I: "Then imagine." She: "I imagine *too* much." One child writes of having a baby. "It was unexpected so its mother put it into a bureau drawer " Edith must go home and is afraid her mother will not let her return for Club. Asks me to write a note saying "Please let Edith come back and read her lovely poems." One says, "Can you tell me the name of the kind of man who sits in a tower and looks out and sees strange mysteries and fortunes and islands far away?" Somebody answers, "A professor." When Jason is teased by a girl who tells him his nose is dirty he runs out of the room like a wild thing, and does not return; is sensitive, gives Christmas gifts to two of the girls which they compare and swap in public. We start a new club in February. Only a few from first group remain; some are graduated and leave for Junior High; others I do not want because they are members of other P.M. groups and there is a division of loyalties. This has made for interruptions the first half-year and distracted attention from our stories. I tell them nobody who belongs to another club may join ours. B: "I know a lady who belongs to 14 clubs." I pass cookies. One boy: "This is what you call a club!" My old children are boisterous and take advantage of their intimacy with me; I cannot check their chatter and get down to group activity. I say at last that the new children appear much readier to have a club than the old ones. This is a mistake on my part; I have hurt the feelings of the first group who want to feel superior to the others and want me to belong to them. They file out silently.

I have not been as satisfied with my results the first half-year as I was at P.S. 33. The children are younger, want noise and activity (physical) after long school day. It has also been harder to hold attention because some are members of another club (poor organizing on part of authorities in beginning), and other club leader often interrupts. Those who got most out of it were George, whose mother is a washwoman and is out all day; he loves fairy stories and is more childlike than most of the others. Marlene never missed a time. Both of these children enjoyed writing and always wrote plentifully. Jason resists and comes irregularly, but loves to tell stories. They are good humored, rowdy as a whole. George shows me a newspaper piece in Harlem paper about a vicar, Mr. X. "That's mah reverend." Thomas sells newspapers in the afternoon. A sweet small boy. He must sell ten papers before stopping. Out of each 10 cents sold, he gets three. Once he earned thirty cents for shovelling snow. George says he worked last summer in the five-and-ten. They took him, he says, because he was a good boy and honest. They tell me about gangs, other boys who sometimes steal your money. "A boy say to me 'Nigger, give me yo' money.' So I say 'Nigger, I will not.' I call him Nigger 'cause he call me Nigger." They say some of the drinking parents train the children to steal or some of the parents are out at work an' the boys can't get home into their own house. Ain't got a key. When their mother come home she don't know where her boy is. Maybe dead.

I show them pictures from Murray's Thematic Apperception Test* and let each choose one for a story. "O, that's a love picture. That's a pity picture," etc. George chooses a sex

*Henry Alexander Murray developed the "Thematic Apperception Test," a series of picture cards which his subjects were asked to interpret.

picture—a man forcing a girl against door. Richard chooses a family scene out of which he writes of robbery and murder. No suggestion of this in picture of three quiet people. Later I show a Lynd Ward woodcut and ask each to tell what it suggests; it is a male figure standing among stonelike forms, abstract stones. "A mummy." "Old man looking at a tombstone." "George Washington Carver at his grave—he's a colored man." Thomas tells story of an old man so tired he thought he'd go to the graveyard to visit his relatives. Went from grave to grave and talked. To his father: "Remember that day I killed you, Father? I only liked Mother that day." He didn't want his father to come back cause he'd have to kill him again. He said "I killed my father an' he's still living. Oh!" He opened the graves and talked. His mother and sister say "All right, join us." He loved his mother but his father used to take his mother away. And when he was little and wanted his father his father didn't play with him. So he just wanted his mother and sister and to be with them when he was dead. The next time: George chooses same sex picture eagerly but pretends he is not interested in love. Says, "You started me writin' love stories. I don't like to. But I started a picture I called 'Persuading Love' and I want to finish it. But I don' *like* love stories." Seizes the picture and kisses it. "Why don't we go on with the story Edith wrote about being in love with Alan Ladd?" His story ends with jealousy of his brother whom he has often criticized. The brother steals his girl. Says, "Mah mother'd beat me for writing a love story." "Doesn't she want you to?" "She knows I don' like them!" He is going to be in a Tom Thumb wedding. The bride is eight years old. "What an awful looking girl! I'm the groom. I sent out a lot of invitations to my wedding." I say, "You all write about robbers and crime. Why?" Thomas: "It's my hobby."

We talk of religion. "Our superintendent goes to Church because he doesn't want to give us heat and being in Church gives him a good excuse." "The war's been goin' on two years.

Men are awful. Mah mother says it's time for God to step in and steal the whole show."

A Tom Thumb wedding! George: "Today was the day ah got married. So much people! O Teacher, I felt lak I could kill myself. I didn't like it." "Didn't you like it or *did* you?" "I like it an' I didn't. My heart went jump jump. That thing was just sorrow an' death. Those people thought I was too young to get married. The Reverend decided we should. I had to spend fifty cents for mah bride."

Murray Picture group reactions:* 3GF. Grief stricken. Just been knocked down by a man. Her husband and her had a little quarrel. Been shot. 4. (Everyone exclaims.) That's mine! Love's mystery. She wants him for love cause he don' want her. Both of 'em unhappy. There's another lady out there. 6BM—He's goin' to the army an she don' like it. She's crying. He killed a girl. The mother found the dead girl in the attic and found a gun. The mother is trying to break news to the son that his father is a gangster. He don't feel good about it.

*In 3GF, a young woman is standing alone with her head bent, covering her face with her right hand, stretching out her left arm against a door. In 4, a woman is clutching a man by the shoulders, but his face and body are averted. In 6BM, a tall young man looks down questioningly at a shorter, older woman whose back is turned to him.

9 The Writer: Characters and Fragments

July 1963: A fantasy of papers. Scraps of notes, appercus, *piling up until I am inundated by them, or snowing down until I am buried. The writer buried by his disorganized particles, under a blizzard of fragments.*

Told of Mortimer Adler—use for someone. He tried to prove that by the method of Aristotelian categories he could play Twenty Questions and guess the answers correctly and quickly. They took Mae West's novel and he never got near it. His failure upset him dreadfully. The next day everyone who'd been at that party got a letter—eight typed pages—explaining why the system hadn't worked and why it should have. His wife said he stayed up all that night. He was terribly upset.

Description of a New Englander—a meagre dry man: "He's the salt of the earth. No—he's a pinch of the salt of the earth."

1927: Lunch and dinner with Weizmann*, at Berkeley and Carlton Hotels. What a figure he is, brilliant often, but as often simple and lovable and sad. Perhaps it is part of his brilliance, his powerful personality, to be able to appear thus. No matter; he is very appealing. He looks badly, yellow and thin, and is plainly discouraged. Fond of Jim and I believe of me too; his

*Chaim Weizmann, then President of the World Zionist Organization, later became the first President of Israel.

desire for our confidence and affection seems to me pathetic.
With him to a reception for Kenworthy, M.P. of the Labour
party, son of a lord and a recent "convert." Not a man to trust.
As Jim said, "Can you imagine him dying for his convictions?"
Large, stout, bland, great white expanse of shirt front and
white kid gloves, one on, one held. Gilt wife. Crowds and much
noisy How-do-you-do. All sorts of dressy people. Food—
servants—a Labour reception! What then can the Conserva-
tives be like. Dr. Edar, psychoanalyst and Zionist, kindly
lumbering man. Mrs. Edith Edar, animated, modern, eager on
all new subjects. Bolshevik lady, agent for promoting cultural
something-or-other. Clever and dangerous—ugly red arms,
thin for large woman.

Lord and Lady Samuel* for tea: Portchester Terrace, a most
beautiful house, arched hall ceiling, mantels, spaciousness, big
square garden in back and tennis court—think of it, in London
itself. Sir Herbert a fine Englishman, dignity and kindliness.
Lady Samuel has poise and charm. Ben Avi and wife there,
little man living in reflection of a well-known father, Ben
Jehudah-Rothenberg of the Palestine Power scheme there too,
man of strength, large, impressing one with his might. Smokes
a hundred cigarettes a day. Lots of cake and sandwiches, etc.
Real English home of best sort.

1935: Thurber—drunk-funny. He would surely kill himself
or go batty someday. Desperate, laconic, cynical humor. Dry.
Tells murder stories—coffins fill up with water, even the best of
them—and big green worms. What would be the best way to
commit a murder? You report to police at once if it was
premeditated; that throws 'em off the scent. Stuff wife into
toilet; a body was once disposed of that way. Absolutely. If he
were going to kill his wife, he'd dismember her. If you hit a man
and drew blood, you'd go on and kill him—the sight of blood.

---

*Lord Herbert Samuel was the first British High Commissioner to
Palestine (1920-25) under the United Nations mandate.

His wife, with her thin legs, straight bones and no flesh, her narrow shoulders and blades protruding, sits expressionless and drinks. But you know she likes it.

Corliss Lamonts: They were a grave, clean, good-looking young couple. They were seriously concerned with whatever they undertook, and they threw themselves into a variety of causes: strikes, the education of Indians, help for Fiji Islanders, picking mushrooms, or rinsing dishes. They were sweet and honest and humorless about it. "I wonder," she thought aloud, watching the sea break on the land, "if we ought to enjoy it so much with all the starving people in the world." They were very chaste in their young beauty. Their love making would be an act of chastity too.

Story?

On his mother's wedding day, or at any rate the day she said to Tim, "I'm going to marry Frank this evening at seven," he let the dog in while she was out doing Mrs. Merrill's laundry, and he and the dog jumped all over her bed, dirtying it. Then the next day he spilled ink. "I gave it to him. He's a monster," said Gretchen, his mother, a young woman whose prettiness was spoiled by mouth sores; she had been bringing numerous men home with her for some years. When she went to work at Mrs. Merrill's on the following day, he accompanied his mother; he was silent, wandering around. That evening a dozen apples and some dirt—heaven knows what sort of filth it was—were found in the Merrill's swimming pool. Nobody saw it happen so who knows who did it? Nobody wanted to mention it to Gretchen in fairness to the child, although the whole family shook their heads. The canvas seats of garden chairs were found slashed by a knife. A chair's arm was broken. What does one do when such destructive, hostile acts indicate future trouble? What was best for the boy? said Mrs. Merrill, besides what *could* be done, when there had been that past, that mother? Next week Gretchen announced she would have a baby. Tim, she said, could hardly wait, he was so glad. "He's a good boy—just mischievous like all boys. He doesn't mean it and he doesn't use bad words." Six months later the baby was born. One month after that it was discovered dead in its clothes-basket crib. It had died mysteriously, a pretty baby too.

Contrast Marriage: Mrs. MacDowell*

Delicious, gracious, young, almost blind, eighty-six, never feels her way, runs rather than walks, breakfast at seven, goes to bed at twelve midnight, manages estate herself, books, antiques, caretaker who reports each detail to her, guests, white stockings, black shoes, silk print dress, lavender ribbon around her throat. Met MacD. when she was his pupil abroad. Bought estate when they were young and poor so he could have peace to work. Any sound disturbed him; she would tiptoe in the next room but still he heard, was conscious of not being alone so she built him a cabin and would bring his lunch in a basket. Gave up her own career for him—two careers would not have done—there was never any question for her. Half-way would not have worked—but to give it up altogether was easy.

Later he lost his mind; "His mind was terribly disturbed," she said of his last years. She nursed him. He said, "You have never failed me yet." This image of love was beautiful. Eternal love—passionate, forever, faithful and fine. The child would someday have just such a love. Later remembers it as a dream.

Fragment: in summer resort

I am having my hair washed in a booth; the operator knows me of old, asks me if I am writing at present, says, "What was the name of your last book?" Around the corner of my curtain a face appears, a middle-aged eagerly smiling lady, big hat, white hair, careful rouge. "Oh!" she says. "Pardon me! You are a writer! Would you mind giving me your autograph for my

*Mrs. MacDowell was the founder and governing personality of the MacDowell Colony.

grand-daughter? She collects them! She loves the autographs of famous people!" I twist about to smile at her—for one hand is in a manicure bowl, and my hair is being wrenched up from my head under the grip of the shampooist's fingers. Through suds of soap I smile at her properly. "My autograph? I'll be glad to." "Oh thank you!" she beams. "That's lovely! Glamor, you know."

Ella Davidoff's neck swells and gets red when she's excited. The cords protrude, out of all proportion to her small face. It seems as if her neck will burst, it is so inflamed and enlarged. Of a farm house she becomes excited to buy though she has never seen it: "It would just suit me! No matter how humble! We just put up nice new curtains, Max. That's all."

H—being deeply interested and objectively excited by life, he was rarely touched by it, or close to it (those few moments when it had happened he'd gone to pieces—his divorce), and therefore could afford to be constantly kind to unfortunates who were caught in the toils of it, such as his brother-in-law's cast-off mistresses. There had been several of these extremely pretty girls and he always used to let them weep on his shoulder and gave them sympathy.

Story: Peterborough.
The meddlesome old maid in a colony. Her effect on a group of people. What happens to *her:*
Eva Lynn was cheery, helpful, officious in the littlest ways, vain, dull, a sixty-year-old spinster who wrote juveniles, one very successful, and lectured all over the country in schools and clubs, lived when she was between tours in an old fashioned hotel. Had no home, had supported herself always, one way or another—press agent, actress when she was young, recitations. Of course she should have married, pleasant looking and built for it, should have had her own children. As it was she had

thousands of children she said, in all those schools after an assembly the children knew her, called her Eva Lynn, waited for her to return next year. 900 schools visited in one season! But the colony, summers, was home. The only one she knew. (Licks spoon with honey. Says, like bad child, "I'm not allowed to do this at home!" But where was home? When?) She makes our house a dormitory. Tells us to put out lights. Change sheets. Talks of her damned chipmunk; meddlesome—tries to woo us by bringing out drinks at night. "Port—rum—sherry—whisky," she announces smugly, and tries to possess us by her little favors; the greatest stickler for rules, a letter of the law person. The library rule that no sale-books to be handled. But Julius was in charge of the library. One night he was playing the piano, Peter took up books to read. E.L. ran across the room, told him there was a rule against it. "It isn't *you*, you know, but others might—it's a rule," etc. Peter: "I think you are very officious and ill-mannered." That started things. She is taken aback, can't believe her ears. But the peace is split open. She is now the spy, the informer to Hillcrest. Julius too resents her, for the library is *his* job and responsibility which she cannot resist usurping. New signs appear at library, bigger, with orders about not picking up books. Little whispering groups develop: "Peter was right! It had to be said," or "Did he really say it?" Julius is asked by her if he had permission to stay open longer at night or leave library for some party. J. becomes a cause, gentle, nervous, scratching self, no malice in him, wonderfully well read. Peter a cause too, troubled brow, flying-away eyes, fine intense psychotic. Roberta, going blind, takes them up. Pretty, earnest, humorless, immature although twice married and with children, she gets concerned, talks intensely to us all, gets us involved and worked up too. Says E.L. is a fascist. Poor Julius—terrible to see him victimized. It is like being in boarding school, she says; one cannot work, one's freedom is gone, what can we do! Yet she obeys E.L. and in a way exaggerates the situation by asking permission to do things, when none of us did before. She refuses E.L.'s drinks yet is always in her room asking, "Is it all right to do so and so?" and thus feeling more bound than before. Then one night when she has called me to her room to talk, feeling so upset, saying what power this one old woman has over us all, we are all restrained and castrated by her (is it her own crippled state makes this worse for her?) E.L. calls, "A guest for you, Roberta," and her husband has come as a surprise. But there is a rule against guests in the houses; logic in this rule, for the sake of others, yet of course all rules ought to be possible to break on occasion. E.L. will not let him in. It rains—they may stand on porch together—he may not come in. E.L. is sorry, but as senior she must uphold the rules. Terrible for the young couple, husband impractical and foolish not to have notified R., but there he is, must be bitten by mosquitoes—why not eat. E.L. brings apricot cordial of her own, and a sweater—explains she is only upholding rules, didn't make them. Goes around telling us, "Shocking!" says Elizabeth Jones, "poor young couple." How she who had had the whip hand is subtly ostracized; people don't kiss her good night or drink her port. She begins to sense it, doesn't understand. Says to me, "Have you noticed people turning against Julius?" "No," I say, "Who?" "Well," she mentions Della Joio who left two weeks before. Goes away disturbed. Says to me, "Everyone likes you so much at Hillcrest." "Feels good," I say but not too thrilled, she cannot bribe us anymore. Yet I feel adult, will not let them draw me in. This tempest in a teapot with a war going on. "I don't agree with you," says Roberta, thinking I am walking out on a situation demanding integrity and courage. But no. Understand. Keep balance. Life is full of rules and old maids. Accept or act. Don't become irrational.

E.L. is ruined. They were her children, this was her home: like all children who are overpossessed they have rebelled— they will see to it that her home is taken away from her too, they will join in action and she will not be asked next year. This was her one hearth—the woman who made it too much her home. Owned it. The pity and tragedy for her, yet she brought it on herself. But the opposing gang, Roberta, invited it, too, by submitting as children and letting it rankle, instead of taking it in their stride as adults. The thing was blown up out of all proportion. Until the murder was done. People are very cruel. Very righteous on both sides. All neurotics. The old woman, the schoolmarm; the young puts herself in position of school-girl. But egoism of the old makes her undermine others. Take away from Sol and Julius what is *their* greatest joy—the ripples spread—Roberta, gauche, literal, thinks I am on wrong side and childishly does not introduce me to her husband. I understand yet am offended and see her in new way, as provincial: she thus loses my friendship which she had valued and which could have helped her (my contacts).

"I think it is such a nice group," she says to me while she does her mischief.

Character—John—chef—butler from
the island of Malta:

He is the ARTIST. He can do everything. "Can you drive?" "I can drive anywhere! I understand all machinery!" But when it comes down to brass tacks, he had *one* lesson once in driving. He will make the stove work better, he takes it apart, all the fuses blow out and we must send to the electric company to repair it. But can he cook! Perfect. "This," he says, "is the best pudding on earth." or "My soups, madam, I make the best soups in all the world! In *all* the world." He cooks and serves; his German wife, plain and hard working, cleans for him; he the prima donna, she the drudge. He bears his fine pastries, beaming, to the table. "It's wonderful, John," I say. "Thank you, madam!" proudly. She will be scrubbing up after him in the kitchen. He sends her to pick vegetables for him in the garden. She climbs the ladder high up in the cherry tree to pick him cherries. "Did you get me the peas too?" is all he says when she comes down, "go get the peas." "I know what will happen in the world, madam. I am a prophet. I am the best prophet in the Bible." But he doesn't like the country, so he returns to town. There he can see prizefights. Baseball games. Le Sport. But before he goes he will make me the best cake, decorated, the most beautiful you have ever seen. Oh yes. He had studied (he says) to be an architect. He is an architect. He is a painter. He would write books if only he could spell. His ambition is to run a chicken farm; no, not to work it, he would have many many men working for him. Also he would like to work in the navy yard. "He's funny," says his poor patient wife, "So I don' know, shee. I don' know. Shee, I like the country but John he likes the city. So I don' know, shee."

I offer her the radio. "No madam. I don' like to listen, only to one program, Mr. Anthony, shee, all the people tell him their troubles. On Sunday at ten people come and tell him their troubles. I like that one, that's all."

Characters:
Peg, in her new magnificent house, says: "We're just camping. We haven't enough chairs yet. But then we thought we might as well move in: we were just camping in the hotel too." Being restless and insecure and dissatisfied with herself, having no beliefs or principles, she always feels that she is "just camping," is always getting ready, getting settled, getting established, prepared for something she never does.

Fougeray, the jeweler: worldly, he illustrates the relativity of money as a value. "A woman can buy herself an inexpensive jewel, trinkets to enjoy for a season and then give to the servant. But when a man buys jewelry for a woman it has to be something valuable and costly, something commensurate with his relation to her." How does one standardize expenditures, I wonder. How much does one give to the refugees? the blind?

for a dress? for a jewel? Peg for her house. I for some roses.
Money's meaning to different people.

Marie

Mystic. Cultivated. Soft spoken. Born in Mexico. Little,
dark, looks colored. "I come on Friday the 13th just before
Christmas. Who would have thought it! But I have found the
perfect place and you the perfect cook." "Look at me. Don't I
vibrate health?" "You must demand perfection. If you demand
it you will get it." Seeks Truth. Belongs to study-philosophy
groups. Marks Emerson passages. Ex-Catholic turned—?
Then, tears in eyes, brings me tray: tells me best friend has
died. English man, ten years younger than she: "The Leslie
Howard type." Engineer—rising in world. "I met his friends
last night. They had never heard of me but were glad to know
his private life had been happy." He worried a lot. He had left
life insurance to her and always told his landlady that Marie was
the only one to go through his papers or enter his room—no one
else, although he had partners and led a social life in which he
was rising. She must go off to bury him. "But I am strong. The
Lord is my shepherd, I shall not want." "I could have married
him but I decided I wanted to go on with my studies. I might
have married him some day."

Later, when she returns, she tells me the rest of the story.
They had met sixteen years before. He was the youngest son of
an aristocratic English father and a mother who came from the
lower classes. His father had really been a drifter and a
ne'er-do-well whose family had had little to do with him when
he made his mis-marriage to a Catholic and a girl of no class.
Jack took after his father—charming but weak, and always he
was in conflict between the two sides of his nature. His mother
divorced his father; his father was killed in the Boer War. Jack
in the World War was what was known as a "Bolshy," a radical;
he had no use for privilege and he turned against the ruling
classes. In Russia, he thought, they had found the thing. He

joined the Navy and was sent to Russia, but there he became disillusioned soon: he saw that the ideal was not working. Yet he belonged to radical groups and did not mention his disillusionment. There was plenty that was hard in his life and bad for a boy: he saw service in Scandinavian waters too and none of the things that happened to him—drifting, drink, women—were much good to an unstable boy. Back in England he was arrested with a gang who were radical troublemakers in the Army and Navy; he was thrown into jail to await court martial. The authorities could not know—nor would they have cared—that at heart he was already through with this life, no longer a Bolshy. He couldn't bear the thought of the court-martial. A ship was sailing. He managed to smuggle himself on board. He got to America, without a passport or money, but free. For a few days he washed dishes to earn a living. Found the Sixth Ave. employment agencies and got a job on an estate near New York owned by a wealthy divorced woman, remarried, her spoilt degenerate son—a rich Tobacco Road family. But on the place he met a fine couple and they brought back his balance and gave him a new point of view. He became ambitious, entered business, and now his old radicalism diminished and he became intent on his own success instead. He rose rapidly, being so charming and witty; wherever he went he liked to be the center of attention. Meanwhile he and Marie had met, somehow; her strength, greater than his, buoyed him up. He relied on her more and more: her philosophy, her directness, her lack of conflict; for she obeyed her inner voice. But he was always in conflict: was it success and wealth he sought, or personal integrity, Marie, the old Bolshy in himself? Did he love to drift like his father, seek luxury and riches, or descend to his mother's level? And under those rising years of success lay the sailor's life, the outcast misfit child, the secret disgrace. "Why do you hide your real self?" Marie would say. "Be a man!" and she left him, feeling the difference between them too great, socially, morally. But she came back; he was her best friend still. Then came the alien registration law. But Jack had entered this country illegally. He could not register. What was he to do? He worried; his whole past rose up to torture him. "Give him enough rope," said Marie's friends, "he'll hang himself." On Xmas day he had a sudden heart attack. That night he died.

That one insurance policy was made out in Marie's name, but she had not let him put her down on the others: that way he would not have been free to use the money himself had he wanted it. He left no will. So his partners located a sister he'd not seen in all those twenty years, living in Birmingham. She would inherit his money. "And the beautiful part of the story," says Marie, "is this: that I can give this money to England in her hour of need. Here am I, an obscure cook whom nobody knows. But I am doing this thing. It is my gift to England."

This story needs elaboration of the Marie-Jack relationship. Should she be the cook he met when he was gardener on the Tobacco Road estate?

Carlo Tresca*

They gave him a 60th birthday party. And Carlo's warm personality held them together—his "boys," thin dark youths, shabby men and women, red wine splashed on the white cloths, smoke in the wooden old hall, the firetrap building on 15th St. East, up a steep flight of stairs. Carlo drunk stood on the platform and he made a speech as long as he wanted to, and people talked and laughed while he spoke, listening but talking themselves at the same time, informal and easy and serious and gay. Carlo's face is red and sweating. "When I came to this country," he wanders on, but talking from his heart, garrulous, repetitive, "I see the Statue of Liberty and I think of liberty here and I think: some day I'm going to squeeze that God-damn

*Carlo Tresca, a good friend, was an anarchist vigorously opposed to communism and fascism, publisher of a radical Italian newspaper in New York.

lady. And so later I live here and work here and I squeeze her at last, and she's God-damn stiff!"

This is the revolutionary movement in America: this here, shabby, sparse, in a corner. The Communists have done this. Split the old radicals. And other radicals are in Washington, riding high in the saddle, playing their game of power and of party. This here is the sad remnant of the revolutionary movement in America.

Characters

B.: of a camp director. "She wore shorts and looked like a competent teacher. Her calves bulge tremendously. She is the sort of woman, you know, by whom you wouldn't like to be kicked."

Miss Lewis—runs Littlest Secretarial School. A pink celluloid crescent is pinned over her bosom and false violets on her shoulder. Greek maxims about persistence are inscribed on the wall. She is most distrait and distracted. "My father was a state surveyor. Well, he was just like Socrates. He was always right. So you see. One must gamble in life. Like Columbus. Not that I mind a little gambling, though it's supposed to be the greatest sin. That book, *Grapes of Wrath*, it's the only thing I have against Mrs. Roosevelt. She even talked of it. Such things. In this country anyone can get along with a skill. Persistence! But in the old days we kept our operations and such to ourselves. That was culture, wasn't it?"

A Business Man—character—Harry Kleinert

The diamond in the rough from the West. The tough guy in a refined family. Says to me, "The gift of gab, as you writers say. Whiskey is still to cross the lips of that baby for the first time," referring to his curly-gray-haired wife with her pince-nez. She is from a temperance family. "Listen," she once said, forty years ago when they were first married and he hardly knew her,

"You've been drinking. If I thought I had married a drinking man I'd walk out on you here and now." But he was pretty good at hiding it. He'd come home with the stuff fairly running out of his ears, if you'll pardon the expression, and she wouldn't know. Only one night he'd been out with the boys and when he got home she was asleep already. That night he had had an awful lot. She opened one eye (never let on to her I told you this one) she opened one eye and she said "Get out of here!" and then she went to sleep again.

Abroad she adored everything. She carried her little flat wooden box of paints and she looked briskly to right and to left. He was always several paces behind her, dutifully bringing up the rear. In the spring he always liked to make plans for a trip to Europe and arrange for a good cabin, but as soon as he got to the other side he could hardly wait to be at home again. He was always looking out for somebody to talk business to. "I'm a businessman," he would say. His old workmen called him by his first name.

Nordy's tales of his childhood:*

He was three years old and his brother was five. He wanted to attack his brother so he knocked him down but soon the brother got the better of him and he was beaten and in tears. The hired man came along. "If you want to grow big and strong enough to lick your brother you must eat lots of mouldy bread," said the hired man. After that, Nordy used to go prowling about looking all the time for mouldy bread.

Another time he was told to mind his baby sister. At that time he was seven. Of course he didn't like wheeling her in her carriage. There was a ditch full of thistles across from the barn, and out of the barn a sloping ramp. Nordy started the carriage on the slope, let go; carriage and baby rolled down, just as planned, and into the thistles. When the baby screamed and he walked unconcernedly away, they found him of course. He was

*Nordy is Bror J. O. Nordfeldt, an artist at New Hope.

spanked and they never told him to mind baby sister again.

When he went to school, aged seven, the first day the big children all asked him his name. Of course they knew, for they were all neighbors. But he was shy. He stuck his thumb in his mouth and said "Nobody." The name remained and afterwards all through his school days they called him "Nobody."

He used to go off by himself, deeply drawn in, studying the view. He thought of God and decided there was no God. He thought of God and of the problems of perspective.

Beach Benefit

All summer at the beach there had been talk of some sort of a children's party so when the iceman's wife died the occasion seemed just the thing. A week-old infant had been left bereaved and the mothers on the beach felt that here was a perfect opportunity for a little lesson from life, their youngsters would give a benefit party for the iceman's baby. The children were informed; they were properly awed for they saw the iceman every morning driving from house to house in his cold dripping sawdusty truck or heaving chunks to his shoulder from which a leather apron appended down his back; at once with the help of a committee of seniors a committee of juniors was formed and it was decided to give a picnic lunch on Friday, twenty-five cents admission. Signs were lettered and posted in the general store and post office: "Come to shore at 12:30 Friday, 25¢, benefit iceman's baby". But on Tuesday the rumor got around that the iceman drank.

The mothers sat in a ring upon the sand, oiled and strapless; behind them their offspring squatted, shovelling bottomless holes and patting up slipping fortress walls. One of the women combed sea out of her fair hair with constant devoted strokes, one tilted her browned face like a cup motionless to the sun, but the others attended to the problem at hand, determined or deterred, concentrating and perplexed, as though the arena of striped towels and auditorium of smiling ocean were a conference room. "All I know is we planned it in good faith," cried Rosie who had constituted herself unofficial chairman.

"But he'll drink it up!" Olive protested. Her pure red lips drew a straight line.

Voices of ready conciliation rose together efficiently. "Perhaps he doesn't need it." "He bought fifteen dollars' worth of clothes from Sears Roebuck." "Okay. Let's give it all up."

"Certainly not." Olive, although troubled, was firm about that. "The children have started their project, they must carry it through. Without discipline where are you?"

"Anyhow, we've promised them a party," said Rosie.

"We might give the money to the Animal Rescue Squad," suggested the haircomber.

The idling absorbed face dedicated to sun opened. "Only what about the iceman? The signs say it's for him. It would be deceiving people."

"Not one cent of my money is going to the iceman," declared Olive gravely.

"But a baby is a baby," Rosie exclaimed.

There was stalemate for a moment. Somebody murmured hopefully, "How about a trust fund?"

"How much will our tots raise?"

"Ten bucks,—maybe."

"That could start a savings fund to give it when it's twenty-one!"

Olive frowned at them. "We've got to organize." She had beautiful gray eyes, full of justice.

"Count me out of anything organized."

"Why not divide the money, just a token to the iceman, the rest to the animals that want salvation. Or give it to the baby's grandmother, she'll bring it up, not the father."

"Ah! That's worth considering," Olive mused. Her eyes could become exalted, especially when justice entered.

"It's really simply a party to give the children a good time," exclaimed Rosie.

"I don't look at it that way at all," Olive replied. "They have a good time here at the beach every day."

"What shall we say to them?"

"We can pretend it's going to the iceman and really give it to the Animal Rescue Squad," said the haircomber.

"Why? That would be lying." This came from the tilted face.

"So they shouldn't know he drinks."

"Listen," said Rosie. "They've been sitting behind us all this while. Don't you suppose they have ears?"

The sun-browned face laughed. The sun-browned arms stretched. "Unofficially they know the iceman drinks but officially we're not going to tell them."

"Shall we put the grandmother to a vote?" Olive had been weighing it. "Because not one cent of my money will go to a drunkard."

The first stage seemed now to be arranged. They looked unanimous before proceeding to the next step. "But what sort of party is it to be? Are they each to bring a lunch and pool everything or eat their own?"

"Let one supply a cake, one hardboiled eggs, one peanut butter sandwiches, et cetera, and divide there on the beach."

"You'll have no end of trouble. Suppose there are twelve portions of cake and fourteen children."

"Okay. Let each bring his own cookie."

"Don't be silly."

"And the money is to be given to the baby's grandmother. Remember. Not one penny to that man," Olive stated.

"Don't you drink? You gave a cocktail party last week." The sun-annointed face took momentary leave to cast a bright glance.

"That's different. The man's alcoholic. I'm not going to provide temptation on the pretense of charity."

"It's settled," said Rosie. "They'll have a fine time. Kids love parties. Now let's call a meeting. Children!" The mothers swivelled around in their sandy hollows. The children were lying behind them whispering over unbridgeable fortress walls and bottomless wells.

On Friday Olive in a white dress, eyes shining, stood beside an abandoned life boat, taking in the admission fees. Actually everyone from the cottages along the shore attended. They raised twenty-two dollars and seventy-five cents. The children ate all they could hold. Later Rosie and Olive took the money, wrapped in some blue knitted booties and sweaters that had been donated, to the iceman's house at the end of the village. The iceman was out delivering ice for afternoon shindigs that were finishing the season but Olive stared sternly at the saloon next door to his shack. The grandmother had tears in her eyes. She really thought it was lovely of the summer people to take such an interest. She showed them the baby sleeping in his basket, she pulled back the blanket and there he was, unexpectedly small, sweet, alone. Rosie clucked over him for some time, blinking a bit herself, and Olive glowed bravely while giving useful advice about feeding and training. After a while they walked away slowly.

It was several minutes before Olive's exalted expression faded, but when they passed the saloon again she averted her head as one does from an untoward question and her gaze dropped to the pavement remaining there fixed in a deepening trouble. Noticing her at last, Rosie came out of her own ruminations. "The mite," she said as if in agreement with Olive, and then quite gently, quite reassuringly, yet with proper caution, "That *baby* certainly *seemed* sober," she said.

Character

Babs—pure. Of killing bugs. "Everything has a right to live." West Point boy tells her about a course in hand-to-hand killing. Asks, "Why do you want to be an individualist?"

Peg. She loved culture. Very much. "My French is really not much better than street French. I'm mortified. I can ask where is the restaurant or museum, you know, but what I mean is I couldn't discuss Tao philosophy with a French factory worker." She loved democracy too and knew a lot about those things, culture and democracy, which she explained to the less fortunate. "We must guide the poor who haven't had our advantages" she said. She really did, I'm not making it up, and she smiled sweetly when she said it. Walking down the street, empty and quiet, a store window with canoe on display, Dutchie's Beauty Parlor, fishing tackle, etc., remote from our pressured life which seems to us to be in the thick of things, I say "I wonder about the range of interest here. Are the people in touch with the world around us?" "Oh no. They are narrow in range. Why, I couldn't find Spick brass polish in four stores I went to. It is the best brass polish but they never heard of it. Imagine that, they are very narrow."

Mrs. X: The farmer's wife, my neighbor, who comes in to clean my house.

I'll fix it waxin', like that time they scratched your floor when somebody drugged your table. I dunno who drugged it but there was a awful scratch under it, five years ago, now honest, hon, why should people drug a table, can you tell me that? . . . Me and Floyd try to do our best, hon, an' there's two things we believe in, an' that's being honest, but we can all make mistakes like that time seven years ago when I baked that awful cherry pie, that was the awfulest pie I ever et, soggy, an' to this day I don't know what went wrong." A path is worn on the lawn where Floyd always walks exactly the same way to the door. Mrs. X scowls at the dog: "That Spin! Always runs one way over the grass wearin it out." In hospital to visit her husband after his operation—says to me: "So full! Nothin' but maternities. I talked to one girl she just come in to have her baby, she was in labor in the hall, I sez "How old's your other?" She sez "Two years," I sez "Honest, why don't you young folks control yourselves? Nothin' but pupulation explosions—Ain't you got no thought of others, tell me that, Sister!"—There's a man in

F's ward, he's in for a heart attack. Hon, he makes such a noise talkin' I just walked over to his bed an' I sez "Lissen, Big Mouth, Whyn't you shut up or you'll talk yourself under the ground!" Driving with her, all dressed nicely, she knows who lives in every house along the road. "That's the Larges'. She want after him with a hammer last week. That's Miss Nelson's. Did you ever see such a mess of a yard? I sez to her. "Lissen, sister, everybody talks about what a pig you are. Ef I was you I'd clean that place. I just told her proper." This world's just visaversaring to pieces . . . I wuz lookin' at the newspaper which is not no news is good news these days . . . Did you see on TV how awful it is in Washington, Johnson and Robert Kennedy fightin'? You look in your paper. Johnson sez, 'Lissen Brother, you'll git into trouble peace-feelin' around Europe like that an' Kennedy answers right back, 'Shit, I can do things same as you, Big Mouth.' That's just about what he told him, hon, honest Mrs. M. What are we comin' to? Did you read about that woman was murdered and raped? I and Floyd don't believe in them things. Killin' and rapin', honest hon, you don't know what's goin' to happen to you. You gotta have someone to watch your property or else they comes in and murders and rapes any more and me and Floyd don't go for that an' we never did.". . . "That Gretchen! All she talks is Sex. Sex, sex, hones' hon, that's how these people is any more. I don't even believe her, she says her husband wants to aggrivate her every night, now we're both women, you and I, hon, an' do you believe he'd want to aggrivate her all night long every night? . . . Just smell this here rose. Ain't it the prettiest stinkin-est rose you ever saw? . . . People is so wicked any more it ain't even funny, as the expression goes. I sez to her, "You got the shittenest laziest husband I ever saw.". . . That new cleanin' girl, honest hon, help is the shittenest truck these days. I told her good and proper, her boy friend come, he sez, I'm her husband, I sez, that's the shittenest lie, you're no such thing, there they was smoochin' in the pantry, I sez, Well, they say Frenchmen are

the most lovable men but looks to me like the Germans are, all
this tooty-tooty-tooty. There's a thing these days called Sex
and that's the trouble any more, hon. She says she knows a man
for this job, but I know he's a drunk an' you don't want a damn
drunk like him drinkin' all day because though I don't know
him he's a horseman an' horsemen is drunks always . . . You
ought to see the roses I got, hon. Honest, Miss M., my house
looks as pretty as a funeral parlor. . . . People is so wicked
any more it ain't even funny, as the expression goes. I
sez to her, you got the shittenest laziest husband I ever saw . . .
Birds is what I love. They just holler. . . . Too many cars skids
even when they got chains on in the snow. They have a
chain-reaction . . . Floyd: "I want a job when I'm old I kin get
my Sundays off.". . . "But Floyd, you get your Sundays off
here.". . . "Yes, but I'm always worryin' about Mondays.". . .

Mrs X. again: That boyfriend my daughter had, I don't
excuse her for having them two babies by him but it was his
fault too. He got himself married to another woman, last
month. I sez to him, "Bill, do you love her? Because you ain't
capable of love." Love, love, love, I told him good and proper,
straight out, if you'll excuse me for usin' such a word, hon, but I
did.

A carpenter and a gardener, loving craft. The gardener and
his calf—it follows when he whistles. He will not sell the dead
calf's hide. He buries it. The carpenter makes chairs of good
hard wood. Won't sell them—hides them in the back room.
Makes a gift for the president—sends it—a walking stick or an
ingenious sliding shelf. Gets letters—framed, they grace his
wall. "Ah this chair. It's a beauty. I can't sell it. No." When the
customer urges, he puts a fantastic price—in lumber and work
it is worth $10 according to any regular market value. "Well it
would cost you $60."

A boy and his calf on road, open-faced friendly boy with big
straw hat and his calf on a rope, mouth tied up with rope.

Mowing boys. Always something new near the pond—blue herons, kingfisher diving for fish.

Massive-bosomed women with folded arms across bosoms. High-neck dresses, wrong to expose the flesh, long-sleeved dresses. Mercy prayed for everyone, starting with the president of the U.S. and his councilors right down to Luke.

Barns were part of the houses, built on in els. A middle room, one went in their side door, never front door. Stone fences, every stone represented back-breaking work. Soap bubbles. Big tub. Apple orchard. Octagonal rustic or boarded summer house or band stand. Dark shingles on top, white on bottom. Frog in pond—she'd be conscious of two big eyes looking up at her.

Norman Thomas's father theologically believed in Hell, nothing crude of course like the pool-of-fire variety, but eternal punishment, yes—although there was nobody, no individual in the world he would have condemned to it. Norman couldn't believe in Hell, but he had quite a list of candidates.

Norman slid out of the home without open rebellion. He was a devoted son and tried not to hurt his parents. It was only after his mother's death that his convictions took their later clear turn.

He wasn't tough enough. Essentially shy.

A writer, he had to find his theme and his theme turned out to be peace. He gave up his great work, his big book, to go into direct action. The agony of the artist in whom meaning stales before the *fact* of modern life, from which most turn away.

Story—Norman Thomas

The great man, old, blind, made the trip to the grave of Eugene Debs. Who now remembers Gene Debs? The socialist movement itself—where or what is it in today's more violent and open and speeded climate, of hundreds of thousands marching and shouting and some being clubbed for it, an every-day thing? There at the cemetery of Terre Haute was the grave of Gene, and his successor stood beside it in the little birthday commemoration, among a handful of other old-timers, faithful loyal assistant beside him. The great tree was gnarled and bent, the kind eyes no longer could see yet the kindness remained in them, a permanent expression more twinkle than fire, the fire in the frame evidently found it more difficult of expression than the kindness. A charming cemetery, not as many stones visible as in most, a park-like atmosphere of lawns in this one, and rolling landscape. A brief ceremony under the branches, the great man leaning heavily on his cane, his face reflective, quiet. He brushes his eyes, his brow, with his hand. A minute later brushed it again: a spider hung from the branch above, weaving its silk on a downward thread. It was on the great man's forehead, the thread over his brow. It ran up and down the thread which he could not see. Here in the cold day, the cold earth, with only a few to witness it, Gene Debs and the socialist movement were quietly recalled—the old days. The great man kept brushing at his face, unable to see what was annoying him, what infinitesimal tickle like a feather was touching and withdrawing, what little pest drew his attention, deflected insistently, and refused to be brushed away. There it was now, scurrying from his hand, spinning from his heavy brows and alighting on his nose. It ran from bridge of nose to nostril, wherever his hand brushed the spider was too elusive, the net it spun hung part in air, part webbing his face, a strand here, a strand there. The loyal friend looked over and noticed at last and pinched the spider off. Little threads invisible even to someone with sight still clung to the great man's weathered, ravaged face. The eyes did not look blind but only bloodshot, watering or swimming, yet swimming with kindness it seemed. Tears down his cheeks—

10 The Writer:
The Setting of It

Was it writing—art—or the setting of it she loved, its nest, its retreat: to sit on a porch and watch sun and shadow over leaves, feel sun and shadow on the body, remote so, watching yet apart from the conflicts and fruitions of active humans.

The blizzard . . . I take refuge with friends who live on the main street of the village, away from our drifted country lane. How exciting to stay in somebody else's house: like a trip to a foreign country. New books on shelves in *my* room! At home I have no Maeterlinck set, no James Russell Lowell, no poems of Alfred Noyes or W. E. Henley. I must find out more about Henley. Similarly where is my Proust, my Yeats? These leave gaps. Among my home fields, my woodland, I have no river flowing rapidly past my window, no full majestic Delaware with ice floes borne on its breast streaming by, snow frozen in patches over the hurrying smooth dignified water all of it— from here to the opposite shore—veiled by snowflakes, falling, falling. How strange to sit here, like living here forever, in another person's home, blue knitting on this table, magazines not quite like mine, carnations instead of my forsythia. So I want to write. I look about for hints for my own house's further comfort: a bowl, a lamp for the guest room table? The river has no interruption of near shore from my second-floor window, the view is not of down but of out, a view that omits the short garden below which slopes to steep bank and retaining wall: from my windows it is only the river flowing steadily, a moving map of little lakes and circular white isles of snow-like cells that join, separate, proceed in groups, sunlight bringing out sparks in ice. The motion is inevitable, constant, rapid, splendid, dignified, blue-gray and white-gray. Across the river may be seen the opposite shore of brown trees rising from the breast of water (why breast?), which is curved—male breast, perhaps, for this strong flatness.

Part of the joy of spring is in the waiting for it. When will the cherry show buds, when will it burst into bloom, when will the dove coo her three notes, when will the first violet—the first!—show blue or white in green grass? Not true of other seasons: autumn is a marvel of richness but we do not watch for it day by day. On the contrary, we hold back, cling to each last day of summer. Winter lies ahead. Winter? Well, beautiful too, the dry clean air, a red cardinal on the snow and green pine branch. But I don't believe we hold fast to winter. We are willing to let it go. In spring I adore and mourn each passing day.

The limits of language! At a million points words fail in their capacity to say. In my summer garden are tall lemon lilies and beyond them a clump of white phlox. I inhale those lilies, move on and bury my nose in the soft many-flowered phlox. How describe those scents? The sweet delicate pale tangy vibrance of the yellow deep-challiced lily, pollen on stamens, a subtle aroma that you must bend close to in order to catch at all, and the softer phlox, sweet too and smelling of childhood gardens, frail, no pungence, no needle of perfume, the gentle fragrance of old aunts in black dresses bearing chocolates in their reticules, a tenderness compounded of the small white flowerets wet with raindrops or dew. And peonies, those luxuriant voluptuous petals, many petaled, intoxicating, unutterably soft, the deepest sweetness of all. How can words say it, describe these scents so that they rise with the words? No. "In winter we shall not remember/Warmth of sea water." My poem: "Memory in Winter." I considered calling it "Airy Memory." Midway it has those lines that I like: "While airy memory steals, without a sign,/Bodiless, into the permanence of love. . . ."

A fire in a winter hearth is a positive good
especially if
antique dutch tiles frame the fireplace
logs come from the old fallen apple tree in my meadow
Mantle is mellow pine bearing red candles in pewter

Hold
to these positive goods
especially
if
my friend died, tearing deepest roots
torn torn roots tangle and tear the inner landscape

especially if
outside too
where my soldiers bomb children

I must accept my friend's death but I'll fight my soldiers
Shouting them Evil
Staring at last into flame
Knowing at least that a fire in a hearth is a positive good.

Poet

He stood on a promontory among the boulders of the steep coast, his back to the foot-path above, staring into a small sea pool cupped within the rocks, and I knew he was a poet. He was looking for the word. Head bent, hands in pockets, legs planted on the rocks, motionless, only his black hair, black sweater, only the rear view of him showed. The shore was composed of lichened granite, rugged gray cliffs or pink tumbled stones; from the trodden sandy foot-path above, one could climb down and pick one's way among stones, seaweed, moss, occasional sprigs of golden-rod, even a short mountain ash tree with bunched bright red berries. The wash of the waves and cry of gulls were constant. You know these Maine coasts: most vacationers are inland on the village street buying souvenirs or at the wharf where lobster pots and fishing smacks are an unending fascination; the hardy shore is for solitaries. Two little boys clamber over rough shelves, jump from ledge to ledge. A bit further, around the next turn, two other boys have made a nest for sandwich-eating adventures in a crevice, and near them a girl who has managed to scramble below dangles her fishing rod in the water, occasionally pulls in a perch. On the path I took each day there were few human encounters; there were wild roses and a scent that I tried and failed to define. Then came the man. Sea spray forms small dark pools in the rocks. High tide leaves water far up in hollows and crannies. At one such pool, his back quiet, his head bent, his hands in pockets, the man stood, as though by watching, by long patient profound intense unstirring watching, he could drag from the pool or draw up from the pool its secret name, plumb that pool, know it. And perhaps he would, perhaps he would. Not likely, of course. And the sun would make the pool more azure, a breeze make it glitter, it would never be quite the same. No matter: for him the necessary fact was to find the word hidden in there at that moment, at that time. Mind you, the true word.

I saw him at the curve of the wild rose path where I sniffed the scent and tried to know it: nothing described it, the wild roses and spruce and sea. Has anyone ever been able to describe that sweetness, or the marks on rocks, cracks and lines, rust color and silver rocks, elephant flanks or jagged ridges, rocking and creaking gulls, or for that matter, has a final word ever been said on the lap of ocean on coast, or the sound of silence between waves? Sun on kelp strewn over one table rock was tawny yellow. One could walk and sit and walk every day and on the return never feel tired. At sunset my shadow fell twenty feet below from the foot-path above, following me along the rocky shore, over boulders, and there was my dark shadow walking horizontally and crossing the quiet man, the poet. He had not stirred. An hour later when I turned and returned, he still stood in his fortress, there he was, surrounded by rough walls, gazing at a small tidal pool, in the silence and setting sunlight. It must have been a good afternoon. I hope he found the word.

I have come to my confidence—maybe arrogance—and myself in my sixties. If I were 40 I'd be at the top. I am getting old. I used to feel like 30—now I feel like 40.

It's really not necessary to repudiate feeling. There's no harm or shame in honest and kind feeling. What is so intimidating?

The city is horrible and we spend our precious time, our hours, feeding it. We buy clothes for it, we go to hairdressers for it, we must live up to that thing we hate.

I think in writing; putting down words, sharpening them. In spoken communication with others I think too—outward, then words—developing thought. And in reading I react to the words. In other words, for me the *Word* clarifies cerebration. Whereas in solitude, in introspection, I retell old stories, I repeat old arguments, hold discourses that will never be held in which I am unanswered as I make my cogent points, as I thrust home, irrefutably, the explanation that will prove and clarify and settle. Thus while the daydream proceeds, all is repetition, a foggy sort of non-thought, which moves like a phonograph needle round and round in a groove, leaving me in the end with no sense of accomplishment or progress. But put it down with a pen or say it out with the voice *to* some other one, the audience, the real opposite number, the responding mind, and at once with the word thinking begins.

Scottsdale, 1964: Sometimes I think life takes away even more than does death.

To return to work—to writing—after absence—the very act of pen to paper has a special fiery excitement.

The artist is to the man of affairs as the architect is to the builder. The idea and ideal flow from him. He clarifies and directs thought and emotion. The rest of the world—"action-people"—carry out. The understanding of life—the shape to be applied—come from the artist.

I'm not interested in form for itself, though one experiments with forms to *get through* the experiment into some new reaches, beyond—which can often then be put back into traditional forms. The idea has been freed, of form-shackles; it can later be returned, liberated, into form again.

"There are laws for art and they may be broken. But always deliberately." (Stephen Vincent Benet)

There is an unjust tinge of criticism in people's voices when they speak of the ivory tower. All true art must spring from an ivory tower. The artist does not retire to it to escape life, but to face it. For him to be in the marketplace, distracted and busy with affairs, is to escape, to escape into dilution and alibis and concerns that are not his own—committees, social life, etc. In his ivory tower he faces head-on his art, his problems, his business—no distraction and alleviation. That sound of opprobrium and criticism in the voice comes from those who cannot know or imagine the hardships of the artist's lone truth, his single state: "I met the wolf alone, and was devoured in peace." (Millay)

In a marriage one or the other must submit. But neither of them ever did. (Novel). I once knew an old poet whose wife was a silly chatterbox. He was wise and deep but he submitted lovingly to her while she fussed over his health and made their arrangements. He idealized her, yes, and in his poems she emerges as the symbol of true love. No matter what she really was.

Elderly black Jehovah's Witness, cook: "I always love to come to you and be with you. We clashed together on first sight." "I don't understand the younger sex."

Character
At bottom he was like the perma-frost in Alaska. Under softness, when you plumbed you always reached hard ice.

Characters
One who clips disaster notes.
One who reads obituaries—first dutifully, for condolence notes. Then hopefully, with a fillip of excitement to the page. Will she know somebody on today's list?

Novel
She could wish for the existence of Hell beyond life, of eternal fire and pitiless brimstone, Dante's Inferno for all the wicked of the universe, if only to be sure that her enemy had just punishment in it forever.

As if a bulldozer had ploughed through her abdomen leaving it a hollow shell, an emptiness that felt stone-heavy, and tossing to the side of the road her red heart that lay beating there. The disembodied heart beating alone at the roadside and the dismembered hollowed body had no connecting touch with each other.

Mrs. Quinby, in country, ex-teacher, Quaker, gives me tea, shows me her house. She has seen mine, so different with its old things. She has varnished mission furniture, padded rockers, dark colors. Says (half proud of her respectable house, half ashamed because I have something she vaguely realizes represents some further step in taste), "My husband is a modern. He doesn't like antiques." He is 84!

Character: (David Beck) quotes you falsely back to yourself, putting in your mouth his own secret reactions. "What!" he says, "You don't remember that you said that?" And shakes his head to show what a funny mind you must have, and how you have deliberately put out of it what you preferred to forget. Only thing is, you never said it. "I quoted you yesterday to ———," he says, choosing some friend or enemy you had rather he did not talk to about you. "Yes? How?" "What Jon said to you when your last book was published." "What was that?" "You don't mean to say you forget!" he laughs. "He said after reading the first he didn't know why you bothered to write any others." I gasp—it is utterly invented. But he smiles tolerantly at my irresponsibility—"I couldn't have made it up, could I?"

Ella Davidoff—"I joined the church when I came here to New York—not for religious reasons but to be refined. Genteel people must belong to a church. You never know. Every refined family has a little something, weddings or birthdays or funerals, or at least *something*. I wanted to be respectable. It's for the girls."

Character—or detail, for humor—realism.

Morris Untermyer—spendthrift—gambler. Had $100 bills to be changed to embarrass waiters. Once it took a waiter in a small restaurant an hour to run around the neighborhood to find change—Morris got awfully worried.

Nothing was too fine when he had the money. The old house on the lake had acetylene gas to light it. One summer when it was full of his invited guests, family, electricians appeared; Morris was in Europe but had written that the whole house was to be wired. After that when he came for the weekend every light had to be lit: He liked to walk through the rooms seeing them lit with illumination. But Sadie was as thrifty as he was openhanded. During the week they used the acetylene gas again.

He saw a beautiful fountain—had to buy it. He thought it would look fine on the porch so that is where he had it installed and piped. Next year cousin Elias came from Memphis. Morris insisted on giving him the fountain and they tore it out.

When he was in love with Sadie she had to go abroad to get her guardian's permission to marry him. For he was considered wild and reprehensible. She was beautiful, reserved, queenly. He hired a tug to see her off, following the ocean liner into the bay and waving to her. Then as the great boat turned, he threw a diamond engagement ring up to her from the tug. But it fell in the water.

Eugene growing up between those two. Once in Europe Leon heard Morris say to a servant: "Do you see that boy? He's a prince! Nothing in this hotel is too good for him."

When he won at the races he gave everyone presents. He paid their hotel bills. He stood up in his fiacre in Paris and called to Blanche and Leon* to join him, when he saw them in the streets. "Do you know where we are going? We're going to buy you pearls."

Maude Adams**

The smile remained. She stood, once, the slim girl actress, in her green boy suit, forward upon the center of the stage, a long waving gallant quill in her cocky hat, her hair brown and soft around the intense face, her voice soft too and ringing, carrying; she had looked steadily out over the sea of children, addressing them directly. "Do you believe in fairies?" she had said. Through the years that smile was unforgettable: gentle and intent and loving and strong.

*Blanche and Leon Lowenstein were the aunt and uncle of James Marshall.

**Maude Adams is perhaps best remembered as the creator of Peter Pan in Sir James Barrie's play. She had retired from the stage many years before, and was teaching drama at Stephens College for Women at Columbia, Missouri.

The same smile remained. The old lady in her rather quaint coat of another age, a long brown coat with a deep brown fur collar and skirt touching the floor, the old lady would have been dowdy had it not been for her smile. It was the same: intense, sensitive, eager, responsive, with an integrity and nobility and far-off other-world eternal beauty about it.

She had been the most famous actress. The star. The center of the theatre, devoted to a pure searching art. All the world knew of her rare relationship with her producer. In a sense they were partners in her art: from him she got a perfect understanding and direction which made her great work possible. This was pure and complete love: he was lover and director in one, care for her personal life and for her public performance fused most tenderly and powerfully in him. His was this male role: he motivated her and she answered: her response in a beautiful whole, a perfect integration, where the two needs of her nature blended harmoniously, internal and external fusion, without the waste of friction. This was the ideal fulfilled. He was a great man to have understood her thus, and to have given so much to her, a man of strength and sensitivity and unselfishness and brilliance.

When his boat was torpedoed in the first war and he drowned with it, she died too and went on living. Her heart burst and darkness fell as surely as if violent hands had crushed her body into pieces. Life had no personal meaning and the theatre had no meaning any more; her heart and her art had been too closely linked with him. She could not believe that any other man could ever direct her. She left the stage then forever; for eight years she was ill, in hospitals, unable to experience any sense of life. Slowly at last she began to pull out. She went to Schenectady and worked with Steinmetz, experimenting on lights. Lighting for the theatre was close to her old love but not that love itself—not *so* close that it would hurt her. Later she went to the girls' college where she taught the drama, giving to the training of these young women her love and passion and integrity. She trained their voices; one girl who stammered came each day for two years and had to repeat French syllables after records on the victrola, until at last she was cured. She gave the college her costumes and scenery and the wonderful lights. She produced their plays and trained the girls, and from this young life around her she drew in new life for herself again. At last she was cured: a woman lived and worked once more. But on the opening night of these plays she waited only until all was ready, the curtain rang up. Then she hurried home to her own room. There, alone, she played solitaire furiously all evening while the play itself took itself through to the end. When she had to go into an audience, she always had a cold and was ill the next day, could not stand audiences any more. The eager beautiful smile remained in the old face, above the old-fashioned mantle.

In 1929 I was a reader for a small, newly founded, and short-lived publishing house, Jonathan Cape and Harrison Smith. The following year I became its literary editor. My office, in an old brownstone walk-up house on East 46th Street, located beside a speakeasy, was on the top story. Each morning on arrival, I would fill my arms with manuscripts that had been put in a safe on the ground floor and carry a dozen or so upstairs, where, between conferences with authors, I would go over them as time allowed.

Being a newcomer, our firm received many submissions already rejected by the established publishing houses; several thousand manuscripts a year would come to me for decision, since we had insufficient staff because of the depression. Unjust as this procedure sounds—to me, too, now at this remove—so many turned out to be illiterate or obvious trash that a few pages at the beginning, middle, or end were often enough for the usual verdict.

One morning, during this expectant and disheartening routine, a severely battered manuscript lay among the collection. It had apparently been around—later information showed that it had rolled up thirteen rejections. I opened *The Sound and the Fury* and read: "Through the fence, between the curling flower spaces, I could see them hitting. They were coming. . . ." I read on. The words, even now, bringing back that initial excitement and promise, make me tremble: life overflowed on those strange confusing pages. I read six of them, not entirely comprehending—but this evidently did not matter. It was like a physical assault, a blow between the eyes, a sudden spell, an overwhelming encounter. *The power of words*, I thought. I remember this phrase, this first marveling response to those pages, and when I reread them today the same response returns, the same phrase that then struck: *the power of words*.

Faulkner's name was unfamiliar to most readers, including me, for although three previous books had appeared, they had gone largely unnoticed. I ran downstairs to the publisher's office on the floor below.

"I think I have found a work of genius," I cried to my boss, Harrison Smith, in later years the president of *The Saturday Review*. "What's it about?" he asked with patient forbearance.

"I don't know. I'm just starting it."

"Finish it."

At its conclusion, I still didn't know what it was about. Numerous readings were needed to fathom it. The manuscript was unclear and uncompromising, no concessions; time surged back and forth through mirrors; the inner chaotic truth of the mind took its place beside the truth of surface; the author offered no help; an immense compulsive store of original energy poured out, scarcely to be contained within the sentence bounds. We accepted the novel. My blue pencil went to work and I sent a list of suggestions for clarifying certain passages to Mr. Faulkner in Mississippi, telling him I believed his book was great but could he please—on page this or that . . . ? He wrote back, "Who the hell are you?" Since then I have learned that this is what most authors want to say to the editor who suggests changes in their work.

Later William Faulkner and I met and became friends.

I still have, among files dating from that period and shown from time to time to friends, my earliest report penciled on lined yellow paper, a brief summary scribbled after that first excited, bewildered reading. It begins: "This is probably a work of genius." Difficult, labyrinthine, and unclassifiable though the manuscript was, it seems incredible that numerous publishers' readers could have passed it by.

The letters I received from Bill Faulkner over the years were written in a penmanship as fine as a Paul Klee line drawing, no i dotted, no t crossed; the word "till," for instance, might be four similar minute strokes, a hieroglyph to decipher. He gave me a chronology which I have pasted in my copy of *The Sound and the Fury*, written in this hand of his, of birth dates of Caddy, Quentin, Jason, et al. "Someday I'll give you the whole manuscript," he said.

He was independent and solitary and lawless in the sense that conventions had no false meaning or importance to him, yet he had the old-fashioned courtesy of a true gentleman. Once when he and I had a one o'clock luncheon appointment he appeared at my home at nine A.M. Seated in my living room, talking in that, to me, unlikely hour for rambling conversation, he related quietly that one night his baby became ill and he called the doctor. The doctor said he would come in the morning. The baby grew worse. Bill walked up and down, up and down, holding it. He telephoned again and told the doctor he had better come; the baby was worse. The doctor said he'd be there first thing in the morning. The baby died. "In the morning I went over and I shot that doctor."

His fiction overflowed into a world of fact—or fact over-flowed into a world made whole by fiction—so pent and pressing that it must have been torture; only words gave the necessary outlet to order. Whatever made his style seem impenetrable to certain critics was the very stuff of an in-exhaustible imagination wherein invention could not be contained by ordinary rules. He wrote of violence, but he celebrated life. That same early morning in my living room he speculated, gentle and remote, upon the idea of changing his identity, disappearing, settling somewhere in a desert—could it be done? The desert would be the best place in which to lose oneself, he ruminated in his low voice, out of some subterranean cosmos—could one change one's name, change one's appearance, become a different person? And then we talked of poetry that morning, discussing each other's verse, his comments attentive and constructive.

He drank. The effect on him of the bootleg liquor available in that restless Prohibition period worried his publishers. One evening several of us called on him at the Algonquin. Bill was in bed, a bottle beside him. Unwilling to leave him, waiting for him to be ready for sleep, we remained in our semicircle of chairs while the night wore on. Our host on the pillow discoursed, and the bottle emptied. He proposed that he rise and scour the city for a speakeasy that might still be open where he could buy the assurance of another bottle. We tried to dissuade him, and urged him to sleep. He turned to me, aggrieved, and said, "Lenore, what would *you* do if *you* woke up at three in the morning and found *you* had *no more whiskey?*"

As I Lay Dying, a heartbreaking novel, and *Sanctuary* were published in close succession; these I also edited. They were written in a comparatively straightforward manner and were not as difficult to unwind as *The Sound and the Fury*. If my recollection is correct, they were published with only minor changes. Afterward, when the firm broke up, Bill's and my paths diverged and in recent times we seldom met.

Through the towering reputation of his later years, that of being the greatest American writer of our century, whose work at its best is comparable to Dostoevsky, the same qualities in his work appear that distinguished his first achievement. The viscosity of his prose gives a clearer light than the most limpid simplicity in the hands of lesser writers. Details of his life changed but not the essential man, not the artist. He was said to have built a study in his Mississippi home where, as even his local fame grew, the exigencies of a large network of kinsfolk, of which he was head, would not intrude; someone was always dropping in because he needed shoes or a horse needed shoeing. The study, Bill announced, was to be inviolate, but one day, glancing up from his papers, he saw a cousin in the doorframe, pointing and saying to a neighbor: "Thar he be, writin'." Whether the story is apocryphal or not, one can imagine the solitary man in his study, in his town, in his spirit, where he found his roots and his release, the man whose humanity encompassed a chaos in which his insight revealed humor and tragedy and raw evil and clear goodness and the indefatigable vision of man.

He had a fearless love of the miracle of language and this was his salvation to the passion and compassion that show in every book he wrote. He spoke of man's "puny inexhaustible voice, still talking"—a phrase which brings to mind Proust's last line in which he speaks men "standing like giants immersed in time." Faulkner's voice will talk for a long time. He said, ". . . man will not merely endure: he will prevail." Other writers would do well to follow him from the road of fatalism and destruction to the faith that man will prevail. Bill Faulkner gave new meaning to the power of words.

Character for Story—career woman

D.—attractive—cropped hair and green eyes and matching jewels. Always lots of men and a vocation—Peace? Reporter? Social service Maggie? Political, journalistic Suzanne? Clever so that her efficiency never got in the way of her femininity. Until. Until suddenly her affairs broke up. Is she possessive or torn between desire for sex and desire to be dominant? Married men she didn't want because their wives complicated things—they had double allegiances—she couldn't stand that. Single men always turned to other women too, would not forsake others for her, when an affair bust up she thought it broke her heart and wept, and she went and bought clothes— hat and earrings and gowns—then she felt reestablished, reasserted. Powerful men she had to have; the weak she despised. But the powerful would then dominate *her;* that her ego couldn't tolerate. One famous man has been in love with her for years, he says; asks her to marry him and return from Washington to Georgia. But imagine her buried there—the wife and hostess!

But the problem—Hers and Bromleys. The attractive career girl grown older. Not so many available men any more. Yet a powerful once-attractive woman wants a man still; cannot be a spinster alone. Shall she marry and submerge self? Marry weak dull man? Or what? Always on hunt. Nervous.

Story

Of Tony, small boy sent to boarding school. Hard social parents, love child, but their idea of helping him is to give him the conventional upbringing, sending him away young to a school with reputation. Thus they shift their responsibility— are themselves free—feeling "he will go through all those awful stages and things (i.e. adolescence) with all the other boys. They'll all be shaving for the first time, together." But he astounds them by being violently homesick! At 13 he has not yet achieved their line, their detached sophistication, alas, though they have done their best to be unemotional and impersonal with him, "no silver ties or other unhealthy attach- ments to home"; he is wretchedly unhappy. Weeps. Is ill. Hates his roommate. *Their* child! who wasn't ever supposed to have a problem! Of course they insist that he see it through. It would be giving in otherwise. They tell him to be a man. "Why can't I live *home?*" he begs stormily. "We know what's best for you, darling!" They are miserable too. Have they made a mistake? Impossible. "Think how ashamed we'd feel if you came back now, when the term has started! You don't want to be a baby always, do you?" Yet the year before he'd still gone out with his little sister and the nurse. "I wouldn't be in the way," he sobs. "I could go to a school in town." They persuade him at last. They visit him in two weeks. The tears are over, though he is still pale. But good, no trouble any more.

By Christmas he was over it. They took him out a lot to give him a good time! Shows, basketball games, the circus. They all had a wonderful gay time. They entertained him and loved it, really. They were proud of him. For he never mentioned his late unhappiness at all. He really acted like an ideal guest.

[Characters]

Lena

Drudge 50 years, brought up the sister's child after sister died. Scrubbed and scrubbed over floors and tubs for this boy. To educate him, her one single-track idea. His sad boyhood, with mirthless joyless absent aunt. He M.D. Absent as intern.

She kisses me day after Christmas. I have given gift. Her mind has been wandering, forgetfully of late. She says, "Willie only gets home for a few minutes every few weeks now. Sometimes it's a little lonely." "Have you no friends? Do you go to movies?" etc. "No. I used to. I don't like that much. I go for walks. Sometimes I start to go to people I know on 168th Street but I turn back, always, never seem to get there." "People in your house?" "I know them but I don't go into their places. Better not. We meet in the halls. They're all right but better not go to see them. But sometimes I'm lonely."

She returns that night in rain at eight. "What shall I do? Tomorrow is Christmas and they don't want me to work on Christmas. But my things will all have to be done over if I wait, all that ironing will have to be washed again!" "No Lena. Yesterday was Christmas." "Ach, I don't know what to do. I'd have to wash all night to get it done. When should I come?"

She has obliterated Christmas in her mind. It was spent alone.

Thema

Story of Hal* and the ring.

He had been engaged to a sweet girl, getting more deeply involved and led toward marriage in spite of himself. His old eternal need to extricate himself. Her society family; he could not see himself as part of this big formal group. She was o.k. he told himself, but not this life, this trap. So he met her one night on the beach. He had with him a diamond ring that had been left to him, along with another, in his uncle's will. He pretended to the girl that he had bought this ring for her. "But you don't really love me," he cried. He accused her of not being truly in love with him. And he threw the ring far out into the sea and ran away. Ran and ran from her, to the dock where he boarded a boat that was waiting for him, there in the middle of the night, and sailed away on it, with the two friends who had been waiting, and never saw her again. "Whew, it was worth it," he tells me, "worth a diamond ring to get out of that." "But," he adds laughing, "I always suspected that that ring wasn't a real diamond."

Elizabeth Sparhawk Jones**

She sat at the table, Du Bose Heyward over there and Thornton Wilder there. Then there was a step on the stair, and then Edward Arlington Robinson stood in the doorway and looked at her. He looked at her straight, that quality of seeing you, the real you, in his look, and at that moment her fate was sealed. Somebody introduced them and later he walked away. For two years she never spoke to him or he to her. It began in terror and in silence and it always had in it terror and silence but afterwards friendship too. She loved him for fifteen years.

*Hal is Harrison Smith of the publishing house of Jonathan Cape and Harrison Smith, where Lenore Marshall worked as editor. This incident is the kernel of Lenore Marshall's short story, "Almost Caught."

**Elizabeth Sparhawk Jones, an artist, became Lenore Marshall's friend at the MacDowell Colony.

During this time she never painted; she lived in him and for him. All through the winter months, eight months, she waited for the summer when she would see him. They were never lovers. Yet for them both it was the most intense thing in life. She was terrified always; she used to make lists of things to talk to him about because her mind went blank when she was with him. He was taller than most men. When he looked at you something complete entered you; if he felt pity for you a mantle would descend upon you. He could be wordless with you and say more than other men could say in a million words. Once he said to her: "Never do it unless you can't help yourself." "To die into Poussin." "To paint the air full of things. Things going up, things going down. A mood, a portrait of a woman really."

Elizabeth, the lonely painter, met a beggar on the Left Bank along the Seine, near the book stalls, in Paris. She put a coin into his filthy hand. "Are you not well?" she asked him, looking at him. "Sick," he mumbled. She asked him where he lived, did he have enough to eat, gave him another coin. The next day when Elizabeth took her walk past the book stalls, the beggar was there. He forgot that he had approached her the day before, mumbled, stretched out his shaking hand. A thin rain was falling. "You will get sicker if you are out in this weather", said Elizabeth. She hailed a taxi, took him to a doctor at the clinic where they found all sorts of things wrong with him. Elizabeth adopted him, a dirty old sick man. She went to the hospital to visit him, brought him flowers and a book. When she returned to her home in the United States, she wrote to him, worried about him, returned after a few weeks to bring a gift to him . . . Dostoyevskyan concept, or, what you do to the least of my children you do unto me. You must know the depths. You must be able to embrace evil in order to embrace life. (I don't believe I accept this! I must hate evil in order to love life.) Her pity and fascination with this specimen of the dregs of existence.

Sociological note

Not so long ago you didn't have to be rich to have fingerbowls on your dinner table. Even the middle class considered them essential in the way that all niceties were practically essential. A mild sociological note: you haven't seen a fingerbowl in a home in some years now. In the better homes a slice of lemon or a pansy floated in the crystal bowl. Once upon a time. What has happened to all those little round lace doilies that used to lie between bowl and matching plate? My mother's, delicately embroidered and filmy, now take up space under paper napkins in the bottom drawer. You can't give them away like sweaters or coats to the poor. Now although we moved in varied groups, we no longer move in a fingerbowl group.

1935

Down the hill on a brown young horse a girl comes trotting, and in one arm she holds a feathery loose bunch of yellow flowers. At the curve where the brook is hidden in the woods she walks her horse off the road and into the woods, deliberately, in her cool assurance, with her yellow airy flowers she walks her horse down the sharp wooded slope to the brook and there he bends his head at once and drinks. As I go on, after watching them, a black poodle bounds out of the field, bounding by but not barking at me. Three blonde children, holding hands, are on their way toward me. When we meet and pass the tallest throws back her head and smiles and calls "Hello." This is a lovely place; so many birds sing in the trees and the stone fences amble on gently by the roadside. Yet I move and breathe with my full surcharged heart heavy in my breast, watching and loving the roadside and desperate about some fearful unknown strain that is always running in me.

1960's

Fourth Novel, chance and choice, Affirmation chapter.

When he pulled up the shade each morning there was his

cherry tree, branch against the pane. At the end of March its bark became shinier. Spring came overnight. It was difficult to believe how quickly it could come, after the coldest longest winter behind, with blizzards until the 21st of March and then the next day a snowdrop hanging its white head under a bare forsythia, a purple crocus, hyacinth buds!—as though nature read the calendar, said that's that, and paid no mind to yesterday's weather. There was a sudden assertion of birds, flutings, cheeps, the first color of spring was blue, not green or yellow, but small blue of tiny weed flowers endearing on the hard ground, blue of crocus and chionodoxa and sky. But of course the advent had been going on gradually somehow for weeks in his blood, he had sensed it in his nerve ends. Seizing a pencil he wrote "At February's end the excitement begins/ Willows tentative are lighter/And accompanied by song—" Then he put down the pencil. No.

Regardless of these lines or their potential, no. Whether or not a poem would flow from them, hold, lead on, no. No more, the times are out of joint. "Farewell to willows, violets are dead. The times/days are fleeing. And the times/days have fled." Corny. True.

The mystical novel. Again. This has a science-fiction element (popular-modern), etc. But it is science-fiction of a gentle sort; this makes it different. No horned creatures, no space men, no exploding stars. It is earth's realism, with a mystical suggestion of connections between worlds of strange possibilities. *It says:* Fellow spirits are fellow spirits wherever they are. *It says:* what is life? Trite?—but no! You *cannot escape from your fate. You recognize your self wherever it is. Mars and Venus are no further or nearer than Timbuctoo or the secret in the house next door.* It says: you enter a forbidden world, when you enter another life. Only the very few, the very rare, the sympatico, the understanding, may enter each other's hearts; and only they who have inner purity and power can break the bounds and bonds of their own? . . . Life can be transcended. Lose the self in another. Heal the wounds by entering another soul. It says: we live in the universe and it is vast, strange things surround us, the new power of science *may indeed waft us out of ourselves.* (Like poem.)

We inhabit successive bodies as we live. From birth to death, from infancy onward the habitation changes; while we live we have eternal life, which is consciousness.

Equally, may we not inhabit several worlds, even simultaneously? One spirit co-existing with itself elsewhere, its inner mate. The revelation—breaking through the flesh—the sharing of life—two lives linked by the spiritual oneness—"I have been here before." Comforted and aghast. My flesh cannot contain me (not through sex this time).

The novel is about two women who never meet, whose paths never cross—or only indirectly. They understand each other, or would if they knew each other, in the sense of understanding the same essences. Their experiences are different, except for the inner life. All outer reality rushes away at some crisis or symbol (the story plot) so that the life of one might be interchanged with the other. The nightmare which is the prelude or introduction to the novel, the wind that draws a woman upward by the roots of her hair into outer space, the terrible nightmare suggests other worlds, forbidden to us, the earthbound human beings. At what point in the story did the nightmare occur? After one woman, the woman who had the nightmare, yielded to a man against her will or through supreme love, taking on all difficulties and sorrows, knowingly and forever? After she gave up the lover?—gave up her life, her self, for a *reason*, another person, her child? *The Hill is Level?** . . . The women, the two human beings who never meet, are bound by a capacity to love, are bound by the wound, the gift, the blessing. The sense "I have not lived well," the compassion that makes serving others its own reward and agony. One is famous, the other is obscure. The sense of the

**The Hill is Level* was Lenore Marshall's last novel.

world's danger is present in both. One is a political woman. Is she on the Board of Education? She may step into a crisis situation offering her wealth and time against a sense of doom. One of them is desperately shy; she has a terror of her audiences. She longs under it all for peace and love—personal, universal. It holds to its mystical nature (where is the excitement?) the implication is all . . . Their deaths?

The confrontation of audience with experience . . . Writers today are tempted more than ever to publish their notebooks.

Fearless Hopelessness (Novel) The moderns—
The end of a road. No beliefs. The thing hangs over them, the sword of Damocles.

To deny their wishes diminishes them in this brief mad moment of living: to kill becomes holy, connected with the universal death and violence, or when not holy it is unimportant because everything is unimportant. They have no past, as we have, no standards. They are intellectuals without direction, minds gone mad, but perhaps this is right, and in keeping with the direction of science, for if we are to end on Mars what use is our humanity? Humanity in the old sense is passé. Where do they stem from? Freud, Hitler, Marx, the atom bomb (Einstein). And parents who were failures. The murderous thoughts of this generation, between 20 and 30, are circulating everywhere. In every magazine—stories of killings, stories of no-love, no-belief, but of intellectual prowess all right, the greatest playwright is the man who never has had a play produced; masturbation he says is purer than sex, the self is an exalted polluted bauble, a swollen and diseased and suffering threat, and those young people terrify me. Something *must* be done for civilization or they will destroy it. Violence.

The existentialist antihero; the man of conscience who finds all decisions torture, all choices meaningless. In all sincerity he searches for a truth.

Fearless hopelessness—the youth of 1960's.

Fearless hopelessness is the worst kind.

This avant-garde is not of crusaders. They have no belief. The end—they are at an end. The dramatist has never produced a play, the painter swishes to the right or the left, swish red, swish yellow. Insanity: and this is appropriate; who can wonder or blame? They have not the background of standards we had. Beats for kicks—because no beliefs. This is the job of the psychiatrist—the Bomb of Damocles hangs over them. Space opens; the universe. Is their end-game more realistic than our search for goals?

A Novel; early idea for this.

About a life as lived in diverse ways, according to the one married. The Central Figure shown in youth, aged 22, knowing a group of four friends of opposite sex. In each of four sections the life is lived with one of them—deep, rich, temperamental—dull, frustrated, blocked—tortured, destroyed—at peace, sacrificial, happy—(or others). In preface the turning point must be given that made the relations what they were—i.e. three not married, the one chosen. But in the sections each is given as it would have been. The power of chance. Take a man central figure for once. Know him fully—in youth, in age. His character is deeply the same in each, a growing, a developing,—but some people and conditions fulfill him, others do not. In some he finds other outlets and successes because of frustration in marriage—in some his work is quite different, changed by personal circumstance. Death enters in one marriage. Children in some. Place of residence varies. Age at marriage. But the idea is that the person's potentialities develop one way or the other—chance is important, marriage the most important step—but the basic human being takes what comes his way in his own way. And some strong bent propels us as we go—not only chance. Some of the same events punctuate each chapter (death of a parent?), some never happen (illness of psychosomatic nature). The whole, all the potentialities, are suggested in first section and could be referred to in each, retrospectively the undeveloped material—clay in the potter's hands.

The girl who was college sweetheart. The girl who was his friend's sister. The right girl he met at her house. The stenographer or trained nurse who helped him. Even his career changes. He is a successful lawyer with rich girl; a struggling clerk with the poor one. One eggs him on by ambition, one says "As long as you're ethical," one is very sexy, one hits below the belt—hates men.

In this novel one of the possible marriages would end in divorce. One in death? One in normal love and family. One in continuing agony. One in character deterioration. One in heroism.

What is love? Is it a solace from loneliness and fear? That is a negative, in a way: in the flight from loneliness and fear we create a refuge, fabricate a communism, construct a moment which the fortunate can prolong. It can be a closed-system (?) self-generated, with little relation to the object. But today it is harder than ever because of the Bomb. One of the most difficult things is achieving love or friendship or communication— sometimes they amount to the same thing—in the world we live in. The sense of isolation in which we exist today, the encroaching fear: I maintain it is *in extremis* because of the Bomb. Men were always afraid of death but now they have good reason. It is not only their own—it is all death— Beethoven's and Chartres' and Shakespeare's and El Greco's and unborn children and brooks and fields. Life is on the verge of breakdown, cut off from its roots. Perhaps some of us cling to the wrong person for that reason. Some of the young seem to give up all values and hope, *carpe diem*, beatnik surface mysticism and wildness, indulgence.

Why aren't we screaming in the streets? Incredible that we aren't all insane, a mass insanity sweeping the human race at its prospect of extinction. The insanity takes the opposite form— acceptance. Evasion. No fight in us. Cynicism.

11 The Woman: Dreams and Scrambled Eggs

Scrambled eggs. I was writing a page but it all fell together, became confused, because it was written in scrambled eggs. Not clear and permanent like ink: a mess, falling together, the eggs merging and obliterating.

Interpretation: scrambled, jumbled domestic chores obliterating the clear outlines of art. Eggs are children, whose own lives are scrambled, and whose scrambles overwhelm my own neat would-be permanent page.

Dreams: Sleep is a means to dream. Civilized man finds it difficult to dream awake, to cast off his isolation and detachment and to become part of the cosmic ocean. Tribal Africans, it is reported, need little sleep. They participate in the ocean of being through myth and ritual. We who have lost our simplicity need dreams to break our barriers.

Threw two books out of window. Fear lest this sign of increasing irresponsibility will lead to my total breakdown.

I uncovered a corpse buried under the floor for five years. It stank. I dug it up. When mother came I told her to take it calmly, the news that there had been a murder and a body buried in the room all that time.

Dream: She sought a little secret dive, a restaurant, that she had once known. Found it in a new place, far toward the river,

in a basement, marked on door outside, "For Men Only. Enter
Me." She went in and sat alone at a table. But there were many
other women there.

My generation: The forces in the pre-war years, between
Victoria and Woodrow Wilson, that shaped us, apart from our
immediate families. It was a time of confusion, yet a good time,
compared to many other periods. The old standards and
restrictions of Victorian days had eased. There was the leaning
toward liberty and democracy, which later, after the war,
leaned till they tottered, too far, and in the attempt to give
freedom gave an utter insecurity and relaxing of every standard. Formerly there had been conventions and rigidity. Later
there was the throwing-to-the-winds, disillusion suffered from
the war-to-end-war, prohibition and speakeasies, if things went
wrong one went to a psychoanalyst, one developed a tough
surface, a hard-boiled exterior: but these were not the requisite
qualities for meeting the exigencies of life. What are the
backgrounds and training for meeting life? What will still give
one liberty and space to think and function as an individual, yet
a background of strength and true standards with which to
know and seek reality? What if not honor? What but true
relationships? The backbone of family life? What do we want in
life—to find ourselves in love and in honor, in a work we may do
and a willing positive biological continuance of the human
species: living, positively. How shall we make our decisions?
How meet reality and make it good?

My generation had a hypocrisy about it, coming between
extremes, the earlier conventional, the later disintegration. My
upbringing contained both elements: tried to reconcile the
moral with the free. It suffered on both counts. The moral
seemed firm when it was only a shell, a pretense, a standard not
lived up to. The free broke down the solid foundations of family
life. What Ellen and Jon* have gotten from me is greater

*Jon is Lenore Marshall's son Jonathan; Ellen, her daughter; Steve, Linda,
Cindy, Robby, Laura, her grandchildren.

sincerity. We face the truth together, more boldly, I believe, than my parents faced life with me. They gave me love, but also something sentimental and false that hid a lie. I try to know the truth, and finding it, to make it work.

Children have a talent for cruelty, know how to hurt most, know each other's weak spots, and when they strike, when they must because of their own hurt, they strike to kill. Adele—the orphan cousin. I said, "You have no parents," but later I wept. When burrs were thrown in her hair it was worse than when they were thrown in mine—because she had no parents. El when she wanted revenge took Jon's papers, the world of his own creation. He was beside himself: he defaced with pencil marks her horse show trophies. Each knew the other's weakness: his greatest treasure. The right to wound there was only exercised in moments of desperation. Each too decent, sensitive, and honorable to misuse it, too full of love for the other. But in a moment of desperation, the instinct was there, to kill, infallibly to strike at the vulnerable spot.

Notes of Peter Pan Club: The mother who calls up boys for her daughter. Ellen too timid to invite the lads she hardly knows so I do it. But it would sound odd if I said "I'm calling up for Ellen Marshall"—as if she had a secretary!—or babyish if they thought it was her mother. So I pretend to be Ellen, while she sits beside me in hysterics of laughter and jitters. "Hello Sam?" I make my voice girlish and inviting. "This is Ellen Marshall. Can you come for dinner?" The boy sounds uncertain but pleased. "Why yes, yes. I guess I can. Is it formal?" "Whatever you want to wear. At 7:15." "Why yes. Guess I can." "That's fine." "Well. Shall we call it a date?" "All right." "That's fine that you can come." "Well, it's very nice of you to ask me. Thanks." El beams. "Gee—you certainly have a way with them!" But she has learned not to be too curt—learned that it is easy. Learned that assurance helps.

Ellen—(15) read my novel. Suddenly the terrible adult world opened up before her. For several days she looked wretched, made faces as she read, was silent and cross. Then it tumbled out and with it a depth and maturity never displayed before. No decent people *could* act that way! It was the worst book she ever read in her life (outraging her virginity). Yet she would rather have read it, too, than any other. The tragic intolerance of youth based on its idealism—due to its inexperience, its simplicity, the one-dimensional tuning of life. Yet glimmers of other things turn this black and white. "I feel so young!" she cried in distress sitting up in bed looking so lovely and flushed and curly haired in her polka dot pajamas. "I think that love is the only thing that makes life worth living." "People who love couldn't act that way." "I thought *you* were Gabriele"— "Promise it isn't you—promise that isn't Daddy? You'd never let another man kiss you *that* way?" "Have you ever had an affair? Or Dad? *Promise!* I know it's beautifully written but let's skip all that—I want to talk of what it's about. How did you *ever* happen to write such a book!"

Age 16—after her first big dance at a hotel—when a boy had called for her—she had come home at two o'clock, had had champagne—all the thrills. The next day I asked her to tell me about it. "Oh," she cried, "We had the most marvellous kind of ice cream!" Still a child.

Ellen—sketch of young girl—heroine at end of Part I. She is easily upset if a word of coldness passes between Jim and me. She will jump up and say Goodnight crisply and go to her own room. Though the war absorbs everyone it is her own life that is real to her, that is all. She becomes deeply involved with the worthless boy, Hal. Tries to be fair, says to me hotly, "You're not fair to him. I guess maybe he's insecure or something. Maladjusted." Her generous nature—she will give gifts to us all, beautiful things, yet ride in subway herself, save on dresses or hairdos. She is honest and cannot lie.

Her friend Martha, not so honest yet not bad. While E. plugs ahead and will not miss a day of school though she hates it, Martha will shift from school to school and tell lies. "I am at Barnard," but she is not. "I am going to X's party," but she was never invited. Does she doublecross E.?

E.—older and sweeter now, reproves me for talking brusquely to a salesgirl. "You shouldn't be so sharp," she says, but politely. Formerly she was impressed by crossness. "Dad gets his way because he shouts so," she used to say, "That's how to be boss; that's how one can get things." Now she has softened, is beautifully solicitous of Jon writes him birthday letter when he is 18, "You have improved I must say; people say you are good looking—I don't know. Anyhow—you'll do. Anyway, always be open-minded. And for goodness' sake don't go to war."

A little snobbish, yet gets on with people . . . used to be jealous of me. "Mom had so many boy friends." "Mom, you're beautiful." "Are you tired? Let me bring you breakfast." At 20, of a young man who takes her out a lot but she doesn't think is her type exactly, still, "He certainly knows how to treat a girl." She confides in Martha about him. Martha writes a letter for her saying, "I am a stranger to you but will introduce myself as being Ellen's best friend. Sorry to tell you she fell from a horse and broke her arm. If you would write to her it would cheer her up." But they do not send it.

Modern skeptic: "I can't believe anyone in the 20th century believes in life after death!" "But Ellen! Many people do—there are millions of Catholics alone who do!" "Really?" "And others. I'm not sure that in a way I don't." "Mom! I'm disillusioned! You! You don't want to be a butterfly, do you?"

Happy, popular, loved. Goes out night after night. And practical, sound. A bubble. A fountain, with one foot on the ground. Says: "Family life's nice. I like it."

El asks me about my editor job. She has just been fired from a sewing job and is discouraged. ("At the age of 21, I am a failure!") I try to buck her up, tell her how people I worked with were fired—lots of people get fired. In the depression Al Wiggins was fired and I had to do the work of two people. "Yes," she says, "but what became of Al Wiggins?"

20: El's warmth and depth. Her love is greater and freer than all of ours.

Jon: Age eleven. He is sturdy now, something to hold on to. The brow is clear and candid, beautifully smooth with light brown hair above it and well defined brows marked up from the eyes. His eyes are big and dark brown, thickly shaded with black lashes. They dance, they sparkle with mischief and life; or they are large with thought. Sometimes—not often—they fill with tears, for he is sensitive. Then he is silent, not a word said till the wound is swallowed. He is so beautiful! I love his nose still shaped like a baby's, a pug nose at the nostrils, innocent and straight and small, nostrils like apple seeds. I love him curled on the sofa with his book, or on the floor reading a newspaper, his rear stuck up in the air. His hands are slim, his firm muscular legs have plenty of scratches. He says when we play tennis, "Gee Mom, I do like to see you in good form!" He says happily: "You know, you're still very pretty." He looks to see if my book is on the best seller lists—"Good old Momsie!" he approves.

He is going to be a professional baseball player, "Even under communism the people will need recreation," he says, "So no matter what government they have when I'm a man, it will be O.K. It's just that the government will pay my salary. Then when I'm too old to play I'll be a manager. That's a kind of literary activity, Mom, signing contracts and things." Very polite to guests, very gallant to me, pulls out my chair at meals, carries my bundles, etc. Reads *Quentin Durward*, Baseball magazines, the *Iliad*, boy's adventure tales, many books of the sea, Stevenson, Poe, etc. His great fault is laziness about duties: writing letters, practicing, mowing the lawn. He likes to do things his own way. But never needs entertaining—always busy. Teases the maids, how they love it! Very graceful, spontaneous, kind. Affirmative in his responses—"I get you," when he understands. Otherwise he inquires about things. He wants to know.

Jon (12): "Mum, you give me encouragement and Dad gives advice. The combination makes me feel a lot better. You're wonderful, Mom, you never get angry. You just get sorry if I'm bad and then I feel sorry. Dad takes me by the scruff of my neck and I find myself up the hall quicker than usual. That makes me sorry in a way too but mostly it hurries up the means of transportation."

Jon (14): Wants to give a contribution at Xmas to the 100 Neediest Cases, which he has been reading in the paper. To me: "But I don't want to sign my name. I thought I'd send it anonymously. Or I'd sign it 'In memory of . . .'the way some people do." I ask, "But in memory of whom, Jon?" He: "I thought I'd sign it 'In memory of Czechoslovakia' "—and it is printed thus in the *Times:* "$1.01."

Takes me out after the theatre. I buy tickets; he puts nickels in his wallet. Says "Let's go to Jack Dempsey's for a soda!" Then tells me a story "I read in a comic strip about a boy named Toots. Toots had 20 cents so he took his best girl for a soda—but she went and ordered a banana split that cost 20 cents so poor Toots had to pretend he had a stomach ache and couldn't eat!" As we leave the play I suggest Schraffts. "No," he says, "Let's go to a nice cosy place like Liggett's!"

Age 14: Going to Quebec he and the other boys look for the men's room on the night boat. Can't find it. Finally one bravely pushes open a door. "It was marked 'Men's Homes' " says Jon—"And that was it. I thought it might be sort of reserved for veterans."

Jon is moving his lips silently on words, practicing lip-reading on us; he wants to see if we can guess them. He turns to Jim: says silently "Fuck." "Don't let Mom know," he laughs, "it would shock her. She wouldn't know that word." He is very chivalrous toward me and merry and proud of his manly knowledge. "Bet I know more dirty words than Ellen!" I say, sticking up for El, "Probably she doesn't especially care about knowing dirty words." "Oh," he says, "you amount to something if you know a lot of dirty words." "What do you amount to, Jon?" "You know. If you're president of your class, or a good athlete, or you know a lot of dirty words, then you amount to something."

So pure, so sweet and true. What can I give you as you grow older and beyond me that is worthy of you, my child? My tall, slender, thoughtful, pure-hearted little boy.

Jon and the Somebodies.

Every other Friday evening he goes to dancing class, from 7:45 to 8:30. He is thirteen years old. He gets all dressed up very neatly and carefully. "Don't wait up for me," he says in a man-about-town manner. "I may be home late. Just go to sleep whenever you want. I may be back about 11:30."

At quarter-to-nine he is home, flushed and happy and beautiful, his soft thin cheeks rosy above the neat dark blue suit. "It was all right," he says casually, with shining eyes. "And afterwards we went for a soda." "Who went?" "Oh, Billy and Artie and Mason and I. And a couple of other people." "Any girls go too?" "I guess so." "Who were they?" "Oh, somebody and somebody else. I might have come home even later but I didn't want to." "Oh yes." "Some of the guys went on to somebody's house." "Yes? To whose house, Jon?" "Oh, I dunno. Somebody's. But I didn't want to go. They all piled into a taxi. I didn't feel like paying part of the taxi fare just to go to somebody's house. So I just decided to come home. How about some ginger ale?"

Age 14   He Takes a Girl Home For First Time

This night he returns at 11:30, very stimulated and glad to sit on my bed and talk. "We went to Artie's house after dancing class. Everybody lived uptown so when they all were going home Artie didn't want to stay home alone all by himself so he decided to walk uptown too. And I just decided to keep him company. We walked to 80th Street & West End." That is how he tells me, thinking he is concealing the real excitement from me. Seeing "Somebody" home.

15—Dancing Class

He says he doesn't like girls and will be an old hermit, but he wouldn't miss dancing class for the world. After it is over he sits on my bed at midnight telling me about it. "I had to sit and digest on the side lines for the first quarter of the evening because I had eaten so much dinner. There were others sitting out too. I dunno whether the other boys were digesting too or whether they just didn't want to dance. But sometimes girls haven't partners and then the teacher comes along and wants the fellows to dance with them. So when that happened I just blew my nose. If you take out your handkerchief and blow your nose the teacher hardly ever asks you to dance. Or another thing is to stoop down and tie your shoe lace. He can't catch your eye then."

They dance with two fingers stuck out if they want to be cut in on. That is a cry for help from their friends.

Of another more formal party: "They didn't have enough to eat. And the kids looked dreary-eyed by ten-thirty. So I talked to the drummer."

16—How hard to look at those broadening shoulders now and remember, or connect them with the little fellow in rompers, saying chrrrrrggg in the back of his throat, being a machine. Or the boy of ten saying, "I think when a boy's ten he wants his mother." (Of camp, dismissing it then.) Or even a few years ago, still in shorts, leaping at her in a hug that wants protection still too, simple and unashamed. He adores me still, is my pal. I am the closest friend. But he is protective now, tenderly teases, a raillery, an equality, a conscious seeking my companionship. He flies in his talk: Plato, Jefferson, Poe, baseball, photography—business—makes fun (that is manly) of aesthetic things but feels them (i.e. Ah! Yes! Posies. Pretty posies.) Talks of the war—feels socialism—wants to work. Identifies with Franklin: theme in which he says "Franklin's father had him at the dinner table when there were guests thus encouraging his interest in the deeper side of life." Talks of the bourgeoisie, scorns his bourgeois ancestors, says, "I take after the proletarians." Is delicate, gay, funny, thoughtful. Understands history. Compares present events with ancient days with true sense of history. Writes story for school. Composition about Lena, the old drudge, describes her life. Says to me: "I can bring in a feeling of time that way. She sees people come and go. Do you think I ought to bring in the class struggle?"

The little boy—big boy room. Old toy auto holds playing cards. The autographed baseball he once got, names of famous players inscribed on it. Poker chips. Stamp album. A knife, an Indian drum, *Buddenbrooks*, *Of Human Bondage*, *Ulysses*, *Sherlock Holmes*, banners on wall. The tin plate with a spinning wheel: his precious old baseball game, untouched but still there in its ancient place.

Gallant—native tact: 17—When mother says she comes to us more than we to her: "Never mind, Gran. When you're *old*, we'll come to you."

To me, severely: "You like to think of yourself as young and beautiful and the men falling for you." "Well, what's wrong?" "Oh, it's all right as a compliment if they like you. But it *can* be inconvenient." "Inconvenient to you, as a son?" "Yes."

When I had been gay with some guests. "You didn't act like yourself. Those people! loud! I don't think Dad liked them either." "Did you mind their off-color stories?" "Certainly. And their manner."

"Dad, do you have any influence with the draft board?" "Not much. Why?" "I thought maybe you could have my math teacher drafted."

He has kept from us the fact that he has a boil that has hurt a great deal. Why? "Well, pain is good for the mind." He wants to be manly, discipline himself.

"What are you reading Jon?" "Oedipus—but don't let that put any ideas into your mind."

Boy of 11 (Hardy Einstein, fat, outgoing, eats immensely), of

Jonny who is seventeen and whom he admires hugely: "He's great! You know—he's not too clean, and not too dirty."

He is severe with me if by a shade I err from perfection, from a straight and narrow concept of the young gay sympathetic but immaculate mother. Voices (men's) in the corridor of hotel. I say as he comes in and I'm in bed, "Don't worry, they're not in here." He frowns at me in annoyance at this kind of levity . . . His diary, at 16, summing up for the year, said "On June 18th I took out a girl for the first time. On 25 did so again. Also made baseball team." Writes out what he will say to girls over phone in dating them—"Hello. I'm a slow worker—just got around to calling you. But do you want to go to a movie Saturday night?" Beginning to be less shy about talking of girls to me. "Pretty girls at X? I must go there!" Pretends to be a gay man about town, Writes themes about how he comes home at six in morning from dance, when he has never been up so late, or about the "fine taste of ten-year-old whisky still on my lips." Strong democratic sense. Gentlemanly, tender, gallant. We go for a trip in car together, through the lovely clear country. I say, "Oh I am so happy!" He: "That's good." Quietly.

Jon and I. Story

He is 18 and has taken the car to go out on a visit one evening. Time passes. I am reading, writing. Under her work his image. Suddenly she is conscious of cars passing on the road—not that one. Not he. It doesn't stop. Another. Her ear sharpens to them. It is early; she looks at her watch. Reads. Reads of Katherine of Aragon.

Suddenly "Toot-toot. Toot-toot-toot." Some car far down the road sounds agitated, may be in trouble. Could it be he? No, why? But it could. How silly, he drives well, as boys do these days. What should happen? Well, there's that turn at the brook. She always noticed how the road sloped and softened at the ditch there, one might slide off the road and in the dark turn over into the brook, lose control, the car would plunge into the darkness and its occupant be pinned inside. He would blow horn for help but though people heard that toot they would assume it was another car and not go. There he would lie (crushed, not able to toot the horn again). It was silent. She went on reading and turned the page. Crazy—stop worrying. She read on. You're comfortable, you don't want to go out. (Cold out—autumn) It is really getting late. Suddenly she shook herself; she felt fear. Terrified for him. She got her flashlight, stepped out to the dark porch. A bat flew close over her head. She rushed inside, slammed door, waited; then resolutely out again to her car. But no, she will walk to that sharp bend; two cars might have trouble on the road, and if he came he would be annoyed to see her set out to find him. Be casual. She flashed on her light. The dog barked—she called, Sh! to him. Then she smelled a skunk. This time didn't stop. Walked quicker—the road was dark and rough. Sky dark, starless. Stone rolled underfoot. Here was the bridge—oh darling be all right—she peered, swinging her flashlight over the silent field, that slipping treacherous soft shoulder of road to brook. The light pierced faintly. Oh can I see enough? But nothing, nothing was there! Is it sure? She flashed over the field again while her anxiety lifted. He's just plain late, she thought, as though no other piece of road existed—as though this must be an omen she thought. She turned slowly, walking up hill, then behind her the blast of a horn!—the sweep of headlights. She stepped to side. He is there! He stopped the car. "What are you doing?" he said in surprise. She got in beside him. "Taking a walk. Walking!" she said lightly. "Such a lovely night. Have a nice time?"

Jon 36:

Visit to son in Oregon. Lukewarm about it—such a long way by train. It is for love of Jonny. I think he would like to see me as I want him—but it must be lonely for him, even though it is his choice to live there. I want to see him and to give him a chance to

talk if he wishes it. For—and these pages show it—Mother—
Mince, we must give our love. More peace, thank heaven now.
Perhaps I feel less intensely in all ways. Is that age? Stevie said,
"You haven't got much time." Chicago in a blizzard. One is
lucky to have money—the comfortable train, a hotel room for a
bath. Does my sybarite life weaken? I want to do so much but it
siphons off in fragments; not enough worldly ambition now.
The country going West is all snow—white sky and white
plains—blurred brown trees. *The Hill Is Level* says we live for
the future rather than the present. I do not know if this is
correct.

The pleasant relaxing bourgeois university town. I can see its
charm and its danger. Unless one had a high cause—work and
spirit—one would be lowered quickly yet have a life of more
sense and dignity, perhaps, small routines, neat homes. I seek
great people. Or greatness—it can be in the moment of creation
or communion with nature as much as the person. I have known
four—Mince-Einstein-Judah-Erich.* Impulse to go to be near
Erich. This is one of the highest experiences life can bring, that
sense of greatness that can be caught, and one is uplifted,
extended by it. Jon: bless him. Now the return. Jon is more
relaxed, has met the challenge of a new place, friends, gave
party for me. His friends liked me, invited me to their homes. I
am glad he wanted that. Gentle and attentive—*perhaps* this is
right for him. Hope domesticity will not keep him from his
potential capacity—Cindy: "Next time remember to bring
Bop." She is sweet and sensitive and Lolli is firm. They are
affectionate to each other and full of laughter.

Grandchildren
Linda—Age 6
"Boo! I rushed out at you like a territory!" "Pretend I'm a

*Judah—Judah Magnes (see p. 47). Erich—the psychoanalyst Erich
Fromm. The reminiscences of meetings with Einstein have unfortunately
vanished.

princess and I have a date with the prince across the street . . ."
"How come a butterfly doesn't sting?" "What are grandmothers
for? Kisses and all that stuff." Plays house with Steve—puts
him to sleep. "Lie down I'll have a nice cuddle with you. If you
have a bad dream call me."

Stephen, Age 3.
A real mechanic. He breaks everything he touches. To a
group of adults, shaking hands, "Are you happy? Are you
happy?" "If I fall my face will crack. This is mine face. I haven't
another."

Linda—12 year old girls—Margy her friend
L: I don't like books that are too romantic. The trouble is they
are all romantic when they're written for us teen agers. I wish
you'd write one about something else, a girl who wants a career
and her problems and how she works them out. In middle age
maybe she meets this very bright man, a doctor of philosophy
or of dentistry or something, but first she does a lot for people
and gives her money to good charities. Her parents are
drunkards, so she lives with this aunt, 89 years old, whom she
loves.
Margy: Oh, I know! write a book called "My First Kiss!"
Linda: Or just "First Kiss."
M: Yes! It could have a picture of a boy and girl on the cover,
just to illustrate the idea.
L: I like sad books. This girl goes to a psychiatrist and then
she knows more what kind of life she wants. Not everything
about it but, you know, her general direction. She and her aunt
have a happy time together. She teaches her aunt to dance, rock
'n roll, the unconscious intuition. Right after *The Hill* is
published.

Steve—8—How old are you?
61

Oi oi oi oi oi!
But I'm still pretty lively.
Yes, but you haven't long to go.

Linda—looking at my picture:
Mommygran, you were so pretty. What happened?
I grew old.

Fragments from our time
Picture the telephone wires: New York to Boston. Freshman
grandson on Boston end, holding receiver, gray-haired loving
grandmother at New York end. His "Hello" to her voice is
gentle, delighted, affectionate; he is a long-haired, thin-faced
youth with a newly-grown still sparse beard. What did she
think of the Dylan record he gave her? She is warm, polite; but
of course, says she, she was brought up on Beethoven, Mozart,
Schubert, Bach, etc., who enrich, deepen. He says, "I feel that
way about Dylan. The classicists are super-human. They are
too lofty. Dylan is simple, human, beautiful." At her end
Grandma makes a sighing face and changes the subject. "What
books have you read lately, dear?" "I haven't much patience to
read. I see too many movies maybe. They're good too." She
takes the encouraging approach. "I feel that you are at a point
now when you will get more and more out of books. You
haven't read *War and Peace?*, etc. You are intelligent. You'll
want to know who Prince Andrew was, Natasha, etc." He must
be looking sweetly patient at his end. He says "I'm going West
this summer. I'm going to buy a van and go with some other
boys, to New Mexico maybe, to the Hog Farmers." "You are
interested in hog farming?" "Oh no, that's a name, a group.
They are people who are going to take over the earth." "What
are they going to do with it?" "Give it to others. They're
beautiful. They spread the word." "What word?" she asks.
"Oh, the word. Beautiful things. So far, they have only a few
thousand acres. Taking over the earth is still a dream. They are

the people who fed the Woodstock Festival. Real food." "Who will go with you?" "Doug. We are taking a course together. A beautiful course, in meditation." Her expression now is aghast, but the phone cannot see it; her voice is interested, as though she wished information. Her brows, however, fly up excruciatingly. "On what do you meditate?" "Everything. For hours. We forget the body. We simply meditate. I wasn't too successful the first time. Doug says it's beautiful." She groans, holding the receiver at arm's length, so that the poor long-haired boy will not hear. She says, aiming hard: "What is the difference between meditation and thinking?" Long silence. Ah hah, thinks Grandma wickedly.

Picture them at the telephone, New York to Boston, the long-haired pipe-dreaming youth, the grandmother distorting her features in twists of cartoon despair, trying to bring a beloved boy back to reality.

Linda—Venice: Among all the wonders of new places, it is Linda who stands out, the exquisite girl—modest, independent, helpful, quick, practical. The graceful figure in the church at Torcello, seated on stone altar steps gazing up at the great blue madonna curved over the altar ceiling. The girl, exquisite beyond any former knowledge of mine. If Henry James had not roped off the American girl in Italy as his preserve forever, how one would wish to write a thousand stories of her!

Soft—everything. Softly self sufficient: never what-shall-I-wear or will-you-close-my-suitcase or have-you-a-stamp. She has it all in her light luggage, efficiently stowed away among her pretty dresses, and if I say I must buy thread or cotton, she says "Don't bother, I have plenty." Softly proud, head held high, swinging walk. Softly independent, off she goes for a stroll, alone down the alley of shops or the church crypt, but more often joining us, keeping companionable step. Softly observant and informed: "Like Cézanne," she says of a group of houses, pink and yellow rectangles of walls, and it is precisely right. Softly accurate: it is she who knows history and catches on to the currency and finds her way around strange new cities and knows exactly what she would like to do yet is invariably considerate of our tastes and choices. A waterfall of dark gold hair, clear blue slanting eyes, soft mouth, a fascinatingly shaped face with high cheek bones, a rounded oval. She bounds forward in development, ten miles a day. In soft command of the Medici or church architecture, never pressing her information out of context or relation to people, but only an accurate reference, interested and brief, modest yet precise.

A half-hour in Santa Croce. She is deeply enchanted by the marble lady who bends forward, grieving, in the lady chapel, a large noble figure surmounting a tomb. The sculptor is nameless but she finds this lady and feels her eloquence more than that of the statues with great names attached, where tourists stand in knots. "My lady," she calls her and returns on three separate occasions. I see her there on our last visit: I have been to the Giotto frescoes and when I turn the corner I catch my breath. There sits the girl in silence with her Lady. In rows behind her are five black nuns, kneeling, praying. The golden girl, soft and still, absorbed in the spirit of this place, sits ahead of the dark praying women and the marble lady broods forever whitely gleaming and removed from them all.

Palm Springs—January 1962

Jonny, thank heaven. And his children. That beautiful baby boy, so like him. Some strain of course—and he is sensitive to it, as I am, but on the whole it is a plus experience, lovely to be together as a family. "You have a nice family, Madam," said the waiter. "I work in Nevada. I forgot there were families." La Quinta, the ring of brown mountains, rock cliffs circling a valley, not circling uniformly but brokenly, a steep jagged cliff, then a range with vistas of mountains behind, peaks, running on and on and around, enclosing the valley-desert where elegant palm trees stand at home and alone. The cliffs, a tumble crumble of bare rock, cracked, experienced what color? How does sun color differ from shadows color? The same tone— endless light. These remind me of my favorite mountains, my million Mexican mountains at Taxco and then Taos and the Riviera. The bones of rock, unhidden by green. I am emptied and replenished.

What is the quality of light?

> Range   peak   cleft   rock   tree
> Miles   gate   arc   wall
> Circle   angle   wall
> Gray   blue   pearl   silver   violet
>
> You, longing to share the moment
> Forever to share, long in vain,
> Love flowing inward, flowing outward,
> But having it, even alone.

A good poem.* It says it. I could live forever here. It would take forever to be able to write it all.

Radio on peace—can I do a good job? Worth trying. Silver lizards sail over the blue sky, mementos of jets. Today's mountains—mist in the dip between near mountain and the range behind, and then, higher, touched with snow, the range behind that, the whiff of orange trees, sweet, deliciously sweet. I am in love with words again. Look to the mountain! I could write the Psalms. The unblemished sky—evening light and the brown sudden mountain; it confronts me in its strength as though it were a beneficent brown lion.

Los Angeles—Interviews—broadcast—for peace— disarmament—Amazing! I was good! And they liked me—they liked me a lot. I'm amused at this new confidence. Who am I? But ah, if only I'd had this thing with people long ago!—

*These are excerpts from her own poem "How Will You Show It."

drawing the kind conventional Beckers, radiomen, newspaper men—if only, once, I'd known I had it in me, so that people—draw, close—show their liking. Silly, amusing.

Christmas 1963 and Jan. 1, 1964   Scottsdale
The same supermarket crossed with fake frontier town as last year. Shoddy affluent desert. No zip to this, no beauty, no off-beat. Everything is *on* beat. Christmas reunion great. My Linda beautiful, wise, perceptive, full of promise. As the week passes, she stands out as rare. Robby beautiful as Jonny once, but an unknown still. Unknown year, what will you bring? A low end, no writing; the discontent of spirit that has developed in this atmosphere: is this conventional bourgeois mediocrity of love all that can be achieved? The childrens' attitudes starve me.

Later—train home   Jan. 17.
On the whole plus, because of son. We lifted our relationship, and there was a delicate warm understanding. And a deep deep bond with Cindy and even little Robby: when I said Goodbye he said "Stop going! Stop going!" Cindy showed deep distress. I too, but time to shrug off the other which bogs me down. Train trips revive. Now back to life. A beauty appeared in the mountains. Always the mountains seen from below, distant, many-shaped, sun shadow mountains.

Grand-children
Cindy—7. "D'you know what?" Her voice lifts. Quaint courtesies: "If you don't mind" . . . "I like to be private and have my room to myself, especially to keep out you-know-who." Her sister—"Mommygran, have you noticed how sometimes you and I automatically say the same things at the same time?" "Shall we let Linda in our club?" "Pull the shower curtain around me when I bathe to protect me from all evil." . . . Laura—6. "The lovely flowers! Flowers make me feel

merry, like singing and dancing. Flowers are my only joy!"
. . . Robby—3. "I want someone to sleep with me." "Who?"
"You!" He is so loving, poor beautiful darling.

Alice in Wonderland is fantasy like Kafka. The man into
cockroach and girl into 3-inches-high are fantasies of the same
order, though motivated one from desperate entrapment of
spirit—despair—fatal outlook at man's condition, the other
from pure freedom of gaiety, an imagination both marvellously
free and splendidly courteous.

Cindy—we go to dinner together, happily all dressed up:
"Now all we need is a couple of men.". . . "I've been in all sorts
of places my parents don't even know about." (Goodness! has
she been running down the road?) "Places in books. I've even
been in the year 1620."

Laura—at the door of the apple cellar, stopped short: "The
smell of fresh apples breaks through to your heart."

Cindy—8. "Nobody understands me. I lie awake at night
and think, my mother never will understand, she scolds and
bosses, and my father doesn't either, I've tested him, so I just
keep things to myself. I've tested lots of people and now I keep
my own thoughts. I see other girls and they laugh more and are
happier than I. (Yet she is full of humor and laughter. How
deep is the mortal wound.)

Cindy—age 10. Delicious, relaxed, intelligent, full of humor
and delight. Charming guest for three weeks. I am so relieved
by what she has become—outgoing, self-sufficient, enthusiastic, beautiful. What eyes! Gray with large black irises, very
white whites. "Bop, not that I wish to sound immodest but I do
have magnificent eyes." "Mommygran, you could dye your
hair white." "Why?" "To look more grandmotherly." "But I *feel*
grandmotherly." "You don't look it. That fulfillment still lies
ahead of you.". . . On leaving: "I can scarcely believe that this
wonderland is over."

(July 1968) Laura—10. "All the rest of us may change but not
you." "Why can't I?" "Because you couldn't change for the

better. If you were to change it would have to be for the worse."

Cindy—12. "Sex, the way I figure it, there it is and you just can't do anything about it, so you might as well forget it."

Robby, just 7. "It is hard to give away your thoughts. You can *think* anything but you can't always say it. A writer, because he can't say it in words but only think it, may not express the most important part of the book."

Robert (aged 9) has a friend from one of his incarnations 1000 years ago. King Albert. Once he was a janitor but being lazy he was demoted to King. He wears Bermuda shorts, a dinner-jacket, bedroom slippers, a raincoat made of doughnuts so the rain can get through the holes. He is thrown down the drain but comes out in China where Mao Tse Tung invites him for dinner. He used to sleep in a garbage pail but now eats out of it. He is also an M.P.—a member of the House of Uncommons. He has half a mustache—one side only. . . . "King Henry VIII did a lot for England, really started it on its way as a modern country but his sexual life was deplorable." We drive to Bath.

He mutters, "It's terrible." "What's terrible?" "The state of the world. The storks are on strike. They refuse to deliver Albert's babies. What's more, the babies are going on strike because the storks won't deliver them. And the banks are going on strike because Albert's babies aren't being delivered by the storks and money intends to strike because of the bank's failure to use it. All comes back to Albert." When he went to Mao Tse Tung for dinner Mao ate him up, but Albert got out and away by means of the toilet drain and was next seen in Russia. When he was weighed the scale sank right into the earth but A. climbed out the other side of the earth. He talks of motion, of Newton and Einstein. Einstein was the greatest genius the world has known: he was a philosopher-scientist, he discovered the law of revelation. "Oh, relativity? Some people believe there is a fifth dimension, time, but my mind just isn't big enough to grasp that." "The ocean is so beautiful. Its many colors." He talks of that and of painting. He says poetry takes more thought but painting—when a picture is done—gives him more satisfaction.

To the child: one thing I can't let you know is that problems never end.

It must be even harder being born than dying . . . (One is so inexperienced!)

Robert

The most pure, the most profound soul and mind I have ever encountered. Put soul first, put mind right there too, beautiful and true. I am in awe. I am shaken . . . We have just lunched together. He talked of the death of animals, cows, flies: "Everything has a right to live. I don't believe things should end. I believe people go on in other people. If Mr. Jackson dies he may enter Mr. Johnson and go on." "Dr. Mary Jane?" He laughs, "Then she's a tomboy. That Greek thinker, the great one, should be alive today to teach us still." "Socrates?" "Uh huh. I grieve because people come to an end." His eyes fill with tears which he fights back. "People should communicate more. Speak directly, even to insects. 'Bee, don't sting.' Perhaps there is more understanding than we realize. Not just stupid limited facts but things beyond. The moon landing shows us that. Perhaps we can know about God from space, whether or not he exists, there is so much that we don't know about all around us. We should talk of these matters to each other." "Yes. Can you talk of them to anyone? Your psychiatrist or your parents?" "No. I can talk best to my teacher." "I can talk truthfully to you of these things, Robert. Can you communicate with me?" "I am trying." He looks straight and earnestly at me, his dark eyes full of trouble. "We men have still to invent a time-machine." "What would it do?" "We could grasp the past and the future. A time-machine could *correct* history! The mistakes could be avoided if you had the past again. But it wouldn't be possible. If time were moved for one person it would have to be for everyone, and then you'd sort of have to be for everyone, and then you'd sort of have the present, wouldn't you. Perhaps it's better the way it is. A flower should still be a flower."

Of his poems: "They shouldn't have published them without asking me. I was mad. It made me look as though I'm a different guy.* Editing the paper was something else. I liked that, the poems made me look too big. I'm not like that. One would have been okay." His eyes are large, earnest, beautiful. Another day: "There's something on my mind I really ought to tell you. I'm a v-e-g-e-t-a-r-i-a-n." I discuss it with him, say man has a more developed nervous system than animals, that animal brains are not capable of realizing events in their lives, their fate, pain, etc., etc., etc. He looks at me: "But let me give you an example. Suppose there were a feeble-minded man, a real moron. Would you throw him in your soup pot? . . . When you think about the universe it's wonderful. The whole universe—the most unending geometry shapes it. I'm trying not to draw it but to describe it in shape. The shapes can be any size, millions of them mixed together. The universe is lots of everything; like millions of boxes with everything in them; you explore even parts you already know. You walk along exploring the universe . . . I'm glad I discovered the word supernatural . . . I'm half my parents but only half. The other half is my inmost inside."

Conversation about our Trip:

"The first thing to decide is what to decide" said Robby. Laura: "If we are taking a trip abroad we must make a list. Important things to take. Not clothes. Like a camera and a passport." "We could take toothbrushes. But not toothpaste." Laura: "This is secret. We'll have to plan how to get to you so They won't suspect. Shall we go on the Queen Elizabeth?" "Yes! And we can write a book about our travels on her. It will get the Newberry award. Yes, that will pay for my college education. I must have a college education." Robby: "Oh, I love

*A teacher had published a selection of his poems in the school literary magazine without his consent.

to take part in things. To be part of them like this! Things real and imaginary at the same time. The way I felt when I edited the class paper. We must have a code so we can write to each other about this trip and make plans. I have it! Every third word will count. Two words between will be gibberish." Laura: "One thing to remember about our book—it should be likeable. We've got to remember to get a publisher. Books must be likeable and should have publishers."

12 Grandmother: The Trip

"Geniuses can make dreams come true," said Timmy. "I believe in that. Why not aim for it?"

GOODBYE! SEE YOU NEXT MONTH

INTRODUCTION

What Becky remembered first of all when they discussed it later was that she and Mommygran stood in the ocean, hand in hand, knee deep. Every minute or two an especially big wave rolled in, a comber which shaped up some distance away and could be seen rising, dipping, rising higher than the surrounding waves, a beautiful dense blue wall that gathered a white foam crest as it heaved forward and broke in a giant downfall splash upon Becky and Mommygran so that they leaped, dove, gasped, laughed. Spitting out salt water, Becky said: "Let's make pretend we're shipwrecked. We'd be washed to Europe. I always wanted to go to Europe."

"Yes!" cried Mommygran. "Although it might be more convenient to go by boat."

That's what Becky remembered as the start of the game. Here is the version of Kathy, her twin. Becky called herself a vivacious blonde, Kathy a dreamy brunette. What Kathy remembered later was saying to Mommygran: "I'm thinking of running away from home." Her home, when she was not on this two-week holiday visit, was far off west in Arizona. She repeated: "Running away. From Them."

Mommygran gave her a quick look with one eyebrow shooting up like an umbrella, but she made no reply. She was silent, invitingly.

Kathy said: "Sometimes—" and stopped. She added: "I've discovered that Timmy sometimes thinks about running away too."

This time Mommygran did exclaim. "Timothy!" Because Timothy was a whole year younger than the twins. After a minute she merely agreed reflectively: "Everybody wants to run away sometimes."

"We really do. So what we want to know is, if we run away from Them, could we run away to you?"

"Certainly!" Mommygran breathed out, laughed and kissed her. "Just let me know ahead of time before running. Promise? What a sensible way to run away! One should always pick one's destination carefully. Only remember that it takes a while to get from Arizona to New York, so just let me know when you're coming. I'd want to be at home."

But Tim and Mommygran remembered the game in the room as the particular episode which was responsible for everything that followed.

CHAPTER 1
THE GAME IN THE ROOM

A strip of sandy path separated the larger beach cottage— where the children and their parents and a fat aunt and a skinny uncle were spending the vacation reunion with Mommygran—from her own private neighboring studio cabin where she was not to be disturbed, please, until she emerged to join the merry throng; the best ideas came in solitude at the beginning of the day, she said, so she liked the day to unfold gradually. In the morning as soon as breakfast was finished, the young people rushed across the path, pulled open Mommygran's door, shouted Hi, then knocked, ran into her room, pounced upon her and cried: "May we come in?"

They never knew what they would find. On numerous mornings Mommygran still sat propped in bed against pillows, a book on her knees, gazing outward at the sea, coffee percolator bubbling beside her. Clad in a pink lacy nightgown, overjoyed at their entry, she hugged with one arm while the other extended with her cup, dangerously balanced. On some mornings, however, dressed in slacks or a bathing suit, she bustled, sliced, chopped, spread and mashed at the table, making surprises for the picnic lunch: not plain cheese or peanut butter sandwiches but sardine and cucumber sandwiches, or chicken salad, not plain hard-boiled eggs but deviled eggs with olives, not plain crackers but cookies from her portable oven, freshly baked, an almond in each center, whose aroma blended deliciously with the tang of briny air.

The young people's parents had warned them that Mommygran was getting older, she needed plenty of rest, they must be considerate. Their fat aunt contributed that if Mommygran seemed a bit quirky at times, if she wanted to be left alone, then observe her wishes, indulge her. She'd always been—well—an individualist, given to certain notions, quite harmless luckily. The thin uncle remarked that nobody should—she simply shouldn't—her ideas were getting more— one of these days she'd need —; he shook his head. To hear them one might think that Mommygran was ready for the old folks' home. And in fact Mommygran had announced that one of the topsy-turvy delights of a get-together was— occasionally—to be alone, each person, when he wished, to be able to go his own separate way, to be free, and thus she felt free not to join them until it was time to go to the beach or after she had imbibed a peaceful hour of morning isolation like breakfast coffee. Timmy reported that They sighed in unison, gazed at each other and told him Mommygran didn't want to be annoyed until she gave the word. The children understood this: it meant that they could come to her cabin as early as possible but they were careful to keep the family out of the way. They understood that Mommygran's restrictions did not apply to them. Only to Them.

They brought with them a deck of cards in order to entertain her during the hour of privacy together, which she called reveille or crack-of-dawn; however they discovered that she was ignorant when it came to card games. Rummy? —— Everybody knows Rummy, they said. Nope, she admitted sadly, not she. Then Gin Rummy? Nope, she confessed, it had missed her. The young people decided to teach her. It would come in handy for her when she had nothing to do in New York after they had to return to Arizona because of Father's business. Yet she was not a very apt pupil; a depth of blankness was revealed in her that they had not suspected previously, like a big hole in her otherwise normal nature; she simply didn't remember one card from another. "I'll play you," Becky volunteered. The twins sat on either side of her bed, Mommygran in the middle. Tim prowled and muttered to somebody invisible. "Kathy can tell you which cards to play and maybe tomorrow we'll let you be on your own and play Timmy." But by tomorrow Mommygran had forgotten all the rules and had to be taught again. It ended by Tim and Becky playing with each other while Kathy said: "MG, are you watching?" And Mommygran said: "I believe I am. Oh dear me."

On the following morning when the young people entered with their deck of cards, Mommygran got ahead of them before they could deal. "How about a different game today for a change?"

"What game?" Becky asked. "We didn't bring another."

"There are games that don't require equipment. We can make up games."

The young people settled in their positions so that the bed was covered with a tangle of legs, somewhat sandy. Tim climbed on the further end, hissing mysteriously over his shoulder: "Ssh, ssh!" He said: "I'm glad I discovered the word *supernatural.*"

The twins sat at the sides, Mommygran up at the top. Becky shuffled her cards and Mommygran laid a quick hand on the deck, putting it together as though to say to it: Now be good. The little room of the beach cottage seemed to wait while everybody settled comfortably on the creaky bed, giving a game time to enter. Mommygran suggested: "Let's play we're taking a trip. To Paris! To France!"

"Okay. What shall we do there?" Becky, the vivacious blonde, was always ready to go. Timothy, whose eyes were either bright as Fourth of July sparklers or deep as dark wells, studied Mommygran as though she were the map of Europe.

"We'll go by ship. That way you can have time to practice your *Bon jour* and *Merci*, see the bigness of the ocean more even than from here, no sign of land for five or six days, and play ping-pong on deck as well. We debark at Cherbourg. People will be speaking French fluently because they will *be* French. It may sound like jabber-jabber to you but soon you will start recognizing words. After we reach the hotel in Paris there will be a nice lunch, patisserie for dessert, would eclairs be okay? And wine. You may drink wine over there, everybody does, half glasses for you, but don't tell your uncle, he wouldn't approve if he knew about it."

"That's right," said Kathy. "He'd say the trouble is your sense of values, and also we might be allergic."

"Allergic-ashlergic. Then first of all we're off to Notre Dame. It will bowl you over."

"What is it? Why is bowl over nice? Do you mean knock us down like an auto? Is Notre Dame a sort of machine?"

"The opposite! More like a spirit! Pure embodied beauty. A church with vast stained glass windows and flying buttresses and gargoyles—I'll explain about that afterwards. It is so glorious that the first time I saw it—as a tourist, mind you, not a worshipper,—I went smack down on my knees and I thought, why did I do this? And answered, I'm kneeling to beauty itself. Notre Dame was started in the twelfth century and took almost a hundred years to build. No modern machines created it, just love and labor."

"I've read *The Hunchback of Notre Dame*," said Kathy. "It's an interesting book."

"Ah? It is."

"I've been in all sorts of places my parents don't know about. Places in books. I've even been in the year 1620."

Mommygran leaned over and squeezed Kathy's hand. Kathy leaned over and patted Mommygran's hand.

"Then we'll take a walk, there are bridges across the Seine, we'll explore among the bookstalls on the Left Bank, *le rive gauche*."

Tim asked: "Can all five of us have a little money to buy books?"

"Five?"

"Including you. Not four. Five." His eyes glanced at the twins, Mommygran, his own stomach, and over his shoulder. "Invisibles can be real, you know."

"Yes."

"Who knows, maybe people go on and become something else and are even happier after they die. Maybe my cat is my great-grand-uncle."

"Well. Certainly you may have money for books. Here." She deposited air-made coins in each hand. They pocketed them. She bent down all the way to the end of the bed, rumpled Tim's hair, smoothed his forehead, he smiled at her, she smiled at him, she wriggled back to her place at the pillow end. "Books make a fine way to spend our money. One must break up sightseeing with refreshments, quite often. There are cafés with tables outside on the boulevards, plenty of patisserie, and

an aperitif for me, but not wine for you every time. You'll like
the lemonades."

"Where shall we go next?" Becky wanted to know. "I've
finished another chocolate éclair."

"A walk down the Champs Elysées, Europe's widest avenue.
Then the Louvre, that's a wonderful museum. Then the Eiffel
Tower—or Versailles? Let's make it Versailles. We get off a
bus, and behold, a palace! Set among formal flowerbeds,
fountains, statuary, a real palace with a hundred rooms! We
don't have palaces in the United States because we don't have
kings, and in France they don't have kings any more either."

"We know all that so you can skip it," said Kathy. "Shall we
walk through the palace? I always wanted to see a throne."

"There's a hall of mirrors in which you see yourself from all
directions," said Mommygran "Long ago I read a novel called
Hall of Mirrors by a lady author. And that was about aspects of
truth through many peoples' eyes, just as in this room you are
shown yourself reflected from different angles."

"That's philosophy," said Tim. "I'm becoming interested in
philosophy."

"It was built by King Louis XIV. Such grandeur! Crystal
chandeliers! Tapestries! But the poor people in contrast were
wretched and hungry. A Queen, Marie Antoinette,—spoiled,
you know,—"

"Wife of Louis XVI," Becky supplied. "She said, 'Let 'em eat
cake', when the hungry people had no bread."

Outside, the rest of the family could be heard knocking
politely on the door. "Are you ready for our morning swim?"
Father called.

"Yes, dear," cried Mommygran. She whispered to the
children, "Then the poor people rebelled and the French
Revolution took place and Queen Marie Antoinette had her
head cut off by means of the guillotine. After Versailles we have
refreshments at another café—"

"Thanks for a nice trip," whispered Kathy in return, her eyes bright from all those éclairs, as she ran out to get her bathing suit.

2

The next morning when the twins and Timothy and their deck of cards entered, Becky inquired: "Do you think you can remember your Gin Rummy?"

"I thought we'd take a trip to England today," Mommygran offered hastily, as they settled over her bed, and when they said, "Fine" she asked: "Are you all down the gangplank? Count the luggage. Every suitcase present? We'll go up to London and first, of course, we'll visit Westminster Abbey. It will take your breath away. Those churches of the Middle Ages——how was it possible to build them? Those lofty ceilings, those great arches——no derricks or cranes or bulldozers, so much for our modern technology. And here you'll find the graves of Britain's greatest——kings, generals, worn stones in the floor inscribed 1300 A.D., maybe, —— poets, there's a poets' corner, you'll find Kipling, Browning, ——"

"Albert is buried there," said Tim. "Only he came alive again."

That was how Albert joined them.

Mommygran's eyebrow lifted, but the twins accepted him. "Albert is Timmy's friend. Sometimes he died, and sometimes he's living now."

"King Albert," Tim stated.

"King Alfred, you mean," said Mommygran. "Reigned from about the year 800 to ——"

"No. Albert. A different king, a friend from one of my incarnations a thousand years ago. Once he was a janitor, but being lazy he was demoted to king. He can be a pest. If he hears we're traveling in England, he'll insist on coming with us. He was at the bookstalls in Paris yesterday."

"Let him come." Becky was a tireless tourist. "Where else shall we go?"

"To see the guards change at Buckingham Palace. To see Big Ben, an immense clock high up in a tower of Parliament. To the Tower of London. That was used as a prison hundreds of years ago. Also you'll see the famous crown jewels there, rubies, emeralds. Some of Henry the Eighth's wives were beheaded in the Tower."

"He had six wives," Becky interposed. "One of my projects on the trip will be to memorize their names and how each died."

"Wham." Tim drew fingers across his throat.

Mommygran sighed. "You're better sightseers than I am. We'd do well to find a pub. Not much chance of patisserie but I'll have a mug of ale and you'll each have half a mug. That is, if you drank up your milk at breakfast. We'll go on to Madame Tussaud's waxworks where there are wax figures of historical characters, and on to Hyde Park where, if it's Sunday, we shall listen to people who stand on boxes, make speeches on all sorts of subjects."

Kathy's chest heaved. "Shall we like London or Paris better?"

Timothy said: "Albert took a trip to China. Mao invited him to dinner. But when he got to the table, Mao ate him. Only Albert got out through the earth and was next seen in South America. I can't prevent him even if I wanted to, from coming along on this trip. That's Albert for you."

"Well!" said Mommygran in consternation. "What a game this is. Do you really want to take this trip, today?"

"Of course!" they cried in unison. "Please go on!"

"In that case we shall be off on a boat ride up the Thames and see Hampton Court. It's a castle."

Nobody was ready when Mother knocked at the door. "Swim time?" She was a cheery mother.

"Yes, dear," Mommygran murmured, and in a lower tone: "We might travel to Italy tomorrow."

"Why do They always interrupt us so early?" said Kathy.

"My plan," Becky muttered, "is to send Them off on an errand tomorrow morning so we'll have more time to travel. Like asking Them to go to the store for watermelon. It's my plot. We haven't had watermelon for three days. They're very nice. They'd probably do it."

3

The next morning, instead of bringing a deck of cards to Mommygran's room, the young people entered waving paper and pencils. "We'd better start making a list of things to pack," Becky began. They all looked thoughtful. "Four toothbrushes. I guess we'd better each have one."

"Five, then," said Timothy. "Drat him!"

"But one tube of toothpaste should do among us all, shouldn't it?" Becky added: "And one deck of cards."

They thought some more. "And a Bible," suggested Kathy.

"Cameras." That one was Becky's idea. "Three diaries. A passport."

"Clothes?" asked Mommygran tentatively.

"Um. Clothes." Kathy wrote this down.

"Pads of paper so we can write a book about our adventures," said Tim. "It might win the Newberry Prize. That will pay for my college education. One thing to remember about our book is that it should be likeable."

Kathy was practical. "We've got to remember to have a publisher."

"My publisher might be interested," said Mommygran breezily. She was an author. "Exactly! You are right. Books should be likeable and have a publisher."

"Oh, I love to take part in things!" exclaimed Timmy. "To be part of them, like this! Things real and imaginary at the same time."

4

The real things went on at the same time as their travels. Across the dunes where marsh grasses bent with the winds and scrub pines rooted in sand, there were beach plums to be gathered. Walk a bit farther around a corner, a promontory, and at high tide a deserted flat island could be seen half a mile off; at low tide you could wade this distance through shallow water and the island became simply a long sand bar, a rise in the ocean floor, a private strip to be boarded for adventure, watching out for jelly fish, your slacks rolled up. You stooped to collect shells, mostly scallops and razor clams. You went clamming, carrying a pail and digging deep with a rake, ripples of the bay wet the rolled-up slacks or bottoms of your shorts, but Father wore hip boots. If you walked in the opposite direction beyond the fishing wharf on which wire lobster baskets were ranged, you came to the bay where great boulders were heaped to form a jetty upon which you could run to the tippy tip, jumping over deep clefts or wobbly rocks, shouldering your fishing rod. Among bottom stones of the breakwater, small pools were left by outgoing tides; climb down and you could play in the tiniest pools, finding a world there, barnacles clinging to stones and little hermit crabs scuttling sideways.

Yet even among these occupations whispers were exchanged about Henry the Eighth's wives and Marie Antoinette's palace. Each day was glorious, of course, the children could scarcely wait to wake up and begin, they could scarcely wait to leap out of bed and rush into each day, the sky blue, the ocean blue-green-purple, the sun bright, the scrub pines smelling hot piney, the surf to shout in, the bay to swim in, every minute brimming over with freedom. All the same Tim, swishing a stick at the littlest of fish about one inch long, in a pool that was a miniature basin of marine life, doing it gently because he believed everything had a right to live, said he was merely pretending to slice off Marie Antoinette's head. Becky referred to clam chowder as almost as good as an aperitif at a cafe on the Champs Elysées. Kathy, slapping together a sand fort, claimed that this was how Westminster Abbey was built, the Abbey was her model. Tim said Albert had rented an apartment in Hampton Court and could be seen wearing Bermuda shorts, a dinner jacket, bedroom slippers and a raincoat made of doughnut holes so the rain could get through. It was all beautiful except that the time flew too quickly.

"I can scarcely believe that this wonderland is almost over," said Kathy, and Timothy, gazing into his pool, said: "All life is a circle."

Despite every moment of pleasure on the beach, they waited impatiently for the next morning and the trip to Europe in Mommygran's room.

5

After several more trips in perfect weather, one morning dawned gray and cold. When fog rolls in at the seashore a frame cottage on the beach becomes damp: doors swell and will not close, walls feel sticky, yesterday's bathing suits have not dried, salt forms lumps, refusing to sprinkle, bread is soggy, varnish smells like varnish. People smell a bit like varnish too, dank, and their hair flops. Outside of the window, impatient iron mountains crash in from the ocean, the highest tide of the season washing over silvery buttons of bayberry bushes, running almost up to the path before each wave sinks forever into sand to be superseded quickly by the next. Where does all that water go after it sinks into sand? Boom, roared the waves, Boom!

Mommygran watched the dark sea. "Summer is ending. How fast summer flies." She opened her arms holding all three children at once in a giant hug.

The young people looked troubled. A problem had appeared with the change of weather. School would start soon. How could one take a trip to Europe and at the same time go back to school, take piano lessons, belong to the Brownies or Scouts, try out for the baseball team, in fact return home to Arizona while Mommygran returned to New York, say Goodbye to vacation ——how was the problem of Time to be solved? Tim thought that if only a time-machine existed one could grasp the past and the future. However, man still had to invent a time-machine. A time-machine, he believed, could correct history. The twins reminded him that the day had come when it was necessary to face the present, to think seriously about arrangements for their trip. There were things to be decided.

"The first thing to decide is what to decide," said Tim.

An atmosphere of depression filled the room, a large empty sense of the Impossible loomed. Rain drummed on the roof. Mommygran turned on all of the lights. The room took on a cheerier appearance. Although she always joined the picnic lunch at the beach and dinner in the family cottage, she had utensils for her own breakfast, all manner of plug-in pots; now she brewed a pot of cocoa. She produced a box of peppermints. People in the little room began smiling.

Becky said: "This trip must be secret. That's the first decision. It's secret from anyone except us in this room."

"Now then," said Kathy, "We'll have to plan how to get to you so They won't suspect. How are we going to get Them to let us come? There will be so many obstacles."

Mommygran said: "Next summer we shall all take a holiday together again. We can go on with our game then."

Kathy shook her head. "You don't know Them if you think it's that easy. How can we overcome all the obstacles? First of all, They'll never let us go abroad with you. They'll say you couldn't handle us. Second of all, They may not even let us come to visit you some year. Uncle Thin thinks the time is coming when you ought to move nearer to us, to be handy in case you can't take care of yourself."

"Does he really?"

"Um. But Auntie Fat, you know, she just presses her lips together. She talked about growing old gracefully. Father said that you were, just in your own way."

"My dear son," said Mommygran fervently. "I can count on his good sense."

"We have to plot." When Becky worried, tears filled her

eyes. She was really worried now. Becky took favorably to conspiracies. "Don't let's joke about this, it takes plotting. However are we going to get to you, and even more, how are we going to get on the ship? Kathy's right, there are just so many obstacles."

"Not for King Albert," said Timmy. "He says the impossible is always possible. That's a good motto." However, he waved Albert out of the room. "Shoo!" he said, so that Mommygran should not be bothered.

"That was thoughtful of you," said Mommygran. "I'm quite used to him. He is always welcome. It is hard to believe that we shall all not see each other for quite a while. We must write to each other often."

"I have it!" cried Becky. "We must write in a code so we can work out this trip in secret and make plans!"

"Oh, I have it too!" Kathy interrupted. "Yes, a code! Every third word will count. Two words between will be gibberish. Like if you want to write The Trip, you could say The piano dog trip. See? Piano dog won't count. Just the and trip. Or, for We are coming, we write We arithmetic ugh are tooth roses coming. That way, if They happen to see one of our letters, They'll never even guess."

"Now all you have to do is figure how to get us to you," said Becky. "The trip should happen next summer and should last about a month, don't you think? Once we are with you, the rest is easy. We simply get on the boat. You'd better buy tickets ahead of time."

Mommygran laughed. "My darlings! What a fairy tale. But your parents will worry if you just vanish. That's how parents are. Don't you think we'd better let them in on our game? After all, they are our closest relatives. We really ought to tell them."

"Definitely not," said Kathy. "It simply wouldn't work. They'd say what madness! They'd come between us."

"But when we get on the ship we can send them a wire," said

Becky kindly. "We shall telegraph: 'Goodbye, see you next month.' "

CHAPTER II

Homecoming contains pleasures often forgotten during vacation. Hello Autumn, changing color, turning brisk, tasting of sappy apples, sweet sun-warmed grapes, juicy pears. If you live in Arizona, hello orange groves, prickly cactus, chains of brown primeval mountains ringing the desert like roaming hordes of dinosaurs. Hello my dear dog, Happy. How did you like living in a kennel? Hello pussycat, Boots. Hello neighbors. Hello my room, my toys, there you are! I had forgotten you. Like New Year's Day or birthdays, homecoming is a time when people are apt to make resolutions for the year ahead: I shall keep my desk clear for school work this season, and not mix compositions or arithmetic papers with bug collections, shell collections, stamp collections, fossil collections, free sample collections, post card collections, dried leaf collections, matchbox collections, decks of cards or bags of candy. I shall keep my dolls one year more. I shall train Albert to look respectable, that rascal has grown half a mustache, one side only, and I shall find out about Einstein because he was a genius who understood the fourth dimension and maybe the fifth which could be Time, but my mind isn't big enough to grasp that. I shall try to make new friends and I'd like to have one good especial friend but not the rough red-haired boy across the street. I shall write to Mommygran who gave us stamped envelopes for letters to her. I shall figure out some way to get to MG at the end of this school year, I simply must, because the trip to Europe would be!!!! I never even dreamed of such a thing before, yet now I dream it all the time. Taking MG along with us would be fun because she's fun and very sensible and such an interesting conversationalist, and besides it would be so educational. Only how are we going to manage it, how can we persuade Them? Is

MG going to be able to arrange it? The first letters from the twins and Timothy to Mommygran all said pretty much the same thing and were full of thoughtful offers: if we can help you don't hesitate to tell us what we can do, no matter how slight.

There were variations in the letters naturally. Becky, who had recently determined to become an actress, stuck dramatically to the code of two gibberish words between the words that counted, regardless of how difficult it was to compose or decipher: Dear dentist pie Mommygran, I pub beer think June steamer of ha ha our ballet class plot thank you night and day. She did wear out toward the end of a sentence but at places that would not give away secrets. Kathy was practical: Here is a list of possible ways to get to you. 1. Run away. (Subhead 1A—We could hitch hike to you. Subhead 1B—We could stow away in a plane. Subhead 1C—You should send us tickets in a sealed envelope marked Personal). 2. You invite us publicly, but not Them, to come to New York. You can say you have not quite enough money for all. When we reach New York, you kidnap us to the ship. 3. Hint and see how They take it. Say They must be worn out from having so many little darlings around. 4. Isn't it about time to be more definite? The year is passing. Timmy wrote: "My allowance has been raised from ten cents to a quarter. So now I can help pay for the trip."

Mommygran answered every single letter, often in code. What she wrote in reply amounted to this: "My *bon jour* dears: I'll *oui non* work gargoyle darling on yippee zowie a Buckingham Palace plan. I'll save my money for it. Be patient. A year is a long time." To which Timmy wrote back: "We trust you."

The letters were of course not entirely upon this most important subject. Everybody wrote things like: How are you? I am fine. What are you doing? Is it cold? I am busy. I have a cat I have a dog. I have a new friend. He has red hair and is not too rough, just nice, and lives across the street. Yet even these communications might be interspersed with sentences such as: My favorite subjects in school are geography and history. Guess why. One letter from Kathy ended merely in a big

When?? How?? Please!! whose meaning surely no parents could guess.

At first Mommygran stuck to the code. Then this tapered off. Careful not to betray their secret, she seldom mentioned it except for an occasional reference such as: Be patient! Another shrewd method of hers was to tell indirect stories of her past travels in her letters; even a mother straightening a child's desk in order to throw out stale crackers that attracted ants, if she happened to glance at a letter lying there would have no suspicion of a conspiracy. The letter might, for example, state that for some reason Mommygran had been thinking of Oxford today, a town of colleges, many of them very old, ivy-mantled, and of Stratford-on-Avon where Shakespeare was born, once she had seen a performance of a play named *Hamlet* there.

Tim answered that he was reading Lamb's *Tales from Shakespeare* and that Albert knew *Hamlet* well, he too had seen the play; so many characters were killed in it that when Ophelia died, Albert called "Two down, eight to go," so the usher put him out of the theatre.

Mommygran replied with a description of the lovely ride from London, glimpses of the Thames and Avon rivers, of gardens full of roses and roses and roses, of ancient peaceful villages, of honey-colored stone walls and stone cottages. Her description of the countryside might have come out of a book, it sounded so nice; it ended with a remark about having told quite a fairy story. By the use of the words fairy and story the children could be sure that she was one grown-up who could keep a secret.

So could they. They were good secret keepers. There was only once some slip that Mother must have caught, for she said: "If you're thinking of a trip with Mommygran, put that notion out of your heads. It's preposterous. We have other plans." This was worrisome. The children wrote four pages about it to Mommygran. Preposterous, they said, was the very word they had feared Mother might use.

There were occasions when Mommygran telephoned long

distance. She said she yearned to hear their voices and then the whole family got on the telephone, one after the other, even calling Uncle Thin, Mother's brother, from the house next door, to say: "Don't overdo." Aunt Fat popped over to ask: "How are you? Are you taking care of yourself? How is New York? I wouldn't mind a week there." "Oh, it's dirty," said Mommygran. Everybody chattered and laughed a lot, saying things like: "Tell me all the news." Mother said: "You sound very gay and active. Are you getting enough rest?" Father said: "This message will sure cost a lot." Mommygran said: "Oh, it's worth it. You sound lovely." Tim even told Mommygran, without giving away any secrets, that Albert had gone to England. Albert, he said, was in Parliament, an M. P., that meant Member of the Parliament, and Parliament, he informed her, was like our Congress, it made laws, it consisted of a House of Lords and a House of Commons, but Albert was a member of the House of Uncommons. Then Father got on the line again to say: "That's enough, Tim."

Becky cooked up a plot. She decided that there should be telephone messages not overheard by Them; therefore she wrote to Mommygran suggesting that Saturday nights were excellent for telephone calls since They were likely to go out; They often had engagements with friends Saturday nights. Kathy, who had a strong sense of honor, added that this would be perfectly honorable since it would leave the coast clear for intelligent conversation about you-know-what. But for weeks Mommygran did not telephone or even write as often as formerly and autumn slid into winter without a single actual step having been taken toward turning the children's dream into reality.

2

Autumn lay behind, winter reigned. Even in Phoenix, Arizona, the air turned cool, coats were worn, oranges and grapefruit and lemons ripened and hung on boughs like bright balls. Mommygran wrote of snow in New York and that maybe she might fly out for a quick visit and a spot of sun some time later. She had stopped mentioning a trip to Europe; one might think Europe had been wiped off the map. She seemed pointedly not to write in code or to answer the children's questions. She seemed very distant, and had lost the special qualities that make one person different from others, a better friend than another. It was rather as though her character had deteriorated. She did not sound like her old self, instead she asked: "Does your adorable kumquat tree have ripe fruit?" Tim painted a picture of a compact small green kumquat tree dangling orange dots which he sent her, and she responded with two lines of a poem for him to go on with: What could be merrier than a kumquat tree/Small fruit bells in a cage of leaves— The children began to increase their letters and their questions to her: what was she doing anyway, why wasn't she getting on with their arrangements? Should they take matters into their own hands? As their letters became more urgent hers seemed to taper off. She seemed like a different person, any person. She sent postcards. "Darlings—Am awfully busy. Shall write more soon. Hope you are fine. Loads of love."

It was difficult. Grown-ups, whoever they were, could be very discouraging and undependable. The twins and Tim decided to write a severe joint letter. They said: "You promised. Of course we love you, but how about?" Then on the following Saturday night Mommygran phoned to them.

She said she had made a discovery.

Their parents were out. For a minute everybody seemed to hug happily one after another over the telephone. Then Mommygran's voice became hesitant, rather odd. "You know," she said, "That game we invented together last summer at the beach. You remember?" It was Kathy she was talking to, with Becky pushing close enough to hear also.

"MG!" cried Kathy, "Of course! What do you take us for? What *game?*"

"*The* game," said Mommygran brightly. "Now I want you to remember how we played it as a change from Gin Rummy. We had a lot of fun playing it, didn't we?"

Tim looked at his sisters' faces. He said: "I'm going to the other phone in the kitchen, the extension phone, so I can be in on this." When he got there all four could listen and talk together. "Albert, this isn't for your ears. Scat!" he said, so there were really four.

"You know," said Mommygran, "We always realized that this trip, or rather a real actual trip, would be a most difficult thing to bring about. So we must not be too disappointed if it doesn't happen. You are having a lovely year and next summer whatever you do you will have a lovely holiday. Don't you agree? So I thought we'd better talk it over realistically. Yes?"

Since the children were silent Mommygran went on: "By next summer maybe you won't even *want* to run off to Europe with me."

This time there were three gasps. Mommygran's voice was not at all like her natural voice, she sounded as though she thought she were an old-fashioned school marm at a blackboard, quite prissy. "How can I explain? I want you to realize the difference between reality and fantasy. Do you know what those words mean?"

Becky nodded. "Fantasy is like dreams, making pretend. Reality is reality."

"All right. Well! People all live somewhat in a make-believe world, yet at bottom they must distinguish between reality and fantasy. I've been thinking for some weeks about this game that we've played and that you must realize that it is something we invented together. Just for fun, yes? A lovely fantasy—to me a game is a game. But I—ahem!—I made the discovery that you might not realize that. You might not distinguish between reality and fantasy."

"Geniuses can make dreams come true," said Timmy. "I believe in that. Why not aim for it? It doesn't take magic. Once the airplane was a fantasy, I guess, but it sure isn't now. Or landing on the moon. You wouldn't say our game is more a fantasy than landing on the moon. Albert believes it simply took persistence. That's all."

Mommygran said: "I've had a great time playing with you all this time. This has been a very good game that we can play again and again. Imaginations can keep us richly supplied all of our lives. We can do more in imagination than we can ever do in fact. So I've been thinking, you see. You *do* see, don't you?"

After a minute Kathy asked: "See what?"

"That not all of one's dreams come true. I thought I'd better point that out to you."

"We knew that," said Tim. "Just what is your idea of reality?"

"Not a gray-haired mad woman of a ripe age leading a covey of children up a gangplank to Europe, like a duck with fluffy ducklings trailing behind."

"Not so fluffy," Kathy corrected, "And not all that gray-haired. You should try for more. You act like an aunt instead of a grandmother. *That* fulfillment is still ahead of you."

"I'm afraid you aren't seeing from my point of view."

"No," replied Becky, "We aren't."

"Albert points out *you* aren't seeing from *our* point of view."

"Oh," protested Mommygran, "I always felt that perhaps I could see things your way."

"Albert says you can when you want to. That's the nice thing about you."

"Of course it would be a glorious adventure, I admit that, I can't imagine anything more wonderful. There we'd be, whisked away as though on a magic carpet from all familiar routines, set down in new lands for a little while, just us, carefree as birds, seeing strange sights, laughing together all day long, having a tremendous adventure, I agree it would be perfect—if it were not next to impossible—but you haven't realized there are a lot of obstacles to this game."

"There always were," said Kathy.

"Next to impossible is not impossible," said Tim.

"I mean that in real life there are obstacles."

"There always are," said Becky.

Tim remarked: "One can try to make good dreams come true."

"Do you really believe one can?" asked Mommygran. "But still, we must remember not to feel too much disappointed when things do not turn out as planned. That's life. One enjoys a game for the sake of playing it, not necessarily to win."

"Albert believes you should try a moon man's point of view or a bug's, bugs may have knowledge that we aren't aware of, you should not just look out from your own rut."

"To me this has been a perfectly lovely game. A game, darlings! When I made the discovery that you saw it differently I had to warn you, you see."

Kathy said: "How many dresses should we take? I have a gorgeous new red skirt to wear in London."

Becky said: "It's like a miracle. It's not every child who plans to run away with a grandmother."

Tim said: "Even if we don't take a trip the main thing is to be together."

Mommygran said: "Oh dear me." Then she said: "Dear you and you and you." Then she said: "I'm hooked."

CHAPTER III

THE OBSTACLES

From this time onward Mommygran was her good old self again, only more so. Gone were her postcards containing dull news such as that the weather was cold and her how-is-school telephone calls. Now between the lines of her letters, as well as in her long-distance voice, it was clear to Kathy, Becky and Timmy that she was once more one of them. She had a purpose. She saw that one could believe in things that weren't just plain every day things, and she saw that one could work for them. She had a mission. Her mind was fixed upon a goal. She sounded as though she had to persuade the twins and Timmy of the importance of their idea, presenting arguments in favor of it as firmly as though they must be convinced. In fact the discovery that she had made, she said, had acquired a new form. It was not any longer that she had discovered that the children had taken her seriously or that she had not properly understood them, although this was true also; she discovered an eagerness in herself that was as urgent as theirs.

Letters now whizzed back and forth from east to west. The postoffice sold a lot of stamps. Mommygran became businesslike. She discouraged ideas of hitch-hiking or stowing away in planes to New York or boarding ships secretly for Europe, announcing that more practical methods of managing adventure must be found.

"But," Kathy asked her twin, "would it really be running away if it's with a grandmother?"

"Why not?" Becky replied. "Especially if it's done in the dead of night."

Their brother added: "Once They went on a trip and left us with Aunt Fat and Uncle Thin. Why can't we leave Them if They left us?"

"True," Becky agreed. "It's only fair. I'd like to try running away. Just for a little time."

Kathy said: "It's not only Europe that makes it like a dream. It's the idea of being on my own. Going off on my own."

Timmy said: "And with Mommygran. We don't see her enough."

The twins agreed. "Grandmothers are not as strict as They are. We can love Them and still want to run away."

Once more Mommygran took to writing in code: "If great guns we ping pong can eclairs tea do please pray this, dear friends, it Marie Antoinette will heads guillotine be crown jewels something roses roses we Shakespeare Thames shall

Albert's mustache never red skirt forget. It would be magic."
She informed Kathy, Becky and Timmy that a few weeks in a
foreign land could teach them as much as a whole year at school,
and that when people see with their own eyes this could mean
more than one hundred lessons out of books. The delight of
seeing for themselves, the delight, she kept repeating—delight
was one of her favorite words—the delight in the wideness of
the world, was the thing she was anxious to give them,—not a
map of France or a photograph of Notre Dame or a page about
Westminster Abbey, but a sight, a smell, a touch of the delight
of reality, for this was reality, wasn't it, the real thing?

She said every day would be like a holiday, they would wear
their best clothes and go to restaurants, and she went so far as to
include Albert in this, warning that he must not spill soup on
his dinner jacket, she couldn't be sending it to the cleaner every
day. If Albert had to spill, he would have to do it on his raincoat
made of doughnut holes so that the soup could leak through to
his skin and not spot his clothes. When the twins rolled with
laughter because she had adopted Albert, it was like a forecast
of all the laughter ahead, a trip full of laughter. She thanked the
children because they would be giving her a gift by coming with
her—*if* they did!—and because they had taught her that a
dream could sometimes come true—*if* it did!—Only the question remained, how were they going to bring it about?

Winter drifted into spring. The cactus flowered in Arizona,
orange crops were picked, sunshine became hotter. Seasons slip
into one another; time passes without recall; people wish that
they had done some of the things they never got around to. The
same regular things kept happening in Arizona, but in New
York Mommygran investigated steamships. She consulted a
travel agent. She wrote down names of the places that must not
be missed. She bought a new suitcase. She reserved rooms in
hotels. The only thing that she didn't do was to inform the
children's parents. The more delightful the trip became the
more she feared the obstacles that They would raise. The

more she worried about how best to bring up the subject, the more convinced she became that They would never permit it.

During a Saturday night telephone conspiracy when They were out having dinner with friends, the children and Mommygran listed obstacles that They would raise and they tried to meet these by giving unanswerable answers. Obstacle 1. Preposterous. Answer 1. Why preposterous? Obstacle 2. MG is too old. Albert supplied Answer 2 to this: he reminded them that he was a thousand years old and he hoped Mommygran would also reach that ripe age; by this measure she was still quite young; anyhow still whole. Obstacle 3. Take only one child. We can't let you have all. What shall we do without any? Answer 3. All or none! You can have a nice rest. Obstacle 4. MG, we are proud that we have responsible children, but are *you* a responsible person to lead an expedition? Answer 4. Yes, I am. Obstacle 5. Suppose somebody gets sick. Answer 5. Call a doctor. There must be a doctor in Europe.

However these unanswerable answers supplied little confidence of success. Everybody admitted that parents possess the final power, and if they happen to be sensible parents it can be a job to argue with them. The more sensible they are the more obstacles may be expected. They could be as hard to handle as ogres. There might be nothing left to do but to run away from them. Timmy had a particular problem all his own. Mother said to him suspiciously: "Listen, have you a secret from me?" Tim felt bad because he answered No. It was a lie. He worried because he had lied to his mother, and he wrote to Mommygran telling her this. Albert, he said, claimed that it was just a white lie but Albert had a deplorable character. So what did Mommygran think that Tim should do, please?

The moment that she read this letter, Mommygran decided that something must be done. They could not stand the uncertainty any longer. She flew to Arizona to pay a surprise visit.

A surprise visit! The parents and Uncle Thin and Auntie Fat

were certainly surprised, much more than the children were. The parents were overjoyed, the children were anxious. Auntie Fat helped Mother prepare a large dinner in a hurry: cream of pea soup (Tim's favorite), roast beef (Kathy's favorite), mashed potatoes (Becky's favorite), carrots (nobody's greatest favorite), tomato and lettuce salad (everybody liked that), and caramel custard (Father's favorite). People kissed and talked and showed off the weather and a new chair. "I'm so glad to be here with you!" exclaimed Mommygran wiping her eyes.

Becky burst into tears. "That's a sign of how happy I am," she apologized. "I always cry when I'm happy. I can't help it."

Timmy who had become interested in baseball, time tables, and maps pulled Mommygran to the back porch where his bike, scooter, bat, and kite were parked. Not only was he bigger this season, but his toys had become bigger too. "I got an atlas for my birthday," he informed Mommygran. "I can name all the rivers in Russia. I'm specializing in Russian rivers."

"Russia!" whispered Mommygran, astonished. "Is that on our tour too?"

Kathy ran from the table and reappeared in her new red skirt. She and Mommygran looked smilingly at each other. "MG," she said, "have you noticed how sometimes you and I automatically think the same thing at the same moment?"

Timmy said: "It's hard to give away our thoughts. We can *think* anything but we can't always say it. Albert was once that old Chinese philosopher—do you know his work?—the one who described ideas. He said in a million years we'd still be looking for perfection. A Chinese philosopher said that but I thought of it previously too."

"That's enough, Timothy," said Father.

"I see," said Mommygran.

"One of the things I like about you is the way you say 'I see,'" commented Tim.

"Oh," exclaimed Mommygran blushing with pleasure, "I see."

Everybody laughed at her. Tim explained kindly and clearly: "The thing is that we can say Uh huh to each other."

"You see," said Mother fondly, "they really love you."

"Oh yes," said the twins. At this they winked at Mommygran encouragingly, and then choked with laughter.

Tim added a helpful thought. "You are all your past experience. Old people can be as gay as children because they have all that past gaiety of being children in them. Who knows, maybe there's reincarnation."

"Preposterous notion, Sonny," said Uncle Thin. "You mustn't fall for every theory."

"Bedtime," said Mother.

"No!" said the twins. They said No every night at eight-thirty o'clock.

"Mommygran must be very, very tired from her journey. We want to take good care of her. She needs her rest," said Auntie Fat.

"She certainly does. Enough sleep is most important," said Uncle Thin. "Dear Mommygran, you're not as young as you used to be."

"I don't know about that," said Father. "In some ways, younger."

"Just don't overdo," said Uncle Thin.

"Nor underdo," said Timmy.

As Kathy and Becky and Timmy kissed Mommygran good-night, each one whispered in her ear: "Are you going to try?" "Good luck! Oh gosh!" "Don't get scared!" Mommygran looked shaky. Becky returned for one more kiss and to whisper: "It's a crisis."

After the children were tucked into bed and Uncle Thin and Aunt Fat had gone home, Mommygran at last sat alone facing Them, forgetful that she must be very, very tired and that enough sleep is most important and that she wasn't as young as she used to be. Father sharpened four pencils, Mother darned

Father's socks, Mommygran cleared her throat. "I am here on a mission," she began. "I am going to tell you a story."

The parents looked curious. Mommygran paused, then began again: "Did you ever want to run away?"

"Which of us?" Mother asked. "From which?"

"Did we what?" Father asked.

Mommygran shook her head, floundering around for a better beginning. Suddenly it seemed to come. She leaned back in her chair, smiled reminiscently, and said: "It all started almost a year ago. Last summer at the seashore the children and I invented a game. I was stupid at Gin Rummy, you see, they couldn't teach me, and so instead every morning when they came to keep me company while I had breakfast we played that—"

Sometimes Mommygran interrupted her story by saying: "And so we wondered——" or "And so they decided——" or "And so it is really they who should get the credit——". Another time she said: "You may think that it sounds a bit crazy, I realize, for somebody to sail off with a covey of your children——" to which Father replied: "Crazy. Pure madness. You never did have a narrow imagination, my dear." To which Mommygran answered: "Lots of crazy things are good things when you think them over," adding: "If you just go ahead and tackle them, they may not be crazy any more," and then very cheerfully, hinting hard: "It sounds like a fairy tale, doesn't it? Everybody loves a fairy tale." She also said: "And so what do you think about it?"

Toward the end, Mommygran said: "The children thought we ought to tell you about it in advance."

"Well, I should hope so," Mother murmured.

Finally Mommygran finished. The parents were looking very serious. They looked at Mommygran in a puzzled way. Mommygran suddenly looked frightened. "What do you think?" she asked.

Father said: "You'd better let us talk it over alone with each other. We shall have to consider this overnight."

Mommygran said: "The children are waiting for your verdict."

Mother said: "It's really quite a preposterous notion, you'll admit."

"Preposterous," Mommygran mused, "but isn't that all the more delightful?"

Breakfast the next day was a subdued, rather quiet, meal. The family seemed to concentrate on their plates as though they had never before seen oatmeal or as though an egg made them uneasy and nervous. Whenever the twins glanced up at Mommygran it was in a mute, waiting way like dogs. Waiting, in fact, described the general mood. Timmy spilled milk and Mommygran spilled orange juice. The cat scratched the atlas that Timmy had carried in as a reminder, and had to be scolded. The children rushed off to school as soon as possible, unable to bear another minute of suspense, almost forgetting their lunch boxes in which Mother had packed peanut butter and cheese sandwiches and left-over roast beef and bananas; however, she was absent-minded about remembering cookies. Father said he had to dash to the office, no time for anything now, he would see them all tonight. Tonight, he repeated with what seemed like unnecessary sternness. Uncle Thin and Aunt Fat came over from next door, the coffee scarcely dry on their lips, Uncle Thin hurried after Father to the office. The women talked of this and that, which never makes very interesting conversation. Mommygran had become silent. Then Mother and Aunt Fat went to the kitchen and talked in low voices while Mommygran took a walk.

The day passed somehow in this manner, with comings and goings. School people returned from school, Father returned early from work. He talked to Mother behind the closed door of their room, came out with a solemn expression on his face. When the twins and Tim made signs to Mommygran she shook her head to show that she was in the dark as much as they, with no news yet, no result, no verdict; she shrugged her shoulders in a gesture of helpless resignation to them.

Retreating to the yard, Kathy whispered: "It looks bad. He is putting it off."

Becky whispered: "He looks guilty."

Tim whispered: "Who could be so wicked?"

Becky whispered: "Our own parents! You never know."

Kathy whispered: "We have a problem with Them. They don't realize we are growing up."

At last Father clapped his hands, announcing that there was to be a conference. He told everyone to draw up chairs in a ring. He seldom called conferences, which he called Good and Welfare Meetings, except for extraordinary occasions; every one could tell by the way he hemmed and hawed and coughed that he was hunting for a way to break the news. The twins and Tim pulled their chairs close together. Mommygran sat bolt upright. She passed a box of peppermints around as though sucking peppermints might relieve everybody's feelings. Then Father spoke.

"Children, your mother and I have heard that you have kept a secret from us for many months. It isn't a surprise to you to hear that your grandmother has invited you to go on a trip all the way to Europe with her but it certainly came as a surprise to us. A complete surprise. So you've got to understand our point of view."

All around the room breath was drawn in. The sound of it could be heard. Father continued: "Uncle Thin puts it this way and it describes some of our feelings: he points out that it is a preposterous idea to burden Mommygran ——"

"Burden!" shrieked three voices. "We wouldn't be a burden," and Kathy shouted: "We'd keep her company. We'd love to. I shall wash Timmy's socks."

"And," Father went on, "that Mommygran isn't —— well —— as young as she used to be. But your mother and I have been talking it over and we have decided ——"

"What?" yelled Kathy and Becky and Timmy.

"That we believe everybody doesn't have to be that young. And so we hope that you will want to go because a trip like this would be a wonderful opportunity for you."

"You did it!" screamed the twins and Tim and rushed at Mommygran, almost knocking her down.

"*You* did it," cried Mommygran, blinking and laughing. "I can scarcely believe it."

"Why not?" Mother asked. "How could anyone fail to see ——"

"What?" they chorused.

"That it's such a wonderful opportunity."

CHAPTER IV

When they recovered from their shock it was as though they had been lifted up by a magic carpet and put down in a new place. Everything was now changed. There was no more game. There were no more Theys. There was no more pretend. Everybody believed. They could barely believe that now they were really believing. Behind them was a fairy tale which had led them to the wrong conclusion. Like all fairy tales it had been made of the waving of a wand and of wings and of enchanted lands and sometimes of imaginary ogres and of disbelief. Now the fact was made of stuff as solid as today and it was made of the most unexpected parents, the most marvellous parents, who saw things in the natural proper right way.

A whirl of activity set in. Mommygran flew back to New York to make arrangements, to say Okay to a real ship, the *S. S. France*, and real cabins and real dates and places and tickets. All the same some long ago experience that sometimes filled her eyes or some grown-up caution in her felt called upon to issue warnings such as: "But we must not set our hearts too, too much in life! Do you know the old saying, 'There's many a slip 'twixt the cup and the lip'?" It was as though she herself were creating Obstacle 6, acting as though the adventure might still not work out and preparing Kathy, Becky and Timmy not to be too broken-hearted if things went wrong. "Anything can happen!" she reminded them and herself.

"What could possibly go wrong?" cried Father. "It is all almost too good to be true." He got passports for the children since these have to be carried in a foreign country so that each traveler can be identified as a United States citizen, and the passports needed little photographs pasted on them, so the whole family trooped to a photographer who took three pictures saying "Smile!" Vaccinations came next so the family trooped to their Doctor Spick who put three smears of serum on three arms saying: "It won't hurt." Then Uncle Thin made a suggestion. "They'd better have typhoid inoculations. Maybe the water won't be pure everywhere."

"We shall be drinking wine," said Becky. This turned out to be the worst thing to say, for Uncle Thin exclaimed: "Wine! Whoever said you could have wine at your age!"

"Booby!" whispered Kathy to her twin.

"Another crisis," groaned Tim.

Mother and Father laughed and said: "Just a little wine. Water and milk, too." But they trooped back to Doctor Spick.

"It's terrible," said Timmy. "The state of the world. The doctors are on strike because they refuse to inoculate Albert. Children are on strike because the doctors are on strike and won't make them well. Parents are on strike because the children are drinking wine instead of impure water. And the banks are on strike because when the parents strike nobody is earning money. It all comes back to Albert."

Nobody likes shots even though the prick of the hypodermic needle lasts only for a minute, but Kathy, Becky and Timmy stuck out their arms bravely because they wanted to do everything right for Europe.

They were to sail in four weeks from Wednesday. On the

Wednesday four weeks before the date of sailing, Kathy came home from school with a sore throat. She had fever. Her head hurt. She had red speckles on her chest. Dr. Spick examined her and gave her medicine and a lollypop. He ordered her to bed. "It is chicken pox," he said. "It will last about ten days. But we must also count the time for the others to catch it. That can take twelve days to nearly three weeks, which is called the incubation period. Then the one next to catch it has to stay home for another ten days to get well. Then it may take another nearly three weeks for the third to catch it from the second and come down with it. Then that one has to stay laid up for another ten days."

When Becky and Timmy heard this they cried. Kathy didn't cry because she didn't hear it because she was tight asleep in a room by herself, having been given ice cream and a pill. She had been feeling so sick that she didn't even think about Europe. Becky and Tim added up nearly three weeks and nearly three weeks for catching it for each of them, plus ten days and ten days for having it, and it came to a lot of time. It came to much more than four weeks from Wednesday. It came to almost the whole holiday. It came to a lot more than the time when their ship, the *S. S. France,* was to sail.

Nobody wanted to break the news to Mommygran in New York. Father said: "She'll be so disappointed! It was such a preposterously great plan. This is very bad news. *You* tell her, Mother."

Mother said: "Oh dear, she's been so worried because there's many a slip 'twixt the cup and the lip. It will be very bad news for her. No, *you* tell her, Father. Tell her gently."

Becky said: "Boo hoo, Poor Mommygran. I bet she'll cry too."

Tim said: "Boo hoo. Somebody has to tell her the bad news."

So Father put him on the telephone and Tim said: "There's many a slip 'twixt the ship and the trip."

It was as kind a way as any of breaking the bad news.

Kathy felt miserable all that night. She hurt and itched. Mother said: "Oh dear. It is so sad to see her miserable. It is sad when somebody is sick." Father said: "It is preposterous that they must miss this lovely experience. I wanted the trip for the children more than anyone did. They will be missing a great opportunity." Becky and Timmy clung together as though their loss made them feel very close to each other. "I'd have washed your socks for you every night, Timmy," said Becky. "I'd have reminded you to pack your tooth brush whenever we moved to a new place."

"Thank you, Becky," said Tim. "I'd have lent you Albert."

"Thank you, Timmy," said Becky.

"I can't imagine how Albert will take it, Becky. Be kind to him. At present he is living with a walrus in a castle in Iceland, but his heart was set on the Tower of London where some of his wives perished. He's in good company there, King Henry the Eighth. Henry did a lot for England, he started it on its way as a modern country, but his married life was deplorable."

They talked about some of the things in England that Mommygran had described to them and that they would miss. They discussed King Henry the Eighth and his six wives to comfort each other.

The next morning Kathy felt a lot better. She had a red rash on her arms and chest but nonetheless she felt better. She sat up in bed, isolated from the others in order to try to keep them from catching her chicken pox, and she played Gin Rummy with herself as though she were two people. But Becky woke up with a headache. Mother guessed it was probably from disappointment. By lunch time Becky's throat hurt. After lunch Tim developed a headache. By mid-afternoon, his throat hurt. Mother ran from room to room with the thermometer and orange juices. Before supper Becky and Timmy each had two red itchy speckles on their chests. Mother telephoned to Doctor Spick and asked him please to come over right away.

After supper Mother and Father telephoned to Mommygran. Father said: "We have the most wonderful news for you! *All* of the children are sick! Isn't that great?"

Mother said: "They all have chicken pox together! So now it will take only about ten days or so until they are all well. We don't have to wait for weeks and weeks to see who may catch it next and then give them still more time to recover. They are all very miserable right now. Hurrah!"

Father said: "If you sent back the tickets and got back your money, hurry up and get the tickets again. You can all go on the trip."

Mother said: "Everybody will get well together soon because everybody is sick together now. It's just great. All three of them are sick. And they're very happy about it."

Mommygran was overjoyed. "All three of them are sick! Poor darlings. That's just great!" she cried.

Four weeks from Wednesday actually came. Mommygran met the plane from Arizona at Kennedy Airport. She had her big suit case with her and she was wearing a new pink dress and carrying a new box of peppermints so that she could occasionally pop one into her mouth to contain her excitement. She was smack up in front of all the greeters who had come to meet the plane from Arizona. When Kathy and Becky and Timmy spotted her they ran forward beginning to laugh and knew that they were going to go right on laughing for one whole month. "Have a peppermint!" exclaimed Mommygran because there was really nothing else possibly to be said.

"Fellow spirit!" cried Kathy.

Baggage and all, they whisked down the highway crowded with cars to New York. In the city tall skyscrapers stared down at them with thousands of windows like eyes winking at four people who were beginning their sightseeing, who looked to the left, to the right, upward, upward, crying: "Oh look!" and laughing because they simply could not stop laughing. The city's maze of stony streets and crossings, of traffic, of red lights, green lights, shops, billboards, newspaper stands, theatres, markets, warehouses, apartment houses, brownstone dwellings, noise, dirt, pedestrians hurrying, seemed like a story-book setting, a picture passage for four travelers who felt that they themselves were part of a story. Through Central Park they went, its shady trees, lakes, playgrounds where there were slides and sand boxes and swings. When they rode between rows of run-down dark tenements, they saw boys and girls dangerously playing ball on the streets because there were no playgrounds in their neighborhoods nor other places in which to play. "We are so lucky," Becky sighed, "I wish they could have all this too, that we're having."

"Yes. I wish it," Mommygran agreed.

"I wish," said Kathy, "that they could all be as happy and lucky as we are."

"I do too. Some of them will, some day, but unfortunately not many. I guess people are lucky when they can open their worlds a little further, wherever they are."

Tim reflected. "Nobody would have guessed a month ago that we'd have such luck either. All of us will have our ups and downs. I intend to work to help the downs when I grow up, and not live like Albert."

Kathy inquired: "MG, were you always so happy?"

"No." She paused. "But I am now." She paused again. "When bad luck comes sometimes we have to accept it, but be sure, too, to welcome good luck when it comes. Now are we sure we are really here, four lucky people? Because we are arriving at the Hudson River and the dock!"

After a moment of gazing in the air, Timmy remembered to come down to earth. "Five people," he reminded them.

"You don't always have to invent, Tim," Becky murmured. "Some wonderful things are real."

They arrived at the dock. Other passengers also were arriving, baggage was being seized by porters and carried aboard, the porters were pushing and puffing with heavy loads. And there was the ship. The *S. S. France.*

From the dock against which it was roped and chained, the

only part of the ship to be seen was one huge white side like the flank of a white elephant. This was dotted with rows of portholes, the cabin windows. Levels of decks were visible, one above another, rising higher and higher, and above these, at the very top, funnels or chimneys from which smoke began to rise as the engines below were turned on for the ship to get ready to sail. Mommygran, Kathy, Becky and Tim stood in the line which moved forward as passengers, one by one, showed their passports in order to be allowed to board the ship. After their passports were inspected by an officer, they again moved forward following the line of people. And here was the gangplank.

Now sailors appeared or ran past, many of them chattering in French. The children's smiles seemed to grow wider every minute; it looked as if their faces would pretty soon not be large enough to hold their smiles. Kathy, Becky and Timmy all held hands and Tim reached for Mommygran's hand. There they stood, smiling and smiling at each other. "The game is coming true," whispered Kathy. "This minute."

At the foot of the gangplank, the shore end, a French officer waved them up. "*Bon jour, Madame,*" he said to Mommygran, bowing and beaming, because she beamed at him. "*Bon jour, mon petit,*" he said to Timmy, and patted his hair and beamed. "*Bon jour, chérie,*" he said to each of the twins, beaming at them too. "*Bon voyage.*"

"*Merci,*" said a voice pitched higher than Tim's normal voice. It practically squeaked with excitement. "That was Albert," he explained, laughing at himself. "He made it! He never talked before."

Then they marched up the gangplank.

At the top of the gangplank, the bridge between shore and ship, between home and sea and Europe, Mommygran turned and looked at the children who followed closely behind her. "One, two, three," she counted. "I feel like a duck with ducklings. Have I feathers?"

"Yes!" they shouted.

There were stewards and stewardesses in the corridors to

direct passengers to their cabins. A band was playing lively music. Kathy, Becky and Timmy rushed up to the outside deck so that they could watch the waving visitors who crowded the pier, watch the gangplanks being drawn up, watch the little tug boats which would help to pull the big *S. S. France* away from her moorings. There was a loud Boom from a funnel. The whole great ship quivered with movement.

The sun was setting in the western sky, making it golden and lighting up the good-by faces on the dock. Further out in the west, further than eyes could see from here, were Mother and Father ——no Theys, no Thems, but Mother and Father who wanted them to go on this adventure. Kathy, Becky and Tim were not exactly running away because this turned out to be much better.

For a minute as the ship inched away from shore, the twins gasped and cuddled close to Mommygran. "Another good part of going away is the coming back home," said Kathy.

Becky wiped her eyes. "I sort of miss them already, only we shall have so many stories to tell them when we get back."

Timmy said: "It's happening!"

Mommygran said: "You did it. It was all of you who did it."

The ship turned slowly in the Hudson River, backing away from the pier and now was pointing her nose toward the harbor. There was water ahead, water behind, water between the giant ship and the dock. The waving people lining the edge of the dock were looking smaller.

"I can't believe it. Here we are. I can't believe it!" said Mommygran.

"Neither can I!" cried Kathy, Becky and Timothy together. Then they all looked at each other and began laughing again in disbelief and belief and waving wildly at the waving vanishing people on the shore and Mommygran blew a kiss in the direction of the west. They all blew kisses. "Dreams can come true. Thank you! Good-by," she called. "See you next month."

The end.

13 A Good Death

"When you are young you hope for a good life. When you are old you hope for a good death."

Making a Will

Having decided to make a new will, after some years, and read the proposed draft drawn up by my best of lawyers, I have decided that a simple basic English course is what every law school needs. Nothing advanced—I have in mind an elementary course the purpose of which is simply to introduce the budding attorney to the sentence. For certainly the legal documents that we now have are designed maliciously to confuse the poor testator who thought he was merely leaving his estate to his children and after them to their children, that's all, with gifts to some charities, of course, and a keepsake or bequest to Mamie and Joe. The lawyer, however, has concepts larger than these; he examines your instructions, but his function is to save you taxes, and by thoroughly confounding you, your executors, your trustees, your beneficiaries and the law itself, to assist your ritual atonement by the labyrinthine guide-lines of his jealous mistress. The confusion of words is his tool. Listen to this: "22nd"(!) (There were 21 such before). "Wherever used herein, words importing singular shall include the plural, and vice versa, and words importing the masculine shall include the feminine and neuter," (Who's neuter?) "unless the context otherwise requires." How do lawyers get away with that? Any writer must envy such fine assumptions, such a broad claim as words-importing-one-thing-shall-mean-another; students taking college exams please note. And then of course there is "Anything herein-before to the contrary notwithstanding," which again is a handy bit of legerdemain. As for "per stirpes," I have no use for it. It sounds like something dermatological. Then, of course, if everybody dies, the stirpes and all, there must be provision for that money to go *somewhere*. Simple! You take a charity and say "In the event of"; this organization then acts as vulture taking care of bits and left-overs of carrion that stirpes had not utilized. By this time the head reels. One might as well have been reading Sanskrit. It is quite impossible to know if one's children have been included or one's wishes respected, or if the lawyer and tax bureau—nay! *federal* tax bureau, etc.—are off on a linguistic binge on which banks, trustees, executors, per capitas and per stirpes have lost the way. Next time I revise my will I'll ask Baedeker to write it and include maps.

Then there is the fact to be reckoned with that "The words 'pass' and 'have passed' wherever used shall have the same meaning as said words shall have under the provisions of the U.S. Internal Revenue Code applicable to my Estate." This puts a new light—I don't know what—on things. I ought to look up that Revenue Code maybe. But look what comes next: something about "Such legacy may be satisfied by distributing in cash or in kind or partly in cash and partly in kind"—see how much leeway somebody is getting! How cunningly words are manipulated to keep me from knowing what it is all about!— "And each item of property or interest in property so distributed in kind shall be valued at the date or"—(or again) "Dates of such distribution or at the value determined," . . . "Provided however that"—ah! another loophole!

Life is really too short to make a will.

Dream: She was ill. Her own M.D. away so went to Ernst Wolff (musician) also a doctor but she had no confidence in him. Then she was also examined in the basement of a department store by other strange doctors, none too good, including Ed Liss, psychiatrist. They all agreed she needed an operation. She went back—from Boston or Chicago—by train with Him who took care of her among the strange passengers. In New York she was examined again, saying how had this illness come upon her suddenly, she had been well before when last examined. Now she became depressed. The depression following her early manic courage. She faced the prospect of the operation, life or death. Said: "What is it that's wrong with me? I didn't even ask those others who examined me. Is it cancer?" "Call it what you will," they said, "It is really a fractured book."

All My Dear Dead

There were leopards blowing down the mountain,
I and the sky and the autumn
And the azure and the crimson;
It was a day for wonders.
There were tree crowns marching by the million
Prison walls suddenly tumbled
(I and my bleeding shadow)
Tag-ends of dreams were banished
Seraphim in branches thundered
(I carrying my loveload
I and my yesterdays)
When the whole gold presence blazed.

Then all my dear dead arose and vanished
They were free of my jailer heart,
A kite string strained I loosed it into sun-moted heaven . . .
They were gone, they belonged to themselves, at last we had
    parted:

Light as milkweed silk they blew on their separate ways
(It was a day for wonders)
In the harvest flame, through the translucent haze.

The poem and the novel may say the same thing yet in
profoundly different terms. In "All My Dear Dead," the key
line midway through is "Then all my dear dead arose and
vanished." When this line came to me I stood on an autumn
hilltop looking down at the brilliant tree crowns and suddenly a
sense of strange freedom and peace overcame me, of release
from the past and in relinquishment of a new kind of love. Later
other key lines added themselves "I and the sky and the
autumn," "I and my bleeding shadow." "I carrying my love
load" and "It was a day for wonders." Again a long novel would
be required to convey what a poem says in one page.

To be surrounded by the dead. The living dead. But this is
what happens as one ages. Here a letter turns up from Bob,
dead 20 years; I loved Bob! one thinks. And in it mention of
Ruth—I loved her too and she died even earlier.* Here is
Larchmont stationery—I was visiting there where I wrote this
Darling Bob note which he kept: mother's home—even the
house sold now, the well known paths would stop my feet if I
trod them, hearing echoes on the gravel, seeing forms that are
not there. Only dead feet are meant for these paths. Only dead
figures move here. But I am alive.

The aristocracy of emotion. Father, Mince, Mother, the
spirit of love. I have it too. And my children. And Linda . . .
The putting-in—and thus of course receiving. The core, the
essence that remains in the dying. Unflagging, no physical
weakness weakens the spirit of love and of giving. It took no
planning because it was second nature—no, first nature. The
last effort went into the gift of love, the sharing of strength
when there was no physical strength, only the great heart. I

*Bob and Ruth were her brother and sister-in-law, Robert Marshall and
Ruth Marshall Billikopf.

can't believe in God. I can't believe in a God of punishment. The mind and the heart, the world divides. It is of no use to be profoundly moved by a crisis unless one connects the experience with all of life.

Mince—she found that she could hold champagne on her stomach; first she had tried ginger ale and when that stayed down she called for champagne. When mother arrived there she sat in her bed, wearing her best nightgown, her best lace cover over the sheets, a red rose in her hair, a glass of champagne in her hand. "You must all drink with me!" she cried. "What shall we drink to?" "To the ship," her nurse suggested. "Yes, to the ship!" she exclaimed. (Ellen was launching a ship that day.)* So they all drank, her bright searching eyes upon them.

"I know why they have come," she said to the nurse. "Now let me go to sleep quickly. It's all so beautiful this way. I know you doctors and nurses, you try to give stimulants. I don't want any. This is beautiful this way."

In the beginning of her sleep there were little noises sometimes, a sigh. When the clumsy doctor gave her a hypodermic straight in the coronary vein she cried out through her coma. But soon the sleep was impenetrable. I stood in the door of that sweet house, looking in at the light quick shallow breathing, the thin shoulder moving swiftly up and down, up and down. Her body grew more rigid. In death the thin face had a severity and yet a peace, the humor and wisdom of a lifetime fixed there, and nothing now could reach her, all communication had ceased to her, I could no longer say . . . The severe thin line of her mouth seemed to judge mankind as she had judged herself and all of life. It was over now. In courage—but more—in gaiety—she had given herself to death when the moment came, as though it were life.

She must have made up her mind to get as much pleasure as possible from those last months. When she was strong enough

*The United States Navy had named a freighter after Lenore Marshall's father-in-law Louis Marshall, and Ellen was to launch it.

she walked through her door into the garden, under the sweet grape arbor dripping aith clustered green bunches of grapes, and down to the little round pool where her chair was placed. There she lay and every least small thing gave her pleasure, the lives of her friends concerned her deeply, she wrote of art to the painters, encouraged and criticized as keenly as ever, writing her letters, loving her flowers, singing old songs with her nurses. At dawn if she woke she would rise and go with the night nurse for a walk around her house to look at the hills. The day she lapsed into a coma she managed to get to the door, supported by her nurse: to see the sunlight on the birch tree in the garden.

She said to her nurse: "Lenore understands me better than anyone else in the family. She is more my child than she is her own mother's." I felt that too. But it was mother she loved most. The extrovert sister, companion, protector of her lonely childhood, the cool handsome thicker-skinned woman, kind and active and musical and successful, with whom was often argument in the past but never difference, always love and friendship, whose children even became somehow like her own.

Story—subtle—of nuance and suggestion.

Mince was dying. It struck to my heart. I would have done anything for her—she was my artistic soul, the true shining creature of purest integrity. And I was afraid. All my old terror of breakdown awakened, my old fears of my own weakness, although too I knew I was strong, scourged by fire yet never consumed, never giving up my own flame and knowledge and inner pledge and pact. Yet I feared: feared for her rather than myself; feared that in some moment of old terror I would break before her and say some word of her death—imagine! I who loved her and would not hurt—but that the ancient terrible pattern, the bitter despair of my own heart, would find vent in the one way that would hurt me most—a breakdown before *her* eyes. Would my face betray me, my eyes show horror and grief, was my strength equal to this test? Sometimes I felt an exhilaration, inspired by her I too could do anything. Yet I dreaded seeing her too although I knew that the inspiration of that dying would light me always.

I wrote daily, in utmost care, trying to give my love as deeply as she would want yet easily too so that there would be no emotional strain. For she too would dread emotion, she had not the strength for it. She would want the warmth and knowledge of love but no tension now to spoil the beauty of life she clung to. My letters must be casual and normal with my love shining through. But could I in my face, my words, my presence before her give that same effect? I wrote that I wanted to come and would come any time. But, I said, we understood each other perfectly: if she were tired and a visit would tax her, we could visit in our letters. For the understanding was there; it was the same for us. I too liked to be quiet when I was ill. And this was true for us both. Yet did I not subtly keep her from sending word to me to come? Did I? Did she read my sorrow and dread between the lines, and not send for me to spare *me* the sight of her, thin and changed and suffering? Did I maneuver this, through love and fear, revealing my reluctance in those considerate words, true and yet weighted by my own selfish desire to be spared—or to spare her from my possible weakness, my possible inability to handle the situation as she would, naturally, philosophically, greatly? She played my game, pretending I was busy and would come later. We both put off the moment of meeting and of farewell until it was too late.

For her, at the end. So be it. Quietly waiting. The months before had been for thought. Now it was only patience, acceptance, receptive waiting.

P.S. Use this—for my children. 1961. To help them.

Too late. This I should have done. I wish I had done. The terrible word spoken forty years ago in utmost innocence, an accidental hurt but the hurt done. Never mentioned later. Never to be undone. The life-work of Mincie's—those beautiful pictures gathered, seen again but for the first time. The grandeur of dying thus, as those two women did, never complaining, never demanding, always giving, always living, with fullness and joy and dignity.

The eyeglasses. The memoranda on scratch pads—a bill added, a reminder to send a gift, have a lamp mended. One's own letters kept, an envelope with one's birthday date that has enclosed a check for the gift one never bought with it. A packet of old Christmas cards. Why? The beautiful warm hospitable room. So many tea parties. The children's drawings kept, the sweater crumpled, crushed gloves from the last time. Ashes. Give me one more chance: why didn't I?

Story. The unknown dead—like *Hall of Mirrors*.*

My strengths break me. They are almost too heavy to carry. Not only do the loads they invite increase with my strengths, but the strengths themselves pouring out to give and to give, leave me drained.

What stands out at this point? Certain faces in memory, over and over. Certain strong deep emotions . . . and mother too.

Slowly I am emptied . . . Cannot really think of Mother yet. The mind snaps back like a rubber band. What is death when I hear her voice? Roses from her summer garden are in my room. It seems cruel that she cannot see her roses, she is a dust like their withered petals. But I see her desperate burning eyes when she looked at me once speechlessly a week before her death. She was loving me then, wondering about all of our future without her. At this I weep. And I, then, trying to be so cheerful, hopeful, casual, dreading the visits that took all my strength yet longing to be with her, inspired by her beauty and magnificence. How can I embody this bigness in my life? After my girlhood I never gave quite enough. What is this book I want to write about mothers and daughters?—

Hall of Mirrors was Lenore Marshall's second novel, published in 1937.

Mother—strange, I was so independent of her before, now I turn to her a dozen times a day and her lack is what is there. To tell her of the baths—of my delights—of the fat boy—the linens. To whom can I say things? It is always too late in life. When shall we learn?

One can never atone. This I have learned. One can only do better another time.

When you glance around it depends on yourself whether you see society or landscape.

1968—Santa Fe Chief

Life here! What is it like? A white frame house alone on the plains beside the railroad track—surrounded by porches— black furrowed soil of Missouri. Speed on—a minute later farmyard, sheds, a man in boots walks past a large hog, opens a barn door, disappears—forever. What will he do this evening, or on Sunday, his life full and satisfied there with his isolated sheds and creatures, is he lonely? Two children run after him but the scene, a Christmas tree red in window, is superseded by fringes of brown woodland ponds reflecting soft bare branches. Whose broken rowboat tied to a tree? Live here? We can only guess. But our imaginations are touched by what we see.

You do not see it like this from a plane.

Yes, to be sure we get there quicker by plane. But sometimes where is "there"? "There" may be here, here where we have time to gather our thoughts, to adjust to space, to look about more slowly and it may be more thoroughly. The train in that case has advantages. If, too, for reasons of necessity such as a health problem, planes are ruled out, the train is like a stable friend.

The train should halt before this escarpment, this jagged bank of rock so that I may search it out, find the exact word which will describe it, words which do not exist.

Sante Fe Train—New Mexico

Tilted castles—scrub bushes growing out of rock—Poem

The great sandstone mounds, not mountains, perpendicular
Ridged bare
Free form giants, primitive thrusts of nature
Nature or prehistoric man, Mars visitors

Deliberate builders of gargantual stockades
Walls of this plain, turret and pyramid,
Island Peninsula dinosaur haunch, wall over wall
Surely fashioned by the gods, the forerunner ones
Leaping over earth's lava, hypotenuses to the sky
Ridged bare and stark, knife sharp or crenelated
Sun hollowed, shadow excavated, three scrub
Bushes. This is the land of space
Large, permanent, Time never touched this land.
Millionfold dome running downhill into buttresses
Spread eagle wings of rock. There was a wooden hut
Leaning on a strong of road. I thought of man
I thought how every day I thought of love
And how man clings like any scrubby bush
Growing persistent from on his barren rock

An ocean god, Poseidon
himself hurling up sea bottom toward the sky
Falling tree form and frozen—I thought of love
And bushes gripping into the earth
Their passionate colors bursting out of rock.
    Return trip—outhouses like upright coffins.

    I have gotten to the point of feeling that fear is worse than
danger.

December 23—1970

The Airplane. The Astrojet—New York to Phoenix—
So here I am. One of the millions who fly. Not too nervous?
I'm not sure. Not on the upper level, and though at the slightest
irregularity I should freeze in terror. A test—another first—
there have been enough! I'm more sure of myself in relation to
people, much more in relation to myself. Leading now on
issues, able to be decisive. But are we still on the ground? We
coast along. Lights seem near.

The earth is our habitat. We are creatures of our earth. Our
feet were meant to press the soil. Suddenly there is a rush of
motion. NO question now: we are leaving the earth.
Moonward, sunward, starward—a steel cocoon of humans
roars into air. How can we be ourselves up there in the
un-earth? Higher—I feel us rise. Well, I'm doing it; I hope to
come back like a human, on earth. "Convenient," they say.
That's not the most important thing. Being natural—our
human selves—that's more important. Yet I have always
adjusted to emergencies—not adjusted—but I've managed to
handle them. Are we up? 30,000 feet? In the realm of
fantasy—unreal. But real people walk to the lavatory, read
magazines, fall asleep with open mouths. We are one of those
jets you see from the ground—a quick light, a noise disappearing. I am in it, frail human borne in the sky. My animal fear as
controlled as the engine, contained in a shape, my body holds
my fear, as the jet holds me.

The symbol suggests the poem. I fly. I am in a jet. I am alive
to meanings—which is the poem, the poem is meanings,
revelations. The poem is the inner meaning told through the
symbol. I am in the sky, the black night sky, I am the lighted
capsule borne through space, through the terror of darkness
and strangeness, the little human, all terror and exhilaration,
the little collection of frail bones.

In the place beyond total destruction
Where I walked, it was white as the moon

I say it was white as the moon.
I walked for a year or ten
As in other places wearing a witty smile
A kind smile too, being kind,
And a kind sigh
Among other persons who walked wherever they walked,
Maybe there, who knows.
It was jagged cold as the moon where my footsteps went
My fire burned down all persons.
Except for one child—

My fire had burned down all persons in its path
My fire made ash
My fire licked out every flower, every person
There was nobody left and nothing, my slashing sword
Had sheared off heads, struck to hearts, my heart
carried a whiteness of emptiness like a moon.
In the place beyond total destruction
My fire, my ash, my sword spared only one
    Child
His arms reached me from afar
My arms reached him.
Dear heroes of my past
Dear loves and friends
One by one showing their faces
Murderings made a murderer of me.

Children grow older.

One day children too come to the small betrayal
Offer a first Judas sign the mark of Cain, of manhood.

Yet always then there would be another child.

Live, live for the child!
Let no self turn me aside.

To comfort him at night I could live for another day—
until he moved away.

Hearts on the shore, heart shaped shells
In the place beyond total destruction
Crack under bare feet—

While there is this one child in the world I shall walk
I walk with the child.

Heaven is an antique shop
Cranberry glass and lustre cups and dust
where we walk hand in hand among the bric a brac
The land of death in my dream

I who seldom sinned against others
I would risk hell and eternity for the chance to do,
the chance to undo my sins—
Death draws your friends together for a moment.

Dayton, *1971*

Visiting author. Sense of doing job well. The class of 40 or 50 very responsive—many questions and from almost all. They had obviously read the poems and knew them. "Story" ranked high. They found themes of illness and death. Some said poems showed serenity and love. Spirit. What did I think of formal forms? They said they liked me and my work more than that of other visiting poets, flocked for my autograph afterward, all had the book. I read "Dream" and explained some of the meanings—the impetus behind it; they added interpretations. It was worth the trip, the flying, the health questions. I felt communication—Gary Pacernick a sincere teacher. The bright lights troubled me but they all said I did well. I felt confident of my performance. I gave out and felt myself projecting my personality—anyway one of them—the public—a thoughtful, a gentle one. Plane—in the plane I want to write and scribble at once—ideas. Why? Always thus, the long train trips of the past. Many notes were written in my books. Now here I am; the fifth flight, old, not well, but with a block overcome, something else mastered. I wish I could tell—. Yes, tense, old morbidities hang on, but able now to be fatalistic, to write as I do, now, not to be stopped by this old fear. To take my chances. What was the source of the fear of hurting—myself and others? The terrible fear of doing hurt, so that the one or two times that I found that I had done a hurtful thing have never been forgiven, prey on my mind to this day, the sins. And terror of losing control, the beast raging through the civilized good girl, the loving and compassionate, prevented me from truly entering the world— the inner life became more tensely strung, the outer under strictest rein. Why? The hurts done unto me were manifold, shocking, but they did not rouse this self-castigating sense of anguish. The beast in the jungle never broke out. The errors, sins, were not deliberate—suddenly they jolted me into shock and awareness of what I had done—stupid slips of sense. Who was the beast? What primitive force behind the scream, the jump, the cruel word?

It was always the fairest who were fed to the Minotaur
They drew lots—it was always someone: a
   maiden, a young man
Imagine it—entering the labyrinth, round and round
Slow walking into the jaw ahead, the imagined torture
Step by step maiden or youth traveling a dark trail
Alone in the dark terror where at some point at last
Jaws teeth maw waited. Monster arms that would crush.
And they crushed. The young and fair.
Sent by adieus of the tribe, a parent's tears.

*Post Operative**

The Body as Thing
Self is separate
Those groans not mine. Cries, never mine
Turn, an inch to the side, never. This is happening
to someone. Remarkable Lenore
Wonderful Lenore is separate from this shell
Strong as it must be now inhabits a crushed shell
Rising out of breakage to go where
What matter? Rising separate
The blessed Demerol—(earth down)
The corridor of doors, door after door
Some doors closed for silence, other doors open for air
Room after room
At night I hear them, cough cough
Room with the cough all night, room where a
whimper faint as a bleat turns to a loud
groan. White nurses pass, white rubber soles
past, scamper of aides giggling. And wheels
Someone or something is wheeled on the stretcher
bed, wheels pass by. Across the hall
visitors stand where the moans go softly on
Visitor one step forward through the door
The past is finished. At last. Or almost
Or only a trace. Banish it now at last
The dark blood, long dark year, dark long
moment. This past is finished!
Whittled down to this core of indestructible
strength. I have reached my measure
Larger than the past. Who is this woman
What is she to that girl, what is she to that dust
This woman who found herself in pain? Was it worth

*These last pages were written after an unsuccessful cancer operation.
Lenore Marshall knew that she was dying.

the cost? Well, yes. What did she find? Oceans
of love. Love from the touching hand, love coursing
from fingertips, a full knowledge of love.
This different new love, the old transmuted
And the new discovered—marvels of old grown great
Discoveries of new—who am I to bring forth
Such boundless love, such rocks of sustaining power?
Everything is centered on me. I rise to meet it. I greet
my new love—

    I found myself in love. I found myself in my
words, "Strict terrible
can have/ The full of reach we measure to the
grave/ Only ourselves, our self made one/
Giving back to love its origin."* Let every one
have these words to hold to. The full of reach
we measure. I reached it.

    The corridor. Across the way: there's a dying

My dying mother's face smiled at me from
   the mirror
For years it had stayed in its niche in memory
Coming and going when some moment drew it out
Returning to its place in the honeycomb of mind
Dark eyes hollowed, smooth white cheeks
hollowed; always the glow of love, force of
radiance. Always giving out reaching out until the niche
enclosed it again for a month a day a year.
Today when I glanced up at the mirror across from
   my bed
The face had left its proper niche, in this new
place I received its familiar greeting

*From Lenore Marshall's poem, "Two Poems in One."